Nicollet Island

History and Architecture

Nicollet Island

History and Architecture

Christopher and Rushika Hage

NODIN PRESS

ISBN: 978-1-935666-03-5
Design: John Toren
a complete list of photo credits appears on page 189

Library of Congress Cataloging-in-Publication Data

Hage, Christopher.
Nicollet Island : history and architecture / by Christopher and Rushika Hage.
p. cm.
Includes index.
ISBN 978-1-935666-03-5
1. Nicollet Island (Minn.) 2. Minneapolis (Minn.)--History. 3. Minneapolis (Minn.)--Buildings, structures, etc. 4. Historic buildings--Minnesota--Minneapolis. 5. Architecture--Minnesota--Minneapolis. I. Hage, Rushika. II. Title.
F614.M56N535 2010
977.6'579--dc22
                            2010020146

Nodin Press, LLC
530 North Third Street
Suite 120
Minneapolis, MN
55401

In researching this book on Nicollet Island one individual came up time and time again. For more than thirty years he fought to save the historic buildings and for a home for those that polite society deemed marginal. He offered practical surveyor and carpentry advice helping preserve Minneapolis's architectural heritage. He diplomatically smoothed over conflicts between neighbors. He provided quiet and steady leadership and showed a rare and genuine tolerance for the wide variety of people who have called Nicollet Island home. Without this man, the island's longest current resident, Nicollet Island would not now exist as it does, preserved for future generations. Thus, it is to the Steward of Nicollet Island that this book is dedicated.

To John Chaffee

Acknowledgements

It is with deep gratitude that we would like to thank all the people without whom this book would not have been possible. We would like to thank everyone we interviewed: James Anderson (Mahpiyaduta), David Wiggins, Winthrop Eastman, John Chaffee, Clague Hodgson, Ellen Stewart, Paul McLeete, Cindy Gentling, John Heiman, Mark Lerner, Harry Lerner, John Kerwin, Bob Roscoe, Jeff Siegel, Dorothy Sams, François Medion, Brother Michael Collins, Mike O'Keefe, Kenneth Gieske, and Lisa Hondros. For providing information we thank Chris Stellar, Barry Clegg and Roberta Swanson, Michelle Terrell, and Steven Dornfeld. For providing photographs from their collections, we would like to thank the Minnesota Historical Society, the Hennepin History Museum, the Special Collections at the Hennepin County Library, and the Northfield Historical Society. The staff at the Minnesota Historical Society and Hennepin County Library was unfailingly helpful, but, in particular, we would like to thank Ian Stade and Heather Lawton at the Hennepin County Library Special Collections, who tirelessly tracked down the information we needed. For photographs, we would like to thank Ellen Stewart, Kenneth Gieske at DeLaSalle High School, Harry Lerner, and, for his photographs and sketches, Clague Hodgson. We extend a special thank you to Edna Brazaitis for sharing with us her own research on some of the figures of Nicollet Island's Gilded Age, and to John Chaffee for his interviews, information, photos, and proofreading. Thanks to Judy Richardson for her proofreading and photographs of Sheba and Pearl. We would like to thank Barbara Flanagan, who for many years was an advocate for Nicollet Island, and whose articles and papers provided valuable information for this book. With much appreciation, we acknowledge Todd Grover for his explanations regarding the architecture on Nicollet Island. Thank you to Sam Jones and Esme Evans for their proofreading and editing. Lastly, thank you to our publisher Norton Stillman and our editor and designer, John Toren. Without all these people our book would not have come together as it did.

TABLE OF CONTENTS

Timeline

c. 10,000 B.C. – A giant waterfall, the melt from an enormous glacier, begins receding from the St. Paul/Fort Snelling area, eventually becoming St. Anthony Falls.

Immemorial – Nicollet Island, known to the Dakota Indians as Wita Waste, is used by them as a birthing place. The legend of Anpetu Sapa is born.

1680 – Father Louis Hennepin beholds Saint Anthony Falls, and describes it in a published account of his adventures in North America. He gives the falls its current name.

1805 – Explorer Zebulon M. Pike and party spend a night camping on Nicollet Island.

1837 – The United States acquires the east bank of the Mississippi via treaty with the Dakota Indians.

1836-39 – Frenchman Joseph N. Nicollet, after whom Nicollet Island is named, explores and maps the region.

1838 – Franklin Steele claims 322 acres along the east bank of the Mississippi along with Nicollet Island.

1847 – Ferry service is established near the present day Hennepin Avenue Bridge.

1849 – Franklin Steele completes a dam on the lower end of Nicollet Island to the east bank of the Mississippi.
 – Lumber milling activity begins in earnest.
 – Franklin Steele provides a cabin on Nicollet Island to John and Ann North.

1850 – The Norths are visited by Frederika Bremer, a famous Swedish novelist.
 – The *Governor Ramsey* steamboat, built on Nicollet Island, is launched.

1854-5 – The first suspension bridge is build between the west bank and Nicollet Island. It is the first bridge to span the Mississippi River anywhere along its length.

1857 – Nicollet Island is proposed as the State Capitol.

1858 – The Fourth of July is celebrated on Nicollet Island and described by Frank G. O'Brien.

1861 – Franklin Steele defaults on a loan and Hercules Dousman forecloses on Nicollet Island.
 – Henry David Thoreau visits Nicollet Island and catalogs its fauna and flora.
 – The First Minnesota Regiment is fêted by the ladies of St. Anthony and Minneapolis on Nicollet Island before leaving for the Civil War.

1862 – The Dakota War breaks out. Franklin C. Griswold enlists to fight in the conflict.

1865 – William W. Eastman and John L. Merriam purchase Nicollet Island from Hercules Dousman. Part of the island is offered for sale as a park, and is voted down by the citizens of Minneapolis.
   – Residential development of Nicollet Island begins on the central and northern portions.

1866 – The "discovery" of Apollo's Cave on Nicollet Island.

c. 1867 – The first beer caves are dug on Nicollet Island.

1868-69 – The Eastman Tunnel is dug and collapses, threatening St. Anthony Falls.

1872 – The citizens of Minneapolis and Saint Anthony vote to merge.

1876 – The second suspension bridge across the Mississippi is completed.

1877-82 – The Grove Street Flats and the Eastman Flats are constructed.

1879 – The Island Power Building is built. It receives water power transmitted by an overhead cable, which runs from the falls to the building through the interchannel tower.

1883 – The Minneapolis Park Board is founded due to efforts of Nicollet Island residents.

1883 – Franklin C. Griswold moves to Nicollet Island and builds several houses there.

1888-91 – The third Hennepin Avenue Bridge, featuring a steel-arch design, is built.

1893 – The Minneapolis Conflagration of 1893 starts on Nicollet Island.

1900 – The DeLaSalle Institute is founded on Nicollet Island. (It later becomes DeLaSalle High School).

1906 – The Jager Plan, a civic plan for Minneapolis, in published—the first of many to include plans to transform Nicollet Island.

1937 – The Island Power Building is razed.

c. 1940 – The Grain Belt beer sign is constructed.

1942 – A one block section of the Eastman Flats is purchased by DeLaSalle High School and demolished for an athletic field. The remaining two blocks of the Eastman Flats are demolished in the 1950s to make a DeLaSalle parking lot.

1950-70s – Nicollet Island becomes an extension of Minneapolis's skid row and a hippie colony.

1969 – Minneapolis Housing and Redevelopment Authority (MHRA) designates the island and the adjacent east bank neighborhood as an Urban Renewal area. The approved plan calls for tearing down all the buildings on the island and constructing new high-rise condos.

1971 – St. Anthony Falls Historic District is established.
 – DeLaSalle High School's original building C burns down, and school becomes co-ed.
 – The MHRA begins acquiring buildings on the island, tearing down most of them.

1972 – The Nicollet Island East Bank Project Area Committee (NIEBPAC) is established.
 – Grove Street Flats are condemned as unfit for human habitation.

1973 - The widening of Hennepin Avenue on the island removes all the businesses and skid-row hotels on both sides of the street.
 – MHRA Urban Renewal plan is amended to call for restoring historic houses on the island instead of demolishing them.

1974 - Miller-Dunwiddie architectural study finds that houses north of the railroad tracks are a unique collection of 19th century architecture with much of their historic fabric intact.

c. 1975 - Two donkeys, Pearl and her daughter Sheba, move onto Nicollet Island.

1976-77 – A small amphitheater is built on the south end of the island with Bicentennial funds.
 – MHRA stabilizes historic houses that they own, replicating their original exteriors.

1976 – The Nicollet Island Blind Lizard antique bike and motorcycle rally is founded.

1978 – A large section of the front wall of Grove Street Flats collapses following a heavy rain.
 – The vacant Carlson Store Fixture building, including the former Nicollet Island Elementary School, is destroyed by fire.
 – The Minneapolis Park and Recreation Board begins acquiring properties for the Riverfront Regional Park with state funds, competing with the MHRA for control of the island.

1980 – Restoration efforts begin with the rehabilitation of the Grove Street Flats by developer John Kerwin; restoration of the Nicollet Island Inn, Truck Building, and the Nicollet Island Pavilion follows.

1983 – Settlement is reached amongst competing elements of city government for the restoration and preservation of historic homes. Control of the island is divided between the Park Board and the MHRA, now renamed the Minneapolis Community Development Agency (MCDA).

1984 – DeLaSalle's athletic field loses size due to high school gym expansion. Permission is obtained from the city to enlarge the field using part of the public right of way of Grove Street.

1985-86 – Ground lease for island housing properties is signed by MCDA and Park Board. Private developers, chosen by lottery, begin restoring historic homes. Other houses are moved to the island.

1986-87 – A span of the old Broadway Bridge is floated downriver and re-erected as the Merriam Street Bridge. It spans the lower end of Nicollet Island to the east bank.

1988 – The MCDA and a neighborhood development group restore six buildings as an affordable-housing cooperative.

– Sheba the donkey is evicted and moves to Iowa. Pearl had died several years earlier.

1989-90 – The Hennepin Avenue steel-arch bridge is replaced by a new suspension bridge.

1997 – All historic houses have been restored. The last house project is completed, an architecturally-compatible new home replaces a house that was badly damaged by fire.

1999 – The Park Board constructs three tennis courts and gives DeLaSalle High School a preferential right to use them. In return, the Park Board is given use of DeLaSalle parking lots.

2001 - A sculpture, the "Bell of Two Friends," is dedicated near the Nicollet Island Pavilion, a gift to the city of Minneapolis from its sister city, Ibaraki, Japan.

2005 – Controversy erupts over DeLaSalle's plan to close half of Grove Street, demolish the tennis courts, and build a new athletic field, to be located partly on public park land. DeLaSalle offers to share the field with the Park Board at certain times.

2008 - The new DeLaSalle High School athletic field is completed.

Nicollet Island

History and Architecture

This map of Nicollet Island was sketched from the original plat by Private R.A. Colby, who was stationed at Fort Snelling. Nicollet Island is called Grand Island in this sketch, Boom Island is called Watah Island, Hennepin Island is called Cataract Island, Upton Island is called Rock Island, and Spirit Island is depicted. The military reserve on the west bank is clearly shown and there is a notation for the ferry from the west bank to Grand Island. On the west end of St. Anthony Falls public mills are noted. The St. Anthony east bank area is platted. The map is labeled ST. ANTHONY, MINI-SOTAH TER'Y.

1

Indians, Explorers, Missionaries, Soldiers, and a Sutler

Yet that death song they say,
is heard
Above the gloomy waters' roar

Indians, pioneers, Christian revivalists, Union and Dakota War soldiers, Gilded Age magnates, men of business, artists, hippies, students, and monks have all lived or worked on Nicollet Island since the ancestors of the Indian peoples migrated into the region some 8,000 years ago. This beautiful 48-acre island, which now lies in the heart of Minneapolis, has been at the center of numerous controversies and conflicts, ranging from whether it would become the capitol seat of Minnesota to whether residents should be expelled and the buildings demolished to make the island exclusively parkland. The story of Nicollet Island is the story of Minnesota and its history in miniature.

There are hundreds of islands on the Mississippi River, but Nicollet Island is among the largest, and one of the few with a residential district. It lies just upstream from St. Anthony Falls, and the two are inextricably linked. St. Anthony Falls, the largest waterfall on the Mississippi, held religious significance for the Dakota and Ojibwe Indians who lived in the area. It also supplied the water power that made St. Anthony and Minneapolis first lumber and then flour milling powerhouses, providing the economic impetus for the rapid growth of both cities.

Twelve thousand years ago the falls were situated 12 miles downstream, at or below the site of Fort Snelling. At that time it was an enormous cataract, 2,700 feet across and 175 feet high, draining the melt water from the glaciers that covered northwestern Minnesota. This powerful force eroded the soft sandstone and limestone through which the river flowed, creating the bluffs in St. Paul, and, as it receded upstream year after year, the deep channel that cuts through the heart of Minneapolis. The falls receded about four feet a year, gradually diminishing in height and strength until they were fixed in their present location by human intervention.

Father Louis Hennepin, a Belgian Franciscan priest, was the first white man to set eyes on St. Anthony Falls. In 1680 he and two companions, Michel Ako and Antoine Auguelle, were dispatched by the explorer Sieur DeLaSalle to discover the source of the Mississippi and the fabled Northwest Passage. While exploring, they were captured by Dakota warriors, whom Father Hennepin called the Isatti, and held captive at their village on Mille Lacs Lake for two months. After some time Father Hennepin received permission from his captors to leave and travel to the mouth of the Wisconsin River, and it was during this expedition that he first saw the falls. Father Hennepin writes, "I named it the Falls of St. Anthony of Padua in gratitude for favors God did me through the intercession of that great saint, whom we chose as patron and protector of all our enterprises. The waterfall is forty or fifty feet high and has a small rocky island, shaped like a pyramid in the center."[1] Hennepin seems to have exaggerated the height of the falls, but

In 1680, Father Hennepin offers prayers of thanks, and names St. Anthony Falls after his patron saint, Anthony of Padua.

his description of them as recounted in his book, *Description de la Louisiane*, published when he returned to France in 1683, established them as a landmark for traders and explorers at the continent's heart.

While Hennepin gave the falls the name we use today, the Dakota peoples who lived in the area had named them first. And as the Ojibwe began to arrive in the area during the early eighteenth century, gradually forcing the Dakota further west and south, they, too, named the falls. The Ojibwe called the falls *Kakabikah*, meaning "the sacred (severed) rocks," and the Dakota called them *Minirara*, meaning "curling water," or *Owahmenah*, meaning "falling water."

The area around the falls was sacred to both the Dakota and the Ojibwe. Father Hennepin writes that while at the falls he witnessed an Indian weeping bitterly in an oak tree. The Indian was hanging a beaver robe decorated with porcupine quills on a branch, sacrificing it to *Oanktehi*, a spirit of evil and water who lived beneath the falls. Hennepin quoted the supplicant praying:

You, who are a spirit, grant that our tribe pass by here tranquilly without mishap. Grant that we may kill many buffaloes, destroy our enemies, and bring here captives, some of whom we will sacrifice to you.[2]

More than 175 years later, Frank G. O'Brien, an early settler, in his *Pioneer Sketches*, recalled seeing the falls for the first time in September, 1855, and invoked Father Hennepin's description:

No wonder we all pronounced this the ideal place; no wonder that the Franciscan priest was so charmed with its magnificence that he made haste to give it a most holy christening; no wonder that France and Italy sent their artists to this country to place upon canvas one of the beauty spots of the Western hemisphere.

Time has wrought surprising changes; this poetic and picturesque beauty has been sacrificed to prosaic utility. And yet but for the intervention of man, the falls, would, no doubt, ere this have been swept away and with them Nicollet Island and the prospect of the city, which then existed only in embryo.[3]

The main tribes who lived near the falls in historic times were the Dakota and the Ojibwe. The Dakota were a semi-migratory tribe, though they had well-established villages on the banks of the Mississippi and Minnesota rivers. Before the arrival of the Ojibwe their spiritual center was on Mille Lacs Lake. The Rum River flowed out of it, and its banks were choked with nutritious wild rice. The French referred to the Dakota as "Sioux," a diminutive of *Nadouessioux*, a pejorative French-Canadian term borrowed from the Ottawa term *Nadouessiouak*, which means "snake." The Dakota were skilled hunters, craftsmen, fishermen, and warriors who lived in teepees, but they also practiced farming on the fertile river flats.

The Dakota Indians held the St. Anthony Falls area to be sacred, and birthed children on Nicollet Island.

One of the best contemporary descriptions of the Dakota comes from Samuel Pond, a Christian missionary to the Dakota who arrived in Minnesota with his brother Gideon in 1834. He composed the first Dakota dictionary, translated some of the books of the Bible into Dakota, and wrote the book, *The Dakotas or Sioux in Minnesota As They Were in 1834*, first published in 1908. This was both a sympathetic and critical work of anthropology drawn from twenty years of intimate experience living in a cabin near the Lake Calhoun band. Pond wrote:

In stature the Dakotas are rather taller than people of European ancestry…The complexion of the Dakotas is considerably darker than of Europeans, but is not very dark. Their cheek bones are not particularly prominent, their features are regular, and many of them are good looking. Taken together the race cannot be characterized as a homely race.[4]

Pond goes on to describe a stoic group of skilled hunters of deer and buffalo. In the spring they split their bands; one group hunted muskrat, whose furs they exchanged with white traders, while the other tapped maple trees for their syrup. The Dakota purchased or traded for their brides, occasionally practiced polygamy, and were generally kind to their children unless, according to Pond, a father thought a son displayed effeminacy or a mother lost her wits with a recalcitrant boy. About their religious practices, Pond writes:

The religion of the Dakotas consisted principally, but not wholly, in the worship of visible things of this world, animate and inanimate. Their chief object of worship was Unkteri, the mammoth, though they held many erroneous opinions concerning the extinct species of elephant, and did not know the race was extinct…As they worshipped many other animals, it was natural that the mammoth, which so much exceeded the others in size, should be adopted as their chief god. To his worship their most solemn religious festivals were dedicated. They supposed that the race was still in existence, and, as they were not seen on land and their bones were found in low and wet places, they concluded that their dwelling was in the water. Their bones were highly prized for magical powers, and were perhaps as valuable to them as relics of a saint are to a devout Catholic.[5]

Although the Ojibwe had succeeded in driving the Dakota from the north woods in the course of the eighteenth century, the eastern Dakota tribes were reluctant to abandon the bounteous and convenient river valleys. They often camped on islands as an added protection against the Ojibwe. During the earliest days of white settlement, there were six islands in the vicinity of Saint Anthony Falls: three above the falls (later named Boom, Nicollet, and Hennepin) and three below (later named Cataract, Upton, and Spirit Island). Today, only Nicollet Island remains, as Hennepin and Boom islands have been joined with the east bank, and the other three have been destroyed by erosion or the effects of civil engineering.[6]

Spirit Island took its name from an Indian legend asserting that it was haunted by the spirit of a Dakota woman named Anpetu Sapa (meaning "Dark Day"). Anpetu Sapa's husband was a successful hunter who took a second wife as his fame and wealth grew. Heartbroken, Anpetu Sapa placed their son in her canoe and paddled mid-river just above the falls. Bedecked in her bridal finery of an embroidered robe, a crown of eagle feathers, and strings of beads, she sailed past her frantic husband and onlookers, singing her death song as she went over the falls. It was said that the lament of Anpetu Sapa could sometimes be heard wailing on the wind, and that she was occasionally glimpsed rising from the foam on Spirit Island looking out over the land where she once lived and was happy.[7] Of this legend Pond wrote:

Yet that death-song, they say, is heard
Above the gloomy waters' roar,
When trees are by the night-wind stirred,
And darkness broods o'er wave and shore!
In haste, and with averted eye,
Benighted travelers pass near;
And when that song of death is heard,
Stout-hearted warriors quake with fear. [8]

Nicollet Island was known to the Dakota as *Wita Waste*, meaning "beautiful island." The Dakota enjoyed the natural resources of the island, tapping its maple trees and fishing there, but the island was also used for ceremonies, particularly rites of passage.

The archeological record of the area is scant. A 1989 study noted the 1870 discovery of a burial site on the east bank to the northeast of Nicollet Island, a report of a copper spear point in the St. Anthony area, and a report of a Clovis point found in 1941 on the west side of the Washington Avenue Bridge. In 2008, an undated projectile point was discovered on Nicollet Island. The lack of archeological data leaves us to rely on sources such as the oral traditions of the Dakota.[9]

Mahpiyaduta (Red Sky), also known as James Anderson, the historian and cultural chairman of the Mdewakanton Mendota Dakota band, says that, according to oral tradition, Nicollet Island was used as a birthing place. He explains, "In those days, you could hear the falls for twelve miles, and the roar of the falls would drown out the cries of a woman in labor and protect her from war bands of Ojibwe or predators."

Red Sky believes that, because of Nicollet Island's location in the sacred St. Anthony Falls area, it was used for ceremonial purposes. He believes that the *Humbleacha* or vision quest ceremonies were held there. The *Humbleacha* involved fasting for four days and nights, and prayers to the gods for guidance. Another ceremony Red Sky believes was held on the island was the life ceremony, which celebrated the transitions from childhood to adolescence, adolescence to adulthood, and adulthood to old age. Lastly, Red Sky believes that the *Innipi,* or purification ceremony, took place there. In the *Innipi* ceremony, participants entered a sweat lodge (an *Innipi*) made of willow branches and buffalo skins. It had four doors, symbolizing the four stages of life: childhood, adolescence, adulthood, and old age. One of the doors was left open and a spirit man poured water on hot rocks in the lodge. The four elements—earth, wind, fire, and water—were mixed and the accompanying prayers cleansed the participants, both physically and spiritually.[10]

Rubin and Malcomb Kittoe, both members of an extended Dakota family, spoke with Dave Wiggins, a supervisory Park Ranger with the National Park Service who has studied the oral tradition of the Dakota people for years, about their family's oral tradition. According to the Kittoe family, in addition to being a birthing place, Nicollet Island was a place of peace, where no weapons were brought. Peace accords between the Dakota and Ojibwe were negotiated there. This made sense in that Nicollet Island formed a sort of no man's land between the Ojibwe and Dakota territories. The Ojibwe would have come down from the north by canoe from the Rum River area and onto the Mississippi, and the Dakota would have come up the river. Both peoples would have had to portage around St. Anthony Falls to travel further north or south along the Mississippi. Nicollet Island provided the necessary neutral ground for both tribes.[11]

Wiggins himself also speculated about the significance of the island. In Dakota mythology, the confluence of the Mississippi and Minnesota rivers, several miles downstream from Nicollet Island, was the omphalos of the world, the earth's navel, its center, or *B'dote* in Dakota. Like the *B'dote*, St. Anthony Falls, which they called *Owahmenah*, was a sacred place beneath which the spirit *Oanktehi* lived. Spirit Island below the falls was the nesting place of eagles and may have been considered a nexus between the spiritual forces

Explorer Captain Johnathan Carver visited St. Anthony Falls in 1766 and made this sketch, which was published in his book *Travels through the Interior parts of North America, in the Years 1766, 1767, and 1768.*

represented by *Oanktehi* and *Wakinyan*, the thunder bird. Nicollet Island, just above the falls, fell into the orbit of this sacred area and its proximity made it a natural place of birth or rebirth through ceremonies or treaties.

EXPLORERS AND A MILITARY FORT

In 1766, Captain Jonathan Carver of Connecticut, a veteran of the recently concluded French and Indian War, paid the falls a visit and wrote about them in a bestselling book, published in 1778, called *Travels through the Interior parts of North America, in the Years 1766, 1767, and 1768.* Carver's book

contains a detailed description of the falls:

We could distinctly hear the noise of the water full fifteen miles before we reached the Falls; and I was greatly pleased and surprised, when I approached this astounding work of nature...This amazing body of waters, which are above 250 yards over, form a most pleasing cataract; they fall perpendicular about thirty feet, and the rapids below, in the space of 300 yards more, render the descent considerably greater; so that when viewed at a distance they appear to be much higher than they really are. The above mentioned traveler (Father

Louis Hennepin) had laid them down at above fixty [sic] feet; but he had made a greater error in calculating the height of the Falls of Niagara; which he asserts to be 600 feet; whereas from latter observations accurately made, it is well known that it does not exceed 140 feet...In the middle of the Falls stands a small island about forty feet broad and somewhat longer, on which grow a few cragged hemlock and spruce trees...These Falls vary much from all the others I have seen, as you may approach close to them without finding the least obstruction from any intervening hill or precipice...The country around them is extremely beautiful...On the whole, when the Falls are included, which may be seen at the distance of four miles, a more pleasing and picturesque view cannot, I believe, be found throughout the universe. [12]

This description corroborates the Dakota tradition that the falls drowned out noise for twelve miles. Carver continues with a description of Spirit Island: "At a little distance below the Falls stands a small island, of about an acre and half, on which grow a great number of oak trees, every branch of which, able to support the weight, was full of eagles' nests." [13]

Prior to the French and Indian Wars, France held a dominant presence in the region that later became Minnesota. French voyageurs traded with Indian peoples, receiving valuable furs in exchange for European trade goods. Voyageur songs were heard across Minnesota waters, and French blood mingled freely with Indian blood, giving birth to the mixed Métis people. But by the terms of the 1763 Treaty of Paris that ended the French and Indian War, the area to the east of the Mississippi came under the British crown. France had ceded the area west of the Mississippi to Spain in 1762. In 1800, Spain transferred sovereignty of this land back to France just in time for Napoleon Bonaparte to sell it to President Thomas Jefferson of the recently independent United States, for $15 million, in 1803. The Louisiana Purchase established the Minnesota area as part of the United States. Though Nicollet Island lay neither east nor west of the Mississippi, being in the center of the river, both the island and the falls just below it were now fully within the United States. It was several decades, however, before agents of the new nation succeeded in asserting American sovereignty locally: foreign fur traders and Indians did not concern themselves much with the territorial claims of a nation whose representatives were nowhere to be seen.

In an effort to rectify that situation, in 1805 a twenty-six-year-old lieutenant named Zebulon Pike was dispatched by General

James Wilkinson to proceed upstream along the Mississippi from St. Louis and obtain permission from the Indians to erect military posts and trading houses at the mouth of the Minnesota River (then called the St. Pierre), the Falls of St. Anthony, and other critical points as Pike should deem fit. Lieutenant Pike, a sergeant, two corporals, and seventeen privates made their way up the river in a seventy-foot keel boat, and on September 21 the party reached the mouth of the Minnesota River. They camped that night on the island that now bears his name.

The following day Pike commenced negotiations with the local Dakota chiefs Little Crow and Way Aga Enagee, and two days later the chiefs signed over land extending nine miles up the Mississippi, including St. Anthony Falls and Nicollet Island, and about nine square miles at the mouth of the St. Croix River, for about $2,000 in money or goods.[14] Lieutenant Pike then traveled to the falls, arriving on Thursday, September 26. He took accurate measurements of them, but was not as impressed by them as he had expected to be, given the accounts of previous visitors. Pike writes in his journal: "arrived at the foot of the Falls about 3 or 4 O'clock with my Boat—…I pitched my Tent and Encamped above the Shoot."[15] While camping at the falls, Pike and his party encountered a small party of Dakota. He writes:

28th Septr. Saturday
Brought my Barge over and put her in the river above the Falls. While we were at work at her ¾ of a mile from camp, 7 Indians painted Black, appeared on the Heights:—As we had all left our guns at the Camp, we were of course defenceless [sic]; but it immediately struck me they were the small party of Sioux's [sic] who were obstinate, and would go to War, when the other part of the Bands came in. These they proved to be. They were better armed than any I had ever seen—having Guns, Bows, Arrows, War Clubs, and Spears; and some even a case of Pistols. Just then I was giving my men a dram—and giving the cup full of Liquor to the first, he drank it off; but I took care to give the other but a moderate dram. I then sent my Interpreter to Camp with them to wait my coming; wishing to purchase one of their War Clubs, it being made of Elk horn, and decorated with inlaid work. This, and a set of Bows and Arrows I wished to get as a curiosity; But the Liquor beginning to work he came back for me, and I refusing to go until I brought my Boat he returned, (and I suppose being offended) borrowed a canoe and crossed the river. In the

Afternoon got the other Boat near the top of the Hill, when the props gave way and she slid all way down to the bottom of the Hill again, but without injuring any person. It [was] raining very hard, we left her. Killed one Goose and a Rackoon.

Lieutenant Pike spent a night on Nicollet Island on Monday, September 30: "Loaded my Boat, moved over and Encamped on the Island. The large Boat's loading likewise we got over, and put on board. In the mean time I took a survey of the Falls, the Portage & c." Of the falls themselves, Pike writes: "As I ascended the Mississippi, the falls of St. Anthony did not strike me with that majestic appearance which I had been taught to expect from the description of former travelers."

Pike's expedition continued upstream and eventually reached the British forts at Sandy and Leech lakes, where he reminded the local authorities of their obligation to pay duties on their trade goods. But he lacked the wherewithal to enforce such behavior, and the British fur traders continued to operate with impunity in northern Minnesota until after the war of 1812, when the United States began to truly assert itself in the area.

In 1819, although the Dakota had not yet been paid for the land, Lieutenant Colonel Henry Leavenworth was dispatched to build a fort in the area Pike had surveyed at the confluence of the Mississippi and Minnesota rivers. (The Dakota did not receive payment until 1838.) The following year Leavenworth, who had not begun contruction, was replaced by Colonel Josiah Snelling, under whose command work finally commenced. Between 1821 and 1823, Colonel Snelling's soldiers built two barracks, a water-driven flour mill, and sawmill on the west bank near St. Anthony Falls, almost opposite Nicollet Island. At the time the surrounding countryside was largely prairie, and Snelling's men went upriver to the confluence of the Rum and Mississippi Rivers to harvest trees and float them downriver to the mill. The vast waterpower of the falls had been tapped, foreshadowing the source of growth of the area.

Perhaps the most distinguished explorer to visit Fort Snelling during its early years was Joseph N. Nicollet, a French astronomer, geographer and mathematician. Nicollet had come to America from Paris in 1832 in an effort to rehabilitate his fortunes, which had been lost in the Revolution of 1830 and the accompanying stock market crash. Nicollet's reputation had vanished along with his personal wealth, since many of his friends had followed his advice and suffered the same fate. His plan was to survey and map the Upper

Mississippi region, with the thought that such a map would be of use to the United States government, which had little geographic knowledge of the area. He arrived at Fort Snelling in 1836, and made two important friends straightaway. Nicollet stayed with and got support from the American Fur Company's representative, Henry H. Sibley, in Mendota, and at Fort Snelling he stayed with Major Lawrence Taliaferro and his wife. Major Taliaferro was the government Indian agent, and in his home Nicollet enjoyed Virginian hospitality. During Nicollet's stay with the Taliaferros he played his violin to Mrs. Taliaferro's piano accompaniment and worked on his maps by candlelight during the winter months.

Joseph N. Nicollet was a French astronomer, geographer, and mathematician. In 1836 and in two subsequent expeditions he mapped the Upper Mississippi region. Nicollet Island is named after him.

Nicollet's first expedition was privately funded, but the United States government was impressed with his efforts and paid him to embark on two more under the auspices of the Corps of Topographical Engineers, both of them devoted to the unexplored regions of the Upper Mississippi River. He published the report of his expeditions in his *Map of the Hydrographical Basin of the Upper Mississippi*, a remarkably accurate map covering an area more than half the size of Europe.[16]

As treaties were signed and the topography of the region became better known, the Upper Mississippi became an attractive destination for adventurous men and women from Prairie Du Chien, St. Louis, New Orleans, and cities further east. The region surrounding the Falls of St. Anthony was especially inviting, less for its beauty, perhaps, than for the economic value of the water power it possessed, and the fact that it had already been ceded to the United States. Before long, games were afoot to determine who would end up controlling that valuable real estate.

The first contender was the commander of Fort Snelling, Major Joseph Plympton. Major Plympton took command of the fort in 1837 and immediately ordered a study of the military reservation around the falls. No precise maps of the area acquired by Lieutenant Pike were available, and the military had exercised little control over the area. Consequently, squatters had encroached. When Major Plympton made his report to his superiors about the squatters on the reservation, he received orders to oust them, which he did. The refugees simply moved east beyond the boundaries of the reservation, forming a community that would soon become St. Paul. At the time it was known as Pig's Eye, in reference to the squinty-eyed French fur trader named Pierre "Pig's Eye" Parrant who opened a saloon there.

Having rid the reservation of squatters, Major Plympton next redrew the maps of the area, intentionally leaving out the eastern bank of the Mississippi so that it would be considered Indian territory. He was well aware that treaties had been signed recently with the tribes who lived east of the river which would open those lands to white settlement. On July 15, 1838, news of the treaties' ratification reached Minnesota and Major Plympton moved immediately to stake his claim on the eastern bank, which would have given him claim to half the waterpower of the falls. But the fort Commandant was too late. He had been outmaneuvered by the sutler (general store operator) at Fort Snelling, a twenty-five-year-old Pennsylvanian named Franklin Steele. Although young, Steele was no greenhorn when it came to frontier claims, having

previously made a claim to the St. Croix Falls. Steele had political connections, too, and may have received advance warning of the Senate's actions from influential friends. According to one story, Steele and his men built a cabin on

Franklin Steele was a lumber milling entrepreneur. In 1838, he laid claim to Nicollet Island and much of the land around St. Anthony Falls.

the east bank by moonlight, and when a detail from the fort, under Captain Scott, arrived the next morning to stake Major Plympton's claim, they found Steele eating breakfast with his men. Steele cordially invited the soldiers to breakfast but was rebuffed by Captain Scott who accused him of jumping Major Plympton's claim. Steele coolly replied, "You can put me off by force…but I shall not leave willingly." Outmanuevered, the Captain departed and claimed for himself and Major Plympton some less attractive plots nearby.[17]

Steele arranged for a succession of individuals to hold his claim, as it was necessary to have a continued physical presence on the site. The first was a French-Canadian voyageur named LaGrue, who returned to his cabin from hunting and found it burned down and his wife dead. LaGrue sought to cross the river below the falls but ran into a war party of Ojibwe hoping to ambush some unwary Dakota. The Ojibwe expressed condolences for LaGrue's loss and assisted him in crossing the river the next morning. People speculated as to whether the Ojibwe had murdered LaGrue's wife, but it seemed unlikely as, if the war party was so inclined, than why had they not murdered LaGrue as well? LaGrue himself was never suspected of the murder, and his wife's death, the first of a settler in what was to become St. Anthony and later Minneapolis, remains a mystery.[18]

While the choicest east bank claim had been taken by Steele, the rest of the east bank was open to other claimants. Colorful characters such as Pierre Bottineau made a claim adjacent to Steele's. Bottineau was a Métis, the son of a French voyageur father and an Ojibwe mother. He was born at the Red River fur-trading post, grew up with Indian children and became a great marksman, skillful hunter, trapper, and scout. Bottineau lived a life of action, surviving charging buffalo, blizzards, and Dakota bullets. He guided immigrants, traders, land speculators, railroad survey teams, gold seekers, and eventually General Sibley's military expedition against the Dakota in 1863. In the early pioneer days of Minnesota, the Métis were a regular fixture of pioneer life and men like Bottineau provided a bridge between Indian and settler cultures.[19]

The area that Steele, Bottineau, and others claimed was shortly to become the city of St. Anthony. The wilderness was slowly being tamed. Control of the falls, the banks, and the islands in the river began to pass from the province of Indians, explorers, fur traders, and soldiers to the pioneers.

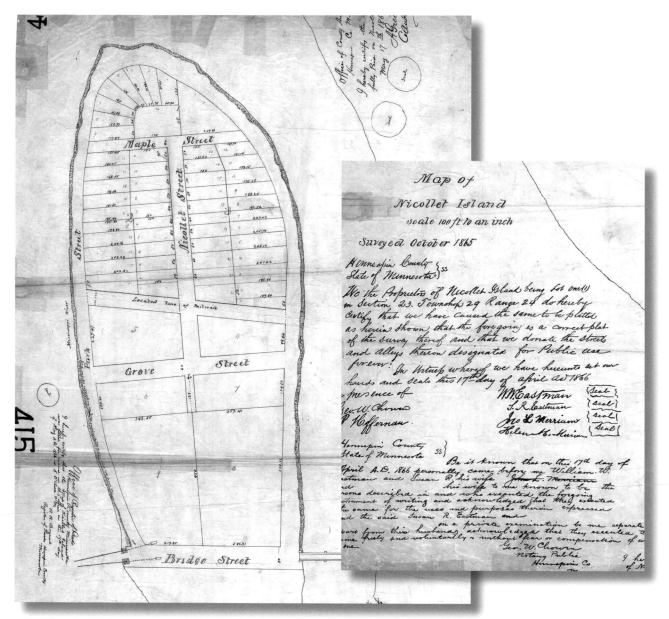

This October 1865 plat of Nicollet Island was surveyed by Franklin Cook for W.W. Eastman, J.L. Merriam, and their wives. The smaller lots on the northern tip are suitable for more modest homes and the larger lots in the central portion permit larger buildings. Of note are the street names of Maple, Nicollet, Grove, Bridge - later changed to Hennepin Avenue, and Park - later changed to Island Ave. Also depicted is the leased line of the railroad, which when the railroad was built would divide the northern portion of the island from the central and southern portions. (The inset magnifies a portion of the lower part of the map.)

2

The Pioneers

When the groves of Nicollet Island
Wore the livery of June

Franklin Steele's pre-emptive claim included 322 acres along the east bank of the Mississippi, all of Nicollet Island, and the waterpower associated with this real estate by virtue of the riparian or water rights. The total claim eventually cost him $1.25 an acre, with Nicollet Island itself figured at about $60 when the U.S. government finally formalized the claim stake by auction in 1848. Upon staking his claim, Steele set about securing the capital and partners for a logging endeavor. After sending a lumberman upriver into central Minnesota to confirm that vast forests of trees were actually available for harvest, in 1847 Steele built a mess hall, blacksmith and carpentry shops, stables, and sleeping quarters for his workers. That same year he established a cable-operated ferry service from the west bank of the river to Nicollet Island at the site where the Hennepin Avenue Bridge now runs. At the time a Dakota woman who netted fish and lived on the river provided passage across for travelers, but Steele wanted something more permanent and searched for a ferryman.[1]

Captain John Tapper was that ferryman. He was a tough, strong man who had been in the Mexican War and worked at Fort Snelling as a mule-skinner for the army. Originally from East Orange, Dorsetshire, England, he was known as "Captain" though he had never been commissioned. The Captain was well known for his lively and humorous conversation and his love of practical jokes, and he appears frequently in early histories of St. Anthony, Minneapolis, and Nicollet Island. Tapper's boat was described by one chronicler as "an imp of a boat that maliciously turned over at the slightest provocation."[2]

Although Captain Tapper was undoubtedly a good ferryman, he did not work day and night. On one occasion Michael Hickey,

Captain John Tapper (right) operated the first ferry between the west bank of the Mississippi River and Nicollet Island. Caleb Dorr (left) was a lumberman who worked for Franklin Steele, and was the owner of the Mississippi and Rum River Boom Company.

plummeted over the falls in the dark, the rescue party (which included Colonel John H. Stevens and Captain Tapper) found him unharmed. Hickey's first thought was not for his own safety, however. Rather, according to Colonel Stevens, "taking the bottle from his pocket and drawing the cork for the first time, he said: "Wasn't it lucky the cratur (meaning the whisky) received no harm in making the bloody trip!"[3]

Franklin Steele knew he needed sharp talents for his numerous business endeavors, so to complete his milling projects he sent for Ard Godfrey, a capable millwright from Maine. The Godreys soon became fixtures in the growing community. Godfrey and his wife, Harriet, offered hospitality to many pioneers in their house, which still exists, and organized the Cataract Lodge of Masons in their home.

The year 1847 also saw the arrival of Caleb Dorr who, like the Godfreys, was from Maine and who boarded with them. The twenty-three-year-old Dorr had worked in lumber mills in the east, and he and Godfrey were engaged by Steele to build a dam across the east channel from the lower end of Nicollet Island to the east bank. By 1849, both

who worked on Boom Island and was given to drinking, could have used his services. Hickey had been drinking and had acquired a bottle of whiskey. He decided to avail himself of one of Captain Tapper's boats, Captain Tapper having retired for the night. Hickey launched the boat but did not make it to the other side. The next morning, a band of Winnebago Indians that was portaging around the falls saw Hickey on Spirit Island. Though he had

Steele's sawmill and the dam were up and running. Many of the elm and maple trees of Nicollet Island were cut down in the course of completing these and other local projects. The millpond upriver of the dam held the logs that Steele's men harvested. From that point they were floated down for processing at the sawmill, which stood on the east bank just upstream from the dam. Steele's logging endeavors were successful, and by the end of 1849 he platted his east bank land, nam- ing it St. Anthony like the falls; settlers soon began arriving in larger numbers. Dorr went on to organize the Mississippi and Rum River Boom Company, which built the first boom across the Mississippi near Boom Island. For the next decade Dorr's company worked cut- ting and rafting timber on the Rum and Mis- sissippi Rivers.[4]

With the east bank under development, Steele saw the value in having a foothold

Pictured are milling operations on the banks of the Mississippi River near Nicollet Island.

on the west bank of the Mississippi, which was still in the Fort Snelling military reservation. He successfully petitioned the government to have his friend and bookkeeper, Colonel John H. Stevens, establish a house on the west bank in exchange for providing ferry service to the government free of charge. Stevens was a veteran of the Mexican War and had been referred to Steele by the fur trader (and future governor) Henry Sibley. Sibley knew that his industrious brother-in-law (Sibley had married Steele's sister in 1843) was always on the lookout for new talent.

Stevens built his house, the first settler home on the west bank, with the help of Pierre Bottineau and Captain John Tapper. He brought his bride, Frances Helen, there, and it was in that home that she gave birth to their children, the first settlers born in what was to become Minneapolis. Stevens planted wheat, corn, and oats on forty acres, and the crops flourished. He and his wife were truly living on the frontier; it was quite a change for his wife, who had been born and raised in New York. Indians and mosquitoes were the Stevens' most frequent visitors. Stevens relates that the mosquitoes proved particularly bothersome for Captain Tapper:

Mosquitoes surrounded the house in such swarms that smoke would not ban-ish them. The windows and doors were barricaded with netting, but that did not suffice to protect us from them. The beds also required bars. With all this protection, Captain Tapper was so annoyed by their depredations that one morning, after a night's duration of suffering, just before daylight he gathered some blankets and took refuge on the brow of the hill back of the house, hoping to get a little sleep before breakfast. He rolled himself in his blankets and was just entering dream-land, when the hot breath of an animal on his face startled him, and thoroughly ended his inclination to sleep. A large tim-ber-wolf, with several companions near by, was in search of a breakfast in the early twilight. With a voice that drowned the roar of the near cataract, Captain Tapper sprang to his feet, and shaking the blan-kets—his only weapons of defense—at the wolves, he made a misstep, rolled down the precipice, and with a single bound entered the door of the house, thinking he was followed pretty closely by the wolves. He declared he would rather be bled by mosquitoes than devoured by wolves.[5]

In 1851, following the signing of the Treaty of Traverse de Sioux, vast expanses of land west of the Mississippi were opened to white settlement; at the same time, the Fort Snelling reservation was reduced, and Colonel Stevens got claim to his land. Hennepin County was organized in his house, the first 100 acres of Minneapolis proper were laid out, the first election was held there, and Stevens was elected the first Hennepin County Register of Deeds. In 1852, the name Minneapolis was adopted in Colonel Stevens's home. A school teacher from New England, Charles Hoag, had proposed in the *St. Anthony Express* newspaper the name "Minnehapolis" from the Dakota *Minnehaha*, meaning "laughing water," and the Greek word *polis*, meaning "city." The matter was settled with a meeting of settlers in the Stevens' house, during which it was decided to drop the "h." Thus the west bank of the Mississippi became Minneapolis, city of laughing waters.[6] Colonel Stevens went on to serve several terms in the Minnesota legislature. His house, which was considered a landmark, was moved twice and now stands in parkland near Minnehaha Falls.

THE ISLAND'S EARLIEST PIONEER RESIDENTS

Franklin Steele continued to search out new settlers and business partners for his numerous projects. In 1849, he recruited John Wesley North to join him on the frontier. North, a lawyer from New York, suffered from ill health. He had been a preacher and was a staunch abolitionist. After being let go from several congregations due to his ardent abolitionist views, North took a trip to Minnesota where he met Franklin Steele. Steele, with his eye for talent, thought a lawyer could be useful for his business interests, and offered North and his young bride the use of his unfinished cabin on Nicollet Island. In November, 1849, John Wesley North and his wife, Ann Loomis North, became the first known permanent inhabitants of Nicollet Island.

The voluminous correspondence of both Ann and John is preserved in the Minnesota Historical Society and the Huntington Library and Art Gallery in Pasadena, California. From these letters we can glean a great deal of information about pioneer life on Nicollet Island. Ann North corresponded at least weekly with her parents and brothers back east. John worked to recruit settlers from the east for the rapidly growing town of St. Anthony. John's efforts paid off, and he recruited as many as a thousand people to St. Anthony during the first year.[7] The Norths quickly came to know the other prominent citizens of St. Anthony and Minneapolis, the communities being small and tightly knit. In fact, on the North's first trip as a couple up by steamboat to St. Paul from Galena, Illinois, on the *Steamer Canada*,

John Wesley and Ann Loomis North were the first white inhabitants of Nicollet Island. They lived in a cabin built for them by Franklin Steele. John was a lawyer, preacher, abolitionist, and state legislator. Ann gave piano lessons to the local youth.

they met Caleb Dorr traveling back to Minnesota with his new bride Celestia.

Ann describes the island vividly in letters to her family:

...and then we are to have as romantic a little spot to live as anyone need ask— This is a very pleasant little village, and has grown amazingly since Mr. North was here before—There are three islands in the river here—The middle and largest one contains about 100 acres—is just above the falls and covered with forest—It is a delightful spot, and near one end of this, Mr. Steele, one of the wealthiest men here is fixing a little house for us—There are to be two rooms, and a garret—That is all—but our wants are so little here that I think we shall get along nicely—.[8]

She corrects the 100 acres to 45 acres in her letter of November 12. Ann writes, "Can you believe it? I have finally had a view of the Falls of St. Anthony—or as the Indians call it Minni ha-hah, which by the way I consider a very appropriate name, for, Anglicized 'tis "Laughing Waters," and certainly it has the most cheerful, merry appearance of any waters I ever saw."

The Norths spent their first winter in Steele's little cabin on Nicollet Island and life there was primitive and full of challenges. For example, in one letter Ann writes, "By the way, if Grandma is at all troubled about our situation, this winter, tell her, we get on the island, at present, by going through the saw mill and following the dam which extends to the island—In winter, we can cross the river on the ice." In a subsequent letter she offers details: "On Wednesday last I crossed the millpond, for the first time on the ice. It is now probably more than four inches thick—and having frozen when there was no wind, is as smooth and clear as the water itself. We could see, through it, the sticks and weeds at the bottom. It forms, too, a very fine mirror—it reflects the stars, and the trees and rocks on the bank, most beautifully. Now the river is frozen, [at] the other side of the island, so that some men went across on the ice yesterday."

Ann writes of the problems of housekeeping and struggling with a house built of lumber so green that the walls of her new home oozed sap. In one letter she remarks that she caught twenty-two mice for want of a cat. This problem was happily solved when Ann's Grandmother Loomis came in the spring with her tomcat.[9] But she writes also of the couple's great felicity and the natural beauty of the island, "This is such a delightful spot—I see new beauties every day—." John writes of his improved health and of what a wonderful housekeeper Ann is. Yet clearly Ann longs for her family and friends, and both she and John entreat their families to reply faithfully. Frontier mail was in its infancy at the time, and Ann writes on December 16 of just having received her mother's letter dated November 11.

Even in the bitter cold of winter, Ann is clearly captivated by the natural beauty of the island: "The temperature last Friday morning was 12 degrees below zero—pretty cold and it is true, but certainly I do not suffer as much as I did winters with you. The air seems pure and bracing. On those cold mornings, the spray from the Falls came up here in most beautiful crystals, almost like a snow storm. The trees were covered with it, and everything about the house and as the sun rose, presented a most splendid appearance." Ann looks forward to spring on the island and comments on the expected abundance of mosquitoes:

This island, all the Fall, had been extremely beautiful. We had flowers till snow came, which was two weeks since…The river is just closed,—a month later than last year. On the west side of the island it presents quite a singular appearance. For several days the ice was floating down on large cakes. It finally became stationary and as the ice came rushing down, it would strike it—and crowd together like packing snow. Consequently, the surface is very white and uneven—Until yesterday, no one had ventured across—On the other side, above the mill dam, the water was perfectly quiet when it froze there being no wind, and the ice is just as smooth and clear as the water itself. When I first crossed it, last Wednesday, I could scarcely persuade myself that we were not going right into the water.

And later:

I think in the summer our little island will be almost a little Paradise. There is an abundance of strawberry vines and raspberry bushes growing about and it is said that in summer there are so many flowers as to give quite the appearance of a garden. It is said there is also a great abundance of mosquitoes—I suppose we shall be obliged to imagine this, "Fairy Land," and them, the "Light-winged Fairies"—

Perhaps, with so much said of the imagination we shall not mind them much.

Matters of bracing cold and pesky mosquitoes aside, the Norths were visited by more imposing predators. "Wolves, foxes and lynx are prowling about—have even been on this island—A fox was caught here, a few days since—and a lynx on the lower island—However, we do not feel that we shall be harmed, at all."

Prior to leaving New York, the couple were forced to decide whether to bring John's law library or Ann's grand piano, and John had wisely deferred to his wife's wishes. Ann's was the first piano in St. Anthony, grand or otherwise. In spite of their relative inaccessibility on the island, Ann was planning to give music lessons. But pupils were hard to come by.

There are two schools here—one taught by a gentleman, the other, by one of Gov. Slade's teachers Miss Backus of Conn. She says she intends to have a large Seminary here, yet. She thinks Mr. Bottineau, a Frenchman who owns a good deal of land here, will give enough for that purpose. I now teach her scholars vocal music and she has engaged me already for teacher on the Piano too, when her great school gets into operation. —O' this castle building is a great business in this new country. —I have no music scholars and probably cannot get any this winter, —it is such a long walk…I think if I were [on] the other side of the river, I might have some."

In spring, Ann's hopes were realized: "Tomorrow I am to have one Music scholar—at $10 For 24 lessons—Rebecca Marshall—Mrs. Godfrey spoke to me, a few days since, to teach her daughter, too—"

Helen Godfrey Berry later reminisced about her days as one of Anne North's piano students: "It was not a very safe or easy trip for me to skip over on the logs, but I got to be quite an expert. My piano came later than Mrs. North's, but was the first new piano brought and bargained for to be sent to St. Anthony."[10]

Rebecca Marshall Cathcart, in *A Sheaf of Remembrances*, published in 1915, also recollects her lessons with Ann North and the hazardous passage to the North home on Nicollet Island. "It is very hard to believe that sixty years ago that island had only one house on it, and that one built of logs; it was also heavily wooded, and in its wild state was very beautiful. There was no bridge connecting it with the main land; the crossing had to be made on the pine logs lying in the mill dam above the sawmills. Mrs. North was a fine musician,

and I had taken music lessons from her, and so I had become quite accomplished in making this dangerous passage every day."[11]

Cathcart also provides us with a description of her first sight of St. Anthony Falls: "The thunder of the falling water reached our ears long before we came to the famous cataract; but when at last our eyes saw the great volume of water that rushed over the precipice, the sight surpassed all our expectations. It was superb; no one can realize now anything of the grandeur of the scene as it was then; no wonder that the poor Indian worshipped the Great Spirit of the cataract. But here again man has destroyed for utilitarian purposes what the savage worshipped….the fall of water at this time was grand, the river not being obstructed with logs and the precipice over which the river dashed not having broken away."[12]

The Marshalls were another important pioneer family. Rebecca notes that, while many of the families hailed from the east, and from Bangor, Maine, in particular, her family was of southern lineage, having come north because of their opposition to slavery. They fit in well with the pioneers from New England. "[M]y brothers were also typical pioneers, with plenty of enterprise and endurance," she wrote. The Marshalls were industrious and William Rainey Marshall and his brother opened the first general store in St. Anthony. [13]

Twenty-two-year-old William Rainey Marshall and John North became friends, and a year after the North's arrival, 1849, were both elected to the first territorial legislature. While they were in the legislature, a proposal was presented to establish the territorial capitol in St. Anthony, which both North and Marshall supported. Proponents of the bill characterized St. Paul as a community made up largely of gamblers, thieves, loose women, and other shady characters, whereas St. Anthony was alleged to be populated largely with industrious New Englanders. St. Paul was by far the bigger community at the time, however. It was where the steamboat passengers disembarked. It was, in fact, the hub of the territory. In the end St. Paul got the capitol and Stillwater got the state penitentiary.

Undaunted, North and others convinced territorial Governor Ramsey that St. Anthony should be chosen as the site of the state university, as part of the land-grant university legislation enacted by the U.S. Congress. These efforts were rewarded when St. Anthony was granted the institution of the University of Minnesota by law in 1851. Franklin Steele made a four-acre donation for the project. North wrote the University charter bill and hosted the first teacher, Elijah Merrill. Merrill ran the school as a preparatory school for about 40 students the first year. The seed of the University of Minnesota and the state college system in Minnesota had been planted.

In addition to his early political achievements, William Rainey Marshall also surveyed and platted the village of St. Anthony and named its streets. In 1861 Marshall founded *The Daily Press* newspaper, combining it with the *Minnesotian*. He also enlisted in the 7th Minnesota infantry regiment, served in the Civil and Dakota Wars, and rose to the rank of brigadier-general. He was elected governor of Minnesota in 1865 and 1867.[14]

In October, 1850, the Norths were visited by the well-known Swedish novelist and feminist Fredericka Bremer, who was a guest of Governor and Mrs. Ramsey. Rebecca Marshall Cathcart accompanied Bremer on her visit to the Norths through the mill dam. Rebecca later wrote that "…Miss Bremer was terrified at the prospect, and Governor Ramsey and my brother had to use their best persuasive powers to get her started on the perilous journey. Fortunately the logs nearer the mill were more tightly jammed, and the noted authoress reached the island safely. Mrs. North entertained us with some of the finest selections of music, both vocal and instrumental, and at the conclusion of our visit we returned to the main shore over the same log jam."[15]

Ann North's version of the visit in her October 20 letter to her parents is different;

she says Miss Bremer was afraid to cross the logs and that Mr. North "paddled her over in a canoe." Ann continues, "She showed herself kind and good, as we always imagined her by offering herself to play a Swedish song— 'a tribute to the God of the Rivers,' she said... Some one asked her to sing...when she replied, 'I never sing only to children and to God in the church—the little ones and the Great One are not critical.' Is not that a beautiful idea--such as her writings are filled with—." Ann does also note, though, that Bremer was "...much pleased with our people, finds the mass much more intelligent than she expected—she supposed the majority were quite ignorant."[16]

Bremer herself writes of the visit, "We drank tea on a considerable island in the Mississippi, above the falls, at a beautiful home, where I saw comforts and cultivation, where I heard music, saw books and pictures—such life, in short, as might be met with on the banks of the Hudson; and how charming it was to me! Here, too, I found friends in its inhabitants, even as I had there. The dwelling had not been long on the island; and the island, in its autumnal attire, looked like a little paradise, although still in its half-wild state." Bremer continues, "As to describing how we traveled about, how we walked over the river on broken trunks of trees which were jammed together by the stream in chaotic masses, how we climbed and clambered up and down, among, over, and upon stocks, and stones, and precipices, and sheer descents—all this I shall not attempt to describe, because it is indescribable. I considered many a passage wholly and altogether impracticable, until my conductors, both gentlemen and ladies, convinced me that it was to them a simple and every-day path. Ugh!"[17]

In spite of such noteworthy guests, life on the island proved too difficult and isolating for Ann, and December 1850 found the Norths settled in a house they had built in St. Anthony. Once they'd left, Captain Tapper took over the cabin and it became known as the Tapper House.[18]

The Norths continued to be influential in the growing community of St. Anthony. John North is known as the father of the Republican Party in Minnesota. He and his close friend William Rainey Marshall presided over the organization of the Minnesota Republicans in 1855 in the North's parlor. North had a restless and adventurous spirit and was always seeking new challenges. In 1855 the Norths moved south and founded the city of Northfield, Minnesota. In 1860, North was the chairman of the Minnesota delegation to the Republican Convention in Chicago, where he was proud to be an integral part of the nomination of Abraham Lincoln. North's strong abolitionist views won him favor with the president, and he was appointed first surveyor general of the Nevada territory in 1861 and then in 1862 was appointed to the Nevada Supreme Court by Lincoln himself. Ann, meanwhile, was kept busy by their growing family; the Norths eventually had six children (only one of whom died in infancy). Their travels took them to Nevada, Tennessee, and finally to California, where North founded the city of Riverside in 1870. John and Ann ended their days in California.[19]

MILLS, STEAMBOATS AND BRIDGES

The year 1851 saw a small grist and flour mill built near the sawmills. Three years later, in the spring of 1854, Captain John Rollins, Rufus P. Upton, M. P. Upton, and John W. Eastman leased the east part of Hennepin Island from Franklin Steele and built the Minnesota Mill (later known as the Island Mill) which was capable of grinding wheat, corn, and feed commercially. John Eastman's brother William soon joined the partnership. This was the beginning of the flour milling industry which in the course of time became the largest in the world.

One of the mill partners, Rufus P. Upton, was also involved in the grocery business. He planted a commercial garden on Nicollet Island where he had a home on Grove Place (now Grove Street). Upton had arrived in St. Anthony from Maine in 1850:

The following spring found me on the first steamboat on my way to Davenport, Iowa, where I made an arrangement with a nurseryman for a quantity of fruit and ornamental trees, shrubbery, and flowers, and also purchased a variety of poultry. The nursery was planted and the poultry yard located on the lower part of Nicollet Island, where is now the long stone building of the Island Power Company. They were hauled to the Island from the east side, fording the river. This was the first nursery in the State. The [sic] most of the fruit trees died and the remainder, after a few years, was removed and was the beginning of Ford's Nursery, half way between this city and St. Paul.[20]

In 1850, the *Anthony Wayne* became the first steamboat to reach St. Anthony Falls from St. Paul. St. Paul had always claimed the title of head of navigation, and reasonably so, as the Mississippi River from St. Paul to St. Anthony was littered with detritus left by the falls as it receded upstream over the centuries. But with the successful voyage of the *Anthony Wayne*, Minneapolis and St. Anthony were now open to navigation, and St. Paul's status appeared to be in jeopardy.

The same year construction began on the first steamboat to be launched *above* the falls. The instigator of this effort, which took place on Nicollet Island, was Captain John Rollins. Rollins had come to Minnesota from Maine along with the Norths and Caleb Dorr. He interested Dorr in steamboating and the keel of a steamboat was soon taking shape. Ann North writes, "The steamboat which is being built on this island is nearly ready to launch and will be ready for navigating the Mississippi above here, in May—.[21] The 108-footer, which was named the *Governor Ramsey*, had its maiden voyage on May 25, 1850, running from St. Anthony to Sauk Rapids. It did brisk business for several years, often carrying supplies to Fort Ripley. Rebecca Marshall Cathcart recalls the maiden voyage of the steamboat:

Mrs. North and I were guests on a little steamboat called the Governor Ramsey, on its trial trip up the river; the boat was built above the Falls, to ply on the upper Mississippi, and it was small and of very light draught. We left St. Anthony one morning, the weather being delightful so that we spent all our time on deck under an awning. Captain Rollins, if I am not mistaken, was in charge of the boat; at evening he tied up to the river bank, navigation being so uncertain that the pilot did not dare to proceed during the night. We reached our destination the next day, and, I think, landed at what is now Saint Cloud; at least, it was below Sauk Rapids.

On the return trip several hundred Ojibwe embarked on the steamboat, making their way to Fort Snelling, as the governor had just arranged a treaty between them and the Dakota. The Ojibwe took a particular interest in Rebecca. She writes:

Indians are great admirers of red or curly hair, and my hair, though brown, curled naturally and profusely, and it was so worn according to the fashion of those days. Several of them came to me and lifted my curls in their hands, saying in their native tongue, "Pretty, pretty." It did not make me feel very comfortable, but I knew that they meant no harm, only admiration, and I didn't resent their familiarity. The homeward trip was charming; the little steamboat stood its trial trip satisfactorily; but it did not prove to be profitable afterward, and it was taken to pieces and transferred to the Red River.[22]

Captain Rollins eventually sold his interest in the steamboat and Caleb and his brother Albert Dorr bought a quarter share each.[23]

A few years later, in 1855, Rufus P. Upton undertook to challenge Saint Paul's claim to being the head of navigation on the Mississippi by purchasing 100 tons of iron, steel, nails, and other items from jobbers in Pittsburg, and offering a price for delivery on the bill of lading of 90 cents per unit weight for delivery to St. Paul, and $1 for delivery of the same items to Minneapolis. When the steamship arrived in St. Paul with his order, Upton hastened on board with a $100 check to encourage delivery to Minneapolis. A number of St. Paul residents also came aboard with tales of the danger involved in such a journey—and offering, naturally, to haul the goods overland, as was the common practice. The captain deferred to his pilot, who, convinced by the $100 check, agreed to make the trip the following day. When Upton returned the following day, he discovered the ever-shady citizens of St. Paul had gotten the pilot senselessly drunk. Not to be deterred, he hired a second pilot and his delivery was made upriver at Cheever's Landing below the University of Minnesota without incident. After this success, Upton continued to boost steamboat navigation to St. Anthony and Minneapolis, first by forming a steamboat transportation company, and later as a committee member of the Minneapolis Board of Trade, which sought to improve river navigation.

While Upton and others worked to make St. Anthony grow, Franklin Steele was struggling with chronic capital issues and continually rearranged his partnerships to remain solvent. In 1851, needing to raise $6,000, he obtained a loan from Hercules L. Dousman, a fur trader and Wisconsin's first millionaire, with the mortgage on Nicollet Island as security on the loan. This loan enabled Steele to proceed with his plans to build sawmills. Steele and his partners incorporated his milling interests and formed the St. Anthony Power Company. In 1853, the St. Anthony Power Company and the Minneapolis Mill Company, which controlled the water power on the west bank, built a dam from Nicollet Island to the west bank to increase the flow of water through the east channel mills.

While commerce was developing all around it, Nicollet Island retained much of its bucolic nature. One observer noted that the island rose approximately fifteen feet at its center and was "rounded as if by the hand of art which seems to be waiting for a handsome mansion." Photographs from the 1850s show sugar maples and elm trees on the island. They also show what may be tree planting or selective cutting around the perimeter.[24]

Frank G. O'Brien, a pioneer writer, provides a good description of Nicollet Island in this period. Writing of his first visit to the island, O'Brien describes leaving the progressive St. Anthony's east bank on a feeble wooden bridge and crossing onto Nicollet Island:

At the roadway going over to the West Side was a tall picket fence, with boards nailed lengthwise along its base, to prevent the escape of a few sheep and hogs that Capt. Tapper was pasturing there. Once over the fence—or under, we should say—we gazed upon a most lovely sight. About half way to the present railroad crossing there was quite an elevation, which formed a perfect half circle, extending from one side of the island to the other and sloping to somewhat below what is now the level of the road. From the top of this elevation down to the fence there was not a tree, but it was a beautiful carpet of green, fresh woven from the loom of nature. At its summit there was a little weather-beaten frame dwelling occupied by Mr. Williamson, who had a general supervision of the island, and whose duty it was to see that the timber was not molested. In consideration he received a free rental of the premises.

Back of this house was a forest so dense with timber and undergrowth, that it was impossible to penetrate it. This was the home of rabbits by the hundred and the roosting place for wild pigeons by the thousands. In the summer of 1856 a noble buck was chased off the upper end of the island into the main channel of the river, and killed in midstream by a rifle ball, his lifeless body being carried over the Falls.

There was a single footpath all around the island, and the only fault lovers found was that they were obliged to walk singly—in Indian fashion. Wild grapes and flowers grew in profusion all around the banks of the island, making the surroundings very picturesque.[25]

Nicollet Island was indeed a place for lovers at the time. It inspired Dr. U. D. Thomas to write the following poem for a young lady who was to become his wife and the mother of their three children. Though Thomas's love was no doubt sincere, only the first verse of his six-verse poem is excerpted here. (The remainder of the poem is found in the appendix):

Fanny Ellis, you remember,
That unclouded afternoon,
When the groves of Nicollet Island
Wore the livery of June,
And we walked beneath their shadow

While the light-winged moments sped,
And our thoughts were bright and cloudless
As the bright sky overhead.[26]

Along with attracting lovers, Nicollet Island also attracted those with an interest in regional flora and fauna. In 1861, philosopher and naturalist Henry David Thoreau visited Minnesota. It was a common notion in that day that the gases leaching from the earth in some climates were responsible for a variety of sicknesses, and Minnesota was promoted as a place of optimal health. The cold, in particular, was seen as bracing and healthful. Thoreau came to Minnesota in an attempt to nurse his health, as he was slowly dying of tuberculosis. An inveterate note-taker, he observed that on Nicollet Island he saw a phoebe, a wood pewee coming up the Mississippi, and a hummingbird. But for the most part Thoreau's island observations capture little of the beauty seen by other visitors:

…Crossing the bridge into Nicollet Island, find the Zanthoxylum Americanum *in flower; the* Turritis brachycarpa? *or* stricta? *in bloom, —or perhaps* Arabis laevigata; *the* Hydrophyllum Virginicum, *just begun;* Phlox divaricata *(variety* Laphammi), *showing raceme not sessile, varying from violet to purple and white; early*
flowering Lychnis, *not out.* Cerastium oblongifolium? *or* nutans? Symphoricarpus *very forward.* Anemone, *pistils few, plant smooth and six to twelve inches high, in flower.* Allosorus gracilis? *The puccoon, as in Michigan and Illinois, the showiest flower now.*[27]

The climate that had attracted Thoreau to Minnesota was also believed to foster the virtue of industry, and, as if to prove the assertion, St. Anthony and Minneapolis were growing at a remarkable rate. In 1854, to further commerce, a suspension bridge, the first bridge ever to span the Mississippi River, was built from the west bank to Nicollet Island. One of the men behind the bridge project was Henry Titus Welles. He had come to St. Anthony from Connecticut in 1853, and was soon involved with Franklin Steele in the lumber business, operating seven of the eight sawmills then at St. Anthony.

Welles and his family soon became friends with other prominent families in the area, including the Eastmans. According to Winthrop Eastman, Welles's great grandson, their two families became connected through marriage when Welles's daughter Harriet married Arthur M. Eastman, son of John Eastman. John Eastman built the Cataract Mills and then, according to family lore, grew tired of the flour milling business. He managed an exchange of his milling business for the hardware business of his friend George Pillsbury. In the end the milling business proved a wise investment for Pillsbury.[28]

In 1855, Welles was elected the first mayor of St. Anthony. He later became president of the first town council of Minneapolis, and was also one of the founders of the Farmers' and Mechanics' Bank and Northwestern Bank, of which he was president for many years. (A few years earlier Welles had established Wells, Fargo and Company in New York to provide banking to California following the Gold Rush.)

Along with the lumber business, Welles and Steele also became partners in the Minneapolis Bridge Company. In that capacity they commissioned Thomas M. Griffith, a New York engineer who had apprenticed under the great American bridge builder John Roebling, to build a span across the Mississippi.

When completed, the bridge was described as "...one of the most elegant, tasteful, and substantial works of art in the West," and "well worth

a visit by every person coming to the Territory." A St. Anthony newspaper called it, "the spider-like creation of a fairy of the Falls." It was six hundred and twenty-five feet in length from tower to tower and cost fifty thousand dollars to build. Initially it was a toll bridge, and the man selected to be the toll keeper was, of course, Captain John Tapper. The bridge charged fifteen cents for a horse, ten cents for a cow, and two cents for a sheep; people were charged three cents for a one way trip, or five cents for a round trip. The bridge may have been unsound from the start as

The first bridge ever to span the Mississippi River was built from the west bank across to Nicollet Island. It opened in 1855 to great fanfare.

signs warned of a ten dollar fine for crossing at faster than walking speed. Yet it served to unite St. Anthony, Minneapolis, and Nicollet Island, allowing the communities to more easily socialize and engage in commerce with one another, and to join in common events and celebrations. [29]

The opening of the suspension bridge was celebrated on January 23, 1855, with great fanfare. The festivities began with a mile-long procession followed by a banquet at the St. Charles Hotel in St. Anthony. The *Minnesota Republican* published this report of the events of that frosty day:

At 1 o'clock, a long procession, formed at the Charles House...proceeded, amid the firing of cannon, the flaunting of banners, and strains of martial music from Lawrence's Brass Band, to Nicollet Island, and thence over the new Suspension Bridge. That superb structure was decorated with evergreens for the occasion, some of which were brought from Lake Superior by W. Q. Allen, and reached here the day before. Each of the four towers was surmounted by the "Stars and Stripes," which were also attached in a miniature form, to the heads of the leading horses, and waved in simple folds from the tall flagstaff horse in the procession.

To one standing on the island, shore, or bridge, this was indeed magnificent... The procession was long in passing, and upwards of one hundred different teams were counted, most of which were double.[30]

This opening of the first span across the Mississippi was notable enough to draw coverage even in eastern papers such as the *New York Mirror*, which published this account of the celebration:

The town was wide-awake on our arrival, and preparations making for the first grand, triumphal march of the East into the West. The procession was formed at the St. Charles, and consisted of a very long line of sleighs, (I dare not say how many as I did not count them, and the reports differ so much). One of mammoth size, with horses gaily decked, went forward with a band of music, and bearing aloft our national banner with its "Stripes and Stars," and then such music of sleigh-bells as followed, I am certain never before rose within the hearing of old St. Anthony.

It was with most singular sensations I looked out upon the scene, watching the procession as it passed on over Nicollet Island to the gates of the bridge, which suddenly flew open, allowing it to pass on amid the cheers of the crowds, the thunder of the cannon, the bugle-blasts of the band, and the sullen roar of the frozen cataract,—under the evergreen arches, and over the first highway which has ever linked the Eastern and Western valleys of the Mississippi.

The structure is a very fine one; strikingly harmonious in its proportions, and corresponds beautifully with the character of the surrounding scenery. Literally, it is a highway in the wilderness, over which Civilization, in her onward march, will bear her lighted torches into the evening land of the West.[31]

Such grand events, and the engineering triumphs they celebrated, were not that uncommon during the early decades of the region's history. When Minnesota applied for territorial status in 1848, its population fell somewhat short of the 5,000 individuals required, but it was not long before hundreds, and sometimes thousands, of settlers were arriving in St. Paul by steamboat every day. A single steamboat sometimes carried up to 800 passengers, many of them young men seeking their fortune, and an oft-heard complaint was that there were not enough women for the all the newcomers. This situation favored the ladies, of course, who had no shortage of suitors, and then, as now, Minnesota was considered a good place to find a man. Unlike earlier phases of American immigration, which had consisted largely of settlers from eastern states moving overland a few hundred miles west, the proliferation of rail lines now made it possible for foreigners to reach St. Paul with relative ease, and English, French, Greeks, Germans, Irish, Italians, Swiss, Jews, and the rare freed black arrived in increasing numbers, bringing with them their religion, language, food, and customs.

With increased population came an increase in trade. Contributing to the boom-town atmosphere of St. Anthony and Nicollet Island was the arrival of the Red River ox carts. These ungainly vehicles had been plying several routes between St. Paul and Pembina (and on to the Selkirk Colony near present-day Winnipeg) since the 1820s in long caravans, carrying furs and buffalo hides to exchange for supplies and trade goods useful in the north. One of these trails came down the old river road on the east bank of the Mississippi within sight of Nicollet Island. The carts were often tended by Métis drivers—a colorful people of mixed European and Indian background. The Métis wore a wild variety of dress, the common elements being moccasins and a bright sash at the waist, and spoke a polyglot language as varied as their Indian and European ancestries. The last leg of the trail heading most directly to St. Paul was the Metropolitan Trail, which covered the distance from Sauk Rapids to St. Paul and ran through St. Anthony.

Caleb Dorr described the Métis and the arrival of the Red River carts:

The Red River carts used to come down from Fort Garry loaded with furs. There had been a white population in that part of the country and around Pembina long before there was any settlement in what is now Minnesota. The drivers were half-breeds, sons of the traders and hunters. They always looked more Indian than white. In the early days, in remote places, where a white man lived with the Indians, his safety was assured if he took an Indian woman for his wife. These cart drivers generally wore buckskin clothes, tricked out so as to make them gay. They had regular camping places from twelve to fifteen miles apart, as that was a day's

The Red River carts were operated by the Métis people. They transported furs from northern Minnesota and Canada to trade for goods in St. Anthony, Minneapolis, St. Paul, and Mendota.

journey for these carts.

As there was not much to amuse us, we were always interested to see the carts and their squawking was endured, as it could not be cured. It could be heard three miles away. They came down the Main road, afterwards called the Anoka road.[32]

In addition to ox or horse carts, the Red River drivers used dogsleds. Ann North gives us a description of the dogsleds used in the winter on the Red River Trails, as well as the summer oxcarts, in a letter to her brothers:

...the funniest, most novel thing I have seen lately, was a Red River train that was down last week—This is made of a long, wide, thin piece of wood (not exceeding ½ inch in thickness), split out—with slats fastening across to prevent its splitting—one end is bent up for the front and held in that position by cords passing from the end which is up, down to the main part of the board—This is drawn by three large dogs—hitched on "tandem"—all the harness they have is a perfectly round collar with a strap on each side passing from it back to the train—The collar looks as though it were made with a hoop of just the right size to fit the neck and buckskin sewed around it like a bag, and then stuffed

with hair or something of the kind—They are obliged to lead the dogs, being unable to guide them in any other way—The train is drawn on the top of the snow, the men walk in snowshoes—Whatever load is carried on these trains is lashed on, as there is no box or anything to hold it in its place. The snow shoes are made, Mr. North says, of a bow, in the shape of those in an ox yoke, with a kind of net-work across, and I supposed have straps to pass over the foot. The mail is carried on such trains from Lake Superior down to the Falls of St. Croix, to which point, in summer, steamboats go. I thought perhaps this might interest you as much as anything I could write, and consequently have given you a pretty full account, though, perhaps not in a very interesting way. The daily ration of these dogs is fish (I suppose of moderate size) eaten at night. It is said that as they sleep their legs are almost constantly in motion, as when walking. The trains in which they come down in summer are not much less curious—being clumsy, two wheeled carts, without a particle of iron about them, and drawn by one ox harnessed to them.[33]

The Métis who guided the Red River carts enjoyed fiddle music, song, and dance, and although the caravans were excruciatingly noisy—the all-wooden carts could be heard for many miles as they approached—when they finally arrived it was an occasion for festivities. Settlers sometimes found themselves challenged by the cart drivers. Caleb Dorr was challenged by a Métis to an endurance dance and he accepted: "One of them challenged me to see who could dance the longest. I would not let him win on account of his color, so danced until my teeth rattled and I saw stars. It seemed as if I was dancing in my sleep, but I would not give up and jigged him down." Dorr recalled another instance of intercultural relations involving his wife Celestia:

Mrs. Dorr was never afraid of the Indians, although they seemed very ferocious to her with their painted faces, stolid looks and speechlessness. One day she was frying a pan of doughnuts and had finished about half of them when she glanced up to see seven big braves, hideously painted, standing and watching her with what she thought was a most malevolent look. She was all alone, with nobody even within calling distance. One of the number looked especially ferocious and her terror was increased by seeing him take up a knife and test it, feeling the edge to see if it was sharp, always watching her with the same malevolent look. Quaking with fear, she passed the doughnuts, first to him. He put out his hand to take the whole pan, but she gave him a jab in the stomach with her elbow and passed on to the next. This occasioned great mirth among the rest of the Indians who all exclaimed 'Tonka Squaw' and looked at her admiringly. When they finished they left without trouble.

Along with dance contests and doughnut brinksmanship, Dorr continued the old Indian practice of tapping the maple trees on Nicollet Island: "We used to tap the maple trees in the forest on Nicollet Island. We had to keep guard to see that the Chippewas [Ojibwe] did not steal the sap." [34]

Red River cart festivities were not the only parties that occurred in St. Anthony. Nicollet Island was the site of many celebrations and gatherings during this period. Colonel John Stevens wrote that in 1856, "the first real, live observance of the Fourth of July by the united twin cities [St. Anthony and Minneapolis] took place in a grove on Nicollet Island." No toll was charged on the new bridge that day for the crowds that turned up. [35]

Of the same occasion the pioneer writer Frank G. O'Brien writes:

July 5, 1856, Minneapolis and St. Anthony held their Union celebration, on Nicollet island. On this occasion the United States flag was first publicly unfurled to the breeze in our city, the National holiday having that year come on Sunday. [O'Brien misremembers: the 4th of July was on Friday that year.]

This flag was made by patriotic ladies of St. Anthony, and presented to the Winslow house. The recipients in token of their appreciation of the gift permitted it to be unfurled for the first time at this celebration, which was attended by ten thousand people, gathered for a pleasant holiday and to express their loyalty to the Union.

As the flag gracefully rose to the top of the staff prepared for it, a salute of thirty-two guns, one for each of its stars, was fired by Captain John Tapper.

The banner was soon caught by the welcoming breeze, and as its folds unfurled, deafening cheers went up from the throats of thousands who loved the dear old symbol of our nation's freedom.

Many who on this day raised their voices in wild enthusiasm for the flag, were ere long, to fight bravely under its folds for the preservation of an undivided Union.

I wonder how many of these ten thousand are living on this official flag day of 1891, to recall with my own pride and enthusiasm, our first flag raising in Minneapolis.[36]

Harlow A. Gale, a pioneer land developer, wrote about another Fourth of July celebration that occurred in 1858:

Great preparations are being made on Nicollet Island. Tables for five thousand, dozen of oxen, tons of cakes and pies, folios of July 4th speeches, American Eagle served up in thirty-two different styles, —hot, cold, living, dead, with feathers, and without, flying and sitting on a tree, the spread-eagle and the calm, domestic bird. Some dust and a great amount of perspiration...At least 9,000 people, half women, gathered on the Island. They came from the towns and the country. All sorts of teams and all sorts of dress, from every nation, too,—Irish, Dutch, Swedes, Norwegians, and so on to Liberia. Music, guns, sports and routes. The free dinner was about half enough for the women. 'Twas the largest assembly of the masses that has ever occurred in Minnesota.[37]

Frank G. O'Brien also wrote about the Fourth of July celebration on Nicollet Island two years later—the first to be celebrated after

Minnesota became a state on May 11, 1858. O'Brien wrote that this Fourth was actually celebrated on July fifth, since the Fourth was a Sunday. Invitations were sent to the citizens of St. Paul and nearby areas by the organizers in Minneapolis and St. Anthony. The celebration was free and the turnout was impressive:

The streets were full of teams [he wrote], and Nicollet Island, where the celebration was held, was literally swarming with people, brimful of enthusiasm, but with empty stomachs, and ready to fill up on "roast ox" and other substantials, with hot coffee, and lemonade that was furnished by the barrel.

There were five tables, each 200 feet long; seats were constructed of planks to accommodate 3,500, and arranged in a semicircle about the speakers' stand. This shows on what a gigantic scale the committee had planned the work. Swings were suspended from trees in different parts of the island for the entertainment of the young people; in fact, every detail that would add to the comfort and pleasure of the occasion had received careful attention. The grounds were beautifully decorated, not alone by Nature, for man had added his artistic touch in the display of banners of great variety, color and shape, with mottoes appropriate to this time-honored, festal day. A level piece of ground, fifty feet square, was selected and floored for the use of such as wished to join in the cotillion, and of these there were many.

At eleven o'clock, at a given signal, Minneapolis citizens, including secret and other societies, formed in grand procession in the open space opposite the Nicollet House on the west side of the river, and marched across the bridge to the grounds near the Winslow house, now the site of the Exposition building, there to meet a similar procession arranged by the citizens of St. Anthony, and made up of civilians, the Union, Benevolent and Turners' Societies, each numbering 150, and bands of music with the respective delegations. There were at least one thousand in each procession, which, added to those already gathered on the island, formed a total of nearly ten thousand, and it was estimated that no less than twelve thousand visited the grounds during the day. At this moment a salute of thirty-two guns, one for each state, was fired from the cannon on the island.[38]

As St. Anthony and Minneapolis developed, there was a spiritual growth as well, as is shown in the construction of churches.

Nicollet Island as seen from an upper story of the Winslow House, c. 1857.

On the east bank of the Mississippi, a stone's throw from Nicollet Island, between 1854 and 1857, the First Universalist Society of St. Anthony constructed a church built with limestone quarried on the island. In 1877 a group of Catholic French Canadians purchased the church and renamed it Our Lady of Lourdes in honor of the Blessed Virgin Mary whom Catholics believed had recently appeared to Bernadette Soubirous in Lourdes, France. Worshippers still attend Our Lady of Lourdes—it's the longest continuously used church in Minneapolis. Less structured revival-style religious gatherings also took place during this era, some of them on Nicollet Island. Pioneers were often devoutly religious people and the natural beauty of Nicollet Island attracted them. In a letter, Harlow Gale described one such gathering:

At six this evening several of us went over to Nicollet Island. An ex-F.W. [Free Will]

Baptist named Ames, a man of excellent heart, great purity of life and honesty of purpose, rather liberal in his religion, preached. This is the second time. A beautiful spot on the east side of the Island and sloping down to the water's edge. A fresh, green turf and scattering oaks; nearly fifteen hundred people present, orderly and attentive. The orthodox clergy refused to read notice of the meeting for which I blame them. Seats only for ladies. I should think there were 300 of them on the seats, besides many sitting in carriages around. I enclose somewhat mutilated copy of two hymns that were distributed through the crowd and sung with good effect; that last one, —isn't it fine? And sung at such a time, in such a place, the rich, mellow light of our sunset glowing through the trees, the up-turned faces of those hundreds of men and women, the freshness of the vegetation and foliage, the hushed quiet of the winds and water sweeping along the shore and only the murmur of the falls below us heard between the verses.[39]

NICOLLET ISLAND AS STATE CAPITOL?

In 1857, the growing prominence of St. Anthony and its twin city Minneapolis placed them in the center of a political conflict regarding the location of the state capitol. The territorial governor at that time, Willis Gorman, was from St. Peter, a town seventy miles south of St. Paul in the Minnesota River Valley. A scheme was floated by some of his supporters to move the capitol from St. Paul to St. Peter. Gorman and other southern Minnesota legislators would have benefited financially from the move as they held stock in the St. Peter Company, which had, in part, built the town. Gorman and his associates also favored setting the as-yet undetermined boundaries of the future state to accentuate its east-west dimension. If Minnesota's northern boundary were established near St. Cloud and the western boundary placed along the Missouri River, as some legislators proposed, St. Peter would be sure to become a powerful railroad hub and a natural site for the capitol, while St. Paul (and Democratic interests) would become marginalized.[40]

The reaction to this effort in St. Paul was predictable and is illustrated by an account in the *Weekly Minnesotian*:

A very amusing proposition is before the grave body now in session at the Capitol. It is no more or less than the immediate removal of the Capitol from St. Paul to St. Peter! So many practical jokes have been perpetrated by this comical body at the

*expense of the people, that this extrava-
gant project for the amusement of their
constituents has failed to excite the laugh-
ter which is due to the intrinsic ridiculous-
ness of the burlesque.*

As a compromise between the factions,
St. Paul Representative W.P. Murray advocated
substituting "Nicollet Island" for "St. Peter"
in the bill, but the proposal failed by one vote.
Two of the legislators who represented the
area, Joel B. Bassett, a mill owner, and J.P.
Plumer, had voted against the proposal, and
they were taken to task by some of the citizens of St. Anthony, who regarded the Nicollet Island plan as a boon. Two well-attended
town meetings were held in St. Anthony to
discuss the issue, and following the general
clamor and chastisement of the first, at the second meeting Bassett was allowed to explain his
vote. Calm was restored as newspaper writers
expressed the belief that the Nicollet Island
proposal had been a ruse by St. Paul interests
to kill the capitol move altogether and that the
governor would not have signed such a bill in
any case. The writers felt that St. Anthony and
Minneapolis were better served by the future of
water power than by politics, and not getting
the capitol would not deter their growth.

As the Nicollet Island proposal faded from
view, the original St. Peter proposal resurfaced.

Representative Murray took offense at a
remark of Representative King of Winona,
called him a liar, and threatened to knock him
down. Ruffians broke into the house of a man
named N.K. Wright in St. Peter who refused
to sell his land to the St. Peter Company, stole
his furniture and threatened to hang him. He
escaped by horse-drawn sleigh and hid in
the woods, while one of his companions was
clubbed by the mob. The vote for the move
proceeded, and the bill was passed by one
vote. Not to be thwarted, a member of the
St. Paul faction, "Jolly Joe" Rolette, disappeared with the bill itself.

Rolette represented the Pembina region
on the Red River. He was a flamboyant,
humorous, and high-spirited character who
cultivated his colorful reputation as an expert
Red River trailsman. He was mostly French
and British in heritage, with only a great-
great-great Ottawa grandmother to provide
him with some Indian blood, but neverthe-
less he sometimes dressed in the Métis fashion
and sang Ojibwe songs and danced Ojibwe
dances.[41]

Councilor Rolette hid the capitol bill in
a bank and then hid himself for five days in
various hotel rooms. The sergeant at arms
who was dispatched to find him was a St. Paul
sympathizer, and he played cards with Rolette
night after night while reporting that the man

could not be found. Five days later Rolette reappeared at the capitol just as the session was ending. The bill was now useless. Rolette was fêted in St. Paul and given a torchlight parade of triumph through the city. St. Paul residents took up a collection and raised the enormous sum of $2,500 for him, most of which he spent celebrating his skullduggery. Investors in the St. Peter Company had been outmaneuvered, to their chagrin, and the proponents of moving the capitol to St. Anthony or Minneapolis were also disappointed, though the bill would probably not have gone into effect even if it has been signed by the governor: the court later ruled that when the legislature had chosen St. Paul to be the capitol, it had exhausted its mandate with regard to that issue.[42]

With or without a capitol, the cities of St. Anthony and Minneapolis continued to flourish, and between them stood the gem of Nicollet Island. A book called *Minneapolis and St. Anthony Falls,* published in 1857, describes the scene:

St. Anthony is an incorporated city, and next to St. Paul, is the largest and most important place in the Territory. St. Anthony and Minneapolis together contain six thousand inhabitants. By an act of the last Legislature, St. Anthony was annexed to Hennepin county, the county-seat being located at Minneapolis.

This place—we speak of two as one, inasmuch as they are naturally connected together as well as artificially, and the remarks applicable to one, will equally apply to the other—will strike the stranger at once as being the most magnificent water-power in the north-west. Indeed, there cannot be a question, but that at this point must be the greatest manufacturing city north of Chicago and St. Louis.

There are now running at the Falls—between the eastern shore and Hennepin island—eight upright, and one gang saw, and a shingle and lath machine. About half a mile above are two steam saw-mills, and on the west side of the river one mill, and two others contracted for, to be erected the present season. There are at the Falls two flouring mills, one of four, and one of two run of stone, a large machine shop, and other machinery of various kinds. Above 40,000,000 feet of lumber will be sawed at the Falls of St. Anthony during the year 1857.

Several large and capacious stores are well stocked with every variety of merchandise which can be required by the immigrant. A large stone hotel is being erected on the bluff opposite the mills, eighty feet by one hundred and fifty, five stories high, which, when completed, will be one of the most elegant and commodious structures north-west of Chicago. Five churches have been erected in St. Anthony, and another will probably be built the present season.[43]

The large stone hotel under construction was the Winslow House. Five stories high with a distinctive cupola, it was one of the most imposing and tallest buildings of the day. But a rival appeared in 1858 on the other side of the river. The Nicollet House hotel was also five stories high; it was built of cream-colored brick above a limestone base and it also featured a cupola. The Nicollet House had storefront rental space, a saloon, billiard hall, and Brussels carpets, lace curtains, and tapestries. Both hotels competed for the patronage of Southerners who sought to escape the summer heat of New Orleans and other southern towns, with its attendant malaria and cholera. At the time the belief was widespread among Southerners that miasma, a kind of bad air from swamps, caused the illnesses that were prevalent in southern climates, and they came upriver on steamboats to enjoy the less humid air, the sights, and the artesian mineral water. In point of fact the artesian water sold in

St. Anthony came from a swamp, but the sights were good nonetheless.

Tensions between the North and South had been growing for years throughout the nation, and it sometimes emerged even during such holidays. In 1860, Eliza Winston, a thirty-year-old slave, was visiting St. Anthony with her owners, Colonel Richard and Mary Christmas of Mississippi. Eliza came with them to care for their five-year-old daughter, Norma, and for Mrs. Christmas, who was in poor health. Winston was staying with her owners at the Winslow House when she attempted to gain her freedom with the help of free blacks Ralph and Emily Grey. The Greys had moved to St. Anthony in 1855, were friends of Frederick Douglas and known for helping slaves obtain their freedom.

Judge Charles Vandenburgh presided at the court hearing, which was a scene of much contention, with both pro-slavery and abolitionist factions present. Eliza had this to say in her court deposition: "It was my own free choice and purpose to obtain my freedom, and I applied to my colored friend in St. Anthony, without solicitation on the part of any other person. I have nursed and taken care of the child of my mistress from her birth till the present, and am so attached to the child that I would be willing to serve Col. Christmas, if I could be assured of my freedom, eventually, but with all my attachment to the child, I prefer freedom in Minnesota, to life long slavery in Mississippi."[44] The court ruling established Winston's right to freedom in a free state and the abolitionist faction was jubilant. According to one account, Colonel King, a resident of Nicollet Island, "…paced the hall, brandishing a huge cane and denouncing in unmeasured terms all who aided or abetted in holding a slave in Minnesota."[45] That night citizens stood guard over Colonel William S. King's *Atlas* newspaper office, anticipating violence from the pro-slavery faction. Instead, the pro-slavery crowd surrounded the Greys' home and demanded Eliza's return to the Christmases, but with the aid of the Underground Railroad she was already on her way to Canada.

Eliza Winston returned voluntarily to the Christmases in Mississippi before the outbreak of the Civil War. The Saint Anthony *Weekly Express* wrote that the incident with Eliza and the Christmases would damage the tourist trade, and in fact the Winslow House was forced to close when it lost its Southern tourists with the outbreak of the Civil War. It reopened later as a hospital but never regained its former glory. The Nicollet House was able to weather the war years and continued as a hotel until 1923.

In 1861, in one of Franklin Steele's frequent financial difficulties, he defaulted on his $6,000 loan to Hercules L. Dousman, giving Dousman claim to Nicollet Island, which in spite of pioneer use remained in large part pristine. An observer of the day noted that the island had "a commanding elevation above high water mark" and was formed "of rock or massive layers of stone, all being covered to the depth of three or four feet with a rich and luxuriant soil. A magnificent grove of native trees surmounts all, giving to the whole island an appearance of unsurpassed beauty. Situated as it is on the river, immediately between the cities of St. Anthony and Minneapolis, with convenient access by means of the very best bridges, the population of both places and the surrounding country look upon it as one of the most refreshing and delightful places of resort in the warm season that can be found in America. This 'gem of an island' as it is so often appropriately termed, has an extent of about forty acres. The native forest upon it is carefully preserved with its original attractions."[46] Dousman did little with the property during the turbulent years of the Civil War, which broke out in 1860 and touched distant Nicollet Island.

Territorial Governor Ramsey was in Washington D.C. when the war broke out and he was the first to offer soldiers to President

Upon the outbreak of the Civil War, the First Minnesota Regiment was mustered and trained at Fort Snelling. They were given a grand sendoff on Nicollet Island by the ladies of St. Anthony and Minneapolis, before being sent to the battlefields of the Civil War.

Lincoln—1,000 soldiers from a territory that had a population of about 172,000. The First Minnesota Regiment was soon in training at Fort Snelling. Former Territorial Governor Willis A. Gorman, a veteran of the Mexican War and a disciplinarian, was named Colonel in the regiment. On May 21, the regiment marched to Nicollet Island where the ladies of St. Anthony and Minneapolis held a banquet for the men. One of the soldiers related his experience to the *Faribault Central Republican* newspaper:

We had dinner in the grove on Nicollet Island, a beautiful place for such purposes. The ladies and gents who had the affair in charge deserve great praise for the manner in which they discharged their duties.

—The tables were supplied with plenty to have fed two regiments, and the materials were all the choicest kind: sandwiches, bread—as white as the fair hands that made it—and butter as delicious as the lips of the ladies who passed it around; but why particularize when everything was excellent—sweet milk and beer as drinkables. So much beer was furnished that after we had drank all we wished there were sixty kegs untapped.

Before partaking of the dinner our Colonel gave the command to 'uncover,' and a benediction was invoked by a venerable clergyman of Minneapolis. Owing to the distance between us I did not hear a word he said. After dinner Col. Gorman, in [sic] behalf of the Regiment, returned thanks to the citizens and committee in his usual happy style. It was responded to by Col. Aldrich of Minneapolis. After complimenting the officers and men, he said, 'Success would surely attend our arms. —We were engaged in a glorious and holy cause—the cause of freedom and humanity.'

Three hearty cheers were given by our soldier boys for the ladies of St. Anthony and Minneapolis, which was sent back with a will by the citizens, including the ladies, the waving of whose scented pocket handkerchiefs seemed to load the air with perfume.

I think it was the happiest thing in the shape of a picnic that I ever attended. The day was fine; the ladies beautiful; the soldiers performed their evolutions gracefully, and everything passed off to the satisfaction of all concerned.[47]

Two months later these soldiers were blooded at the First Battle of Bull Run, where they performed well, facing off against General Stonewall Jackson's men. Colonel Gorman reported that the First Minnesota had lost forty-nine men in the battle, had another 107 wounded, and reported 34 as missing. Under repeated orders to withdraw, they retired reluctantly from the field and held a rearguard position. The First Minnesota had suffered the highest proportional loss of any Union regiment that day.

Other campaigns followed, and the soldiers who entered the field at Gettysburg on July 2, 1863, were seasoned veterans. The First Minnesota acquitted itself well that day. Positioned on Cemetery Ridge, it repelled a Confederate brigade's breach in the line which threatened to engulf the Union Army. The First Minnesota then charged and valiantly sacrificed itself to repel the enemy. Of the 262 men who charged, 215 became casualties, including the regimental commander, Col. William Colvill, and all but three of his officers. The unit's colors fell five times and rose again each time. The 82 percent casualty rate stands to this day as the largest loss by any American regiment in a single engagement in United States history.

Despite the horrendous casualties the First Minnesota had incurred, it continued the fight the next day, helping to repulse Pickett's Charge. The surviving Minnesotans just happened to have been positioned at one of the few places where Union lines were breached during that engagement, and, as a result, charged the advancing Confederate positions one last time as a unit. The actions of the men of the First Minnesota saved the Union Army and changed the tide of the Battle of Gettysburg and the prospects of the survival of the Union itself. The remains of the unit's colors are now on display in the Minnesota State Capitol's rotunda.

Some of the soldiers who fought in the Civil War later took up residence on Nicollet Island. George Brookins built the house at 163 Nicollet Street in 1873, but prior to that lived in Silver Creek Township where he farmed and worked as a surveyor. In 1861, he and some of his neighbors organized a volunteer regiment they called the Silver Creek Rifles, with Brookins serving as a 2nd Lieutenant.

The services of the volunteer regiment were turned down by the government so Brookins enlisted in the Third Minnesota Regiment. The Third Minnesota was captured at Murfreesboro by the Confederate General Nathan Bedford Forrest. They were held as prisoners and released after a few months. They were then called back to Minnesota in 1862 to put down the Dakota Uprising.

As settlers arrived and Minnesota grew, the government had negotiated a succession of treaties with the Dakota Indians, offering equipment and annuities in exchange for land-rights and confining the tribes to ever-decreasing swaths of territory. But as settlers arrived tensions inevitably grew, and they were exacerbated by the dilatory payment of the promised annuities. In 1862, having become dependent on the government and its agents and unable to continue their traditional way of life, with annuities delayed and government Indian agents refusing to make food advances, the Dakota under Little Crow revolted and killed hundreds of settlers. Governor Ramsey sent for 200 mounted volunteers under the command of General Sibley to Ft. Ridgley, a few miles northwest of New Ulm, to defend the frontier settlers. General Sibley had been empowered by Governor Ramsey to deal with the uprising, though the two were political

In 1862, the Dakota lead by chief Little Crow rose up and killed several hundred settlers before being subdued and driven into Dakota Territory by General Sibley's forces.

I had no pull with the sheriff, or anyone. Had just got in from harvesting. Had got an old gun and horse pistols from the arsenal. For a horse the best I could get was a poor old one I took…So I started, galloping bareback down Ft. Snelling Road to Colonel Girard Hewitt's house, about two miles out from St. Paul. He was one of the company, and got me a bridle, and then, or soon after, a saddle. Then, before we had galloped a good part of the way to Shakopee, had got blanket and spurs and fairly well equipped, but a raw and very sore back. (Meaning the horse) but was getting along fast on the road…We rode with all possible speed on our way to the rescue, and got to Fort Ridgley about one hundred miles from St. Paul the second night out, and reported to Gen. Sibley who had arrived to command. We were then known as Capt. Joe Anderson's militia.[48]

rivals, because Ramsey knew that Sibley had dealt with the Dakota and Ojibwe for thirty years as a fur trader and as the first governor of the state. He was respected by the Indians and knew their character well.

A recent Yale law school graduate, a young twenty-four-year-old by the name of Franklin C. Griswold was in St. Paul when the call went out. From Griswold's letter to his family he relates his tale:

With a company of infantry, Griswold's unit was ordered to relieve the frontier and bury the dead. The first day they found and buried over eighty-five settlers, many of them scalped and mutilated. Expecting to return to Camp Ridgely in the morning, the exhausted men made camp for the night in the open. A Dakota war party, on the way to attack

St. Peter and Mankato, ambushed the men instead, attacking from a wooded ravine known as the Birch Coulee.

Joe Bruin, an old Indian and interpreter of St. Paul, told us to go to sleep. We were tired out, and slept as sound as if we had been at home, and thought the Indians had gone west, as appeared from what we had seen out the day before. (Did Joe pick that camping place?) But just before daylight, while yet dark, we were startled, utterly surprised by that never-to-be-forgotten war whoop. The sentries we had outside came running in, firing and yelling 'Indians…' Our Capt. Anderson yelling 'Everyone out and down on your bellies and shoot.' The Indians were then close by rushing for us. Robt. Baxter sleeping in one tent was shot dead raising up to get his pistol. I slept with Thomas Baxter that night. He was seriously injured the first hour of the battle. Bullets whistled thick all about us. The tent was riddled to pieces…most of the killed and wounded in the first charge, so were all but two of the eighty-seven horses, that broke loose and ran away. Horse or man couldn't stand up long before such a rain of bullets, but our quick and desperate fight had—thank God—hurled the Indians back from their charge, and caused them

Franklin C. Griswold was a lawyer and Dakota War soldier. He raised most of his fifteen children on Nicollet Island and was a builder and landlord of many of the houses there.

to retreat to the shelter of a deep ravine, but within constant firing distance.

Most of the soldiers were killed in the battle's first hour. The soldiers hid behind dead horses and their wagons. They dug into the earth with bayonets and tin plates because they could not stand to dig with spades. About 500 braves besieged the little group, now some 60 able-bodied men. Griswold remembered, "The feverish, dying, wounded and suffering crying 'Oh give me water' was the hardest to bear. We were glad to have dishwater left from the night before and water in our canteens, which we used for the suffering. I used most in my canteen for those shrieking out near me. We were here seeing that war is indeed Hell." The soldiers were encouraged by the appearance of Colonel McPhail and 240 men with two six-pound guns who appeared near sundown of the first day, but Colonel McPhail did not deem his force sufficient to break the siege: "Small matter that we could get nothing to eat or drink for nearly forty-eight hours except bits of raw cabbage and dishwater. But it tasted fine. The Indians had us all in except our courage. They thought too much of their own lives to take too much risk in attacking again but kept threatening, keeping us in a continual agony of suspense." An Indian approached the group with a white flag to parley. The Indians offered safe surrender to the "half-breeds" amongst them. The "half-breeds" declined passage and the siege continued and was finally broken only when General Sibley's forces advanced into the area. General Sibley's forces routed the 2,000 or so braves under Little Crow, eventually driving them north to Canada or beyond the Missouri River into the Dakota Territory.

Following the uprising 307 Indians were sentenced to death. Minnesota's first Episcopal bishop, Henry Whipple, a man known for his missionary work with the Ojibwe and Dakota, intervened. Known by the Dakota as Straight Tongue, he published an open letter to President Lincoln detailing the injustices in the system of Indian governance. Whipple personally met with Lincoln and explained the circumstances of the uprising and the suffering of the Dakota. President Lincoln said, "He came here the other day and talked with me about the rascality of this Indian business until I felt it down to my boots." President Lincoln eventually pardoned all but thirty-eight offenders, who were hanged in Mankato. It was the largest mass execution ever to take place in the United States. A hundred and twenty Dakota had died in prison and 350 died in the winter of 1862 at Fort Snelling. The Dakota way of life in Minnesota had ended.[49]

After the uprising Brookins returned with the Third Minnesota to the Civil War and fought in the Vicksburg campaign under General Grant. After the war he returned to Silver Creek and married Zilpha Atwood. They moved to Nicollet Island and had three children. Their house still stands at 163 Nicollet Street.[50]

Griswold eventually attained the rank of 1st Lieutenant and received a command over a detachment of cavalry whose mission was to defend the city of Princeton against any possible uprising of the Ojibwe. The Ojibwe for their part had sat out the war against their traditional enemies, and some had aided the white settlers. Griswold married while still in service and eventually mustered out as a 1st Lieutenant on December 4, 1865. He set up a farm near Minnehaha and Lake Streets and practiced law, specializing in soldier's pensions. His wife, Sarah Elizabeth Putnam, was a widow with a daughter, Annette Dimmick. Together they had four boys, Edwin Franklin, Charles Clinton, Frank Putnam, who died at age three, and William Putnam, who became a great opera singer. Eventually Franklin Griswold obtained a divorce on grounds of cruelty. He later remarried, had many more children, and built several exceptional houses on Nicollet Island which still exist.

In 1865, Hercules Dousman sold Nicollet Island to William W. Eastman of Minneapolis (whom we have already met) and John L. Merriam of St. Paul for $24,000. By this time Eastman had earned a fortune as a lumberman and miller; Merriam was a banker and stagecoach operator. With the end of the Civil War and the sale of Nicollet Island, minds turned from warfare to rebuilding and the era entered what came to be known as the Gilded Age.

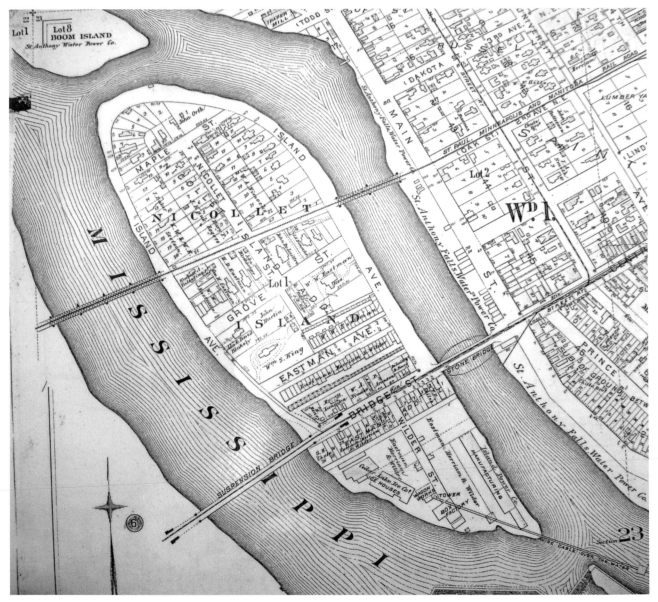

This 1885 map of Nicollet Island shows the St. Anthony Power Company having control over Boom Island and the east bank. On the northern tip of the island itself is a residential neighborhood and a shaft to beer caves marked John Orth. In the central section are several homes owned by prominent families such as the DeLaittres, Kings, and Eastmans. The Eastman and Grove Street Flats are also depicted. South of the businesses straddling Bridge Street are industrial buildings including the Cedar Lake Ice Company Ice Houses and the Island Power Company Building, which got its power through a cable over to Hennepin Island via the interchannel tower (also depicted).

3

The Gilded Age

If the Island satisfied the social and artistic cravings of our parents,
what did it mean to us children? There was no limit to our joys.

Hercules Dousman's sale of Nicollet Island in 1865 to William W. Eastman and John L. Merriam resulted in an offer by the new owners to sell the part of the island north of the suspension bridge. Some sources say that this offer became part of an 1866 proposal to unite the cities of St. Anthony and Minneapolis; other sources say it was a standalone proposal for Nicollet Island to become a park. A citizens' committee debated the merits of using Nicollet Island as a park, and the issue of relocating the state capitol there resurfaced. The northern portion of the island could have been purchased for $47,500, less $8,000 to be paid by the railroad company for crossing rights. Those who stood to gain financially from the deal were in favor of the proposal and so were many local politicians, but most businessmen were against it.

On March 19, 1866 a referendum was held in Minneapolis regarding the annexation of St. Anthony and the acquisition of Nicollet Island. The referendum failed by 85 votes (accounts of the final tally differ) and the residents of St. Anthony never got the chance to vote, as both cities had to approve the proposal for it to be valid.[1]

There was, however, more to the story of *why* the referendum failed, according to Charles M. Loring. Loring was one of the great patriarchs of Minneapolis, an early resident of Nicollet Island, and widely considered to be the Father of the Minneapolis park system. At the end of his long and productive life, Loring recounted in an interview:

And now I'll tell you a bit of history that has not yet been written. Nicollet Island would be a park today if George Brackett had not bet John H. Thompson $100 that a project then before the city to establish *the island as a park would carry hand-somely. Seeing an easy $100, Thompson, as a result of the bet, electioneered so forcefully that the referendum was lost by 83 votes and Nicollet Island never became city property. It has been one of my life-long regrets.*[2]

This may have been one of Brackett's few miscalculations. George Brackett was one of Minneapolis's most prominent citizens, had interests in business and railroad construction, and held municipal offices including fire chief, alderman, member of the Park Board, and eventually mayor. Brackett was also illustrative of the competition between St. Anthony and upstart Minneapolis. Loring recalls:

There was a tall, muscular young fellow who seemed a favorite with everyone, whom they called Brackett. There was a great jealousy between the citizens of St. Anthony and the "upstart village" on the West Side, and occasionally when some of the "East Siders" celebrated, a number would come over the bridge with the avowed intention of "cleaning out" the Minneapolitans. Bridge Square was an open field on which there was many a skirmish between the warriors of the two villages. George Brackett, his brother, and

William W. Eastman was a lumberman, miller, and real estate developer. He and his business partner, John L. Merriam, purchased Nicollet Island in 1865. Eastman built a mansion on the island and encouraged family members to live there.

two Goff boys defended the honor of the younger city, and it was said that they were always victorious. George Brackett from that day to this has been fighting for Minneapolis, and as chief of the fire department, alderman, mayor, and all around progressive citizen has won every battle.[3]

With the failure of the park proposal, the island that had been surveyed by Franklin Cook in October of 1865 was registered in April of 1866 with a nine-block layout and residential area north of Bridge Street, where Hennepin Avenue is now.[4] As Eastman and Merriam turned their eyes toward developing a residential portion of Nicollet Island, they worked out a deal with the Minneapolis Bridge Company so that all residents of Nicollet Island would have free passage over the suspension bridge. Any residents traveling "on foot or on horseback, in buggy, cutter or other pleasure carriage" would not have to pay the bridge toll. This free pass did not include any vehicle used for transporting multiple passengers, building materials, or merchandise. This arrangement with the Minneapolis Bridge Company was part of Eastman and Merriam's attempt to encourage people to settle on Nicollet Island.[5]

It was around this time that the Nesmith Cave incident occurred. This incident involved the "discovery" of evidence of an advanced civilization in a cave connected to a tunnel in St. Anthony, just downriver from Nicollet Island. Mr. Nesmith was one of the party of explorers of this cave and the "evidence" included a spiral staircase, which was discovered under a trapdoor. The staircase led to a tunnel and then a series of successive vaults filled with hieroglyphics, a stone sarcophagus with a human skeleton inside, iron and copper implements, a sacrificial altar, and a colossal human figure. The "discovery" was

John L. Merriam was a banker and stagecoach operator who purchased Nicollet Island with his business partner William W. Eastman. Merriam and Eastman joined in several business endeavors to include the ill-fated Eastman Tunnel project.

covered in the *New York Herald* on December 10, 1866, and was carried by and eventually revealed to be a hoax by several local papers.

The tunnel referred to in the story was real, however, and came to be known as Chute's Tunnel. It became part of a tourist attraction in the 1870s run by Mannasseh Pettengill.

Mannasseh Pettengill leased the St. Anthony Chalybeate Springs near the present-day east bank by the Stone Arch Bridge. The resort he ran there included an observation tower, hotel, photographic gallery, and bath. For ten cents, visitors could take a torchlit boat ride into Chute's Tunnel, which went under St. Anthony Main Street for some 2,000 feet.[6]

While the Nesmith cave hoax garnered national attention, the *Minneapolis Chronicle* newspaper was not to be outdone. It reported the discovery of a mysterious underground six-cubic-foot vault found by railroad excavators on Nicollet Island eighteen days after the report of the Nesmith cave story in the *New York Herald*. Of the Nicollet Island discovery, the story related that on the walls of the vault were "hierogliphics [sic] signifying a knowledge of Hebrue [sic], Arabic, German, and French languages."[7] The hieroglyphics were examined by an educated Frenchman who determined that they depicted a winged race of men of high intellect who were now extinct. Of further intrigue was a door in the vault made of a curious material: "Some say that the bands are platinum. There are nine

bolts, with large heads, each of different color. In the night time they are as brilliant as the stars. The one nearest the lock appears to be a diamond." After much experimentation a secret word was finally uttered, the door opened and a passageway was revealed. Three individuals entered the vault to behold a brilliant light, then the door closed behind them and the light extinguished. The secret word was uttered again and the light relit. To the party's wonder they found a vaulted chamber and "a statue resembling an angel with its two fingers on the right hand of its mouth—this we understood to mean silence…Beautiful lettering and drafting were made upon the walls, representing nine departments." The departments were interpreted as Language, Mathematics, Geometry, Music, Astronomy, Botany, Zoology, Intelligences, and Spirit Land:

In front of each of these departments was a statue of [a] beautiful figure about five feet high, angel in form situated as if viewing the field before it. The floor of the hall was something like crystal. The canopy was so bright that our eyes could not view it.

The different disciplines were analyzed and the men, morally uplifted, exited the way they came, back through the door which opened and closed behind them silently. The party of adventurers found that they had been gone for nine hours.

This hoax, dubbed Apollo's Cave after the signatory of the first day's newspaper article, continued in the newspaper for four days. Though sought after by this book's authors, the cave has yet to be found again.

THE RECOLLECTIONS OF MARGARET CALLADINE

Somewhat more reliable than the "discovery" of an advanced race of flying men was Mrs. Margaret Calladine's claim that the first lot on Nicollet Island was bought by her and her husband George. Born in Hertfordshire, England, in 1827, George Calladine entered the army at age twenty-two and served as a saddler for three years in the Eleventh Hussars. (The Eleventh Hussars later participated in the Charge of the Light Brigade during the Crimean War and were immortalized in the poem by Alfred, Lord Tennyson.) In 1852, according to his wife, Calladine then went to Australia and prospected gold. In 1856 he came to Minnesota out of curiosity, met Caroline Howser, and on December 25, 1860, the couple was married. Upon the outbreak of the Civil War he sold his livestock and raised a company and fought with them as their 1st Lieutenant. He served for three years in the Civil War, fought in several engagements, and

became a provost marshal for General Burnside during the Tennessee campaign. In 1865 Calladine served on the honor guard of Abraham Lincoln's funeral bier in Chicago. His hat, insignia, and jacket remain in the Minnesota Historical Society collection.[8]

During the Civil War Calladine served in the same regiment with his second wife Margaret's father, and after the war went into business with him in Chicago. George and Margaret were married on June 7, 1866, in St. Paul's Church, St. Paul, two months to the day after he had obtained a divorce from his first wife, Caroline. Margaret was born in Montreal and had lived in New York and Chicago prior to her marriage. In an interview for the *Minneapolis Journal* in July 1927, Calladine said, "After living in New York and even in Chicago, Nicollet Island seemed awfully countrified to me...I couldn't get used to it a first. But it was so pretty and green and nice that I soon learned to love it..."

George was in the harness manufacturing business. He and Margaret raised their children Caroline and Margaret in the house they built on East Island Avenue near where the railroad tracks now cross the island. "We thought we were buying a corner lot and it turned out to be right on the railroad track. But I always did like to see the trains go by... There was a wood train and a passenger going

Above is an 1866 etching of Minneapolis, Nicollet Island, and St. Anthony. The character of the two lumber milling cities is clear from the logs in the river and mills on both banks. Several homes can be seen on Nicollet Island, including the Calladine home to the left of the railroad tracks and the two-story Eastman mansion in the central portion.

each way once a day after I had lived there a year. It was the St. Paul & Pacific line. When we first came to Minneapolis we came by boat to St. Paul and took the St. Paul and Pacific to the east side of the river. It wasn't until later that the train crossed over to the west side of the river. I didn't mind the hard work or the loneliness. It was always interesting out here. And the very nicest people lived on Nicollet Island in those days. Colonel William S. King who was in charge of the State Fair for so many years; R. P. Upton; the Eastmans and many others lived there."

Margaret Calladine lived on the island for 43 years and remembered the end of the pioneer days and the beginning of the Gilded Age:

The Pence opera house hadn't been built yet, when I first lived there. My, we had a big celebration when that was opened. The Nicollet house and the Winslow house were the big hotels. Many well-to-do persons came to stay there from the east and south. I used to do all my shopping over in Bridge Square. That's where the best shops were. In order to get from my home on the island to the west side of the river I had to go through a dense wood. I didn't mind that however, although there were plenty of Indians around. They used to have pow-wows and war dances on the upper end of the island and in Bridge Square but I never went out to watch them. The upper end of the island was a great place for church picnics also, in the early days.

Along with residential development, Eastman and Merriam had ambitious plans for commercial undertakings on the island. Through their plans and negotiations, the history of Nicollet Island became entwined with the history of brewing in Minneapolis.

Gluek's Bar and Restaurant, one of the oldest businesses still existing in Minneapolis, can trace its history back to these commercial prospects on Nicollet Island.

The first commercial beer was sold in Minnesota in 1849 by the Yoerg Brewing Company of St. Paul, and other brewers appeared. In 1855, Gottlieb Gluek arrived from Germany. Gluek had learned the art of brewing malt beverages in his home town of Marbach, Germany. In 1846 he went to Dijon, France, to complete his education in French breweries and wineries. Upon immigrating to Minnesota, Gluek worked as a lumberjack to augment the savings he had brought from Germany. He also worked for John Orth, who had founded the state's second brewery in St. Anthony in 1850. In 1857, Gluek established his own brewery, the Mississippi Brewery, at Marshall and 22nd Street NE in St. Anthony, and it flourished. He then brought his sweetheart Caroline Foell over from Germany. They married and had three sons and seven daughters. The sons went into the family business, carrying on their father's legacy. The name of the brewery was later changed to Gluek Brewing Company and produced a variety of beer such as Gluek's Beer, Glix Beer, Gluek's Stite, and Pioneer Beer.[9]

Beer required refrigeration, and in 1867 Gluek purchased for $50 "The Right to

Excavate by Tunnelling from the Shore of Mississippi River on the Northerly Side of Nicollet Island…" from Eastman, Merriam, and their wives.[10] These were the first beer caves on Nicollet Island. A 1947 newspaper article about the Gluek family said, "In those days before refrigeration, the Glueks' kept the beer in caves on the north end of Nicollet Island and in their own ice-cooled cellars. Great, strong, gray dappled horses—there were 110 of them—hauled the casks of beer around the town."[11]

By the 1870s the John Orth Brewery had also acquired tunnels at the northern tip to store beer, probably tunneling in from the riverbank and driving a shaft down from the surface to haul out the barrels. A map of the day shows the location of the shaft marked as "John Orth." Orth and his family hailed from Alsace, a French province where the German influence was strong—in fact, Alsace became a part of Germany in 1870, following the Franco-Prussian War. The Orths were the first German immigrants to settle in St. Anthony and John Orth had soon established a successful brewery which was merged with three other breweries to form the Minneapolis Brewing Company, later the Grain Belt Breweries. The beer caves became outdated with the advent of effective cold storage technology and fell into disuse. However, these successful tunneling projects may have encouraged Eastman and Merriam to undertake a far more ambitious scheme.

Although Eastman sold some lots for residential development, his primary concern was the riparian, or water, rights associated with his purchase of the island. This put him at odds with Franklin Steele's St. Anthony Power Company, and he and Merriam filed suit demanding that the company remove their dams and mills. Rather than fight a protracted legal battle, the contending parties reached a compromise in 1867. The company was granted rights to continue utilizing Nicollet Island and its water power, and Eastman and Merriam were granted the rights to tunnel underneath Nicollet and Hennepin Islands. Eastman and Merriam intended to dig a 2,500 foot tunnel between Hennepin and Nicollet Islands that would provide a tailrace equal to 200 horsepower of water flow for their businesses.

TUNNELS AND TENEMENTS

The following year Eastman, Merriam, and two partners began to tunnel underneath Hennepin Island upriver toward Nicollet Island, with visions of a water-powered manufacturing center on Nicollet Island. Their engineers had worked for almost a year when disaster struck. The soft sandstone underlying the limestone edge of the falls began to give

In 1868 Eastman, Merriam and two partners began a tunnel from Hennepin Island to Nicollet Island in order to tap into additional waterpower. On October 5, 1869 the tunnel collapsed washing away several mills, creating a giant whirlpool, and endangering St. Anthony Falls.

way. At first only a few drops of water from the upper end of the tunnel appeared, but on October 5, 1869, the trickle became a torrent which burst through the tunnel, and Hennepin Island began to sink. A cry rang out in every direction: "the falls are going out," and people abandoned their business and made their way to the falls to see the giant whirlpool that had been created by the collapsed tunnel. Several mills had already been swept downstream. On Nicollet Island, George A. Brackett, the commander of the volunteer fire companies of Minneapolis, stripped off his coat and said, "that water must be stopped." John Jarvis,

yardmaster for the Milwaukee and St. Paul Railroad, stepped beside him and spoke out to the men who had gathered and said, "Boys, let's plug that hole." These men led the volunteers in an effort to fill the whirlpool. Mrs. Calladine remembered, "We were all afraid for our lives. The men had to cut all the trees off the upper end of the island—all the lovely trees. They carried them down to the falls all day long, with six horse teams pulling the big logs. Then they threw them into the hole—and one by one the big trees disappeared in the whirl. We were in great danger expecting the falls to go out any moment. But we couldn't fill that whirling pool." The volunteer force attempted to fill the hole with timber cribs filled with boulders and dirt. These timber cribs filled the first hole, but then more parts of the tunnel collapsed, and they filled those places with cribs as well. By mid-afternoon they had plugged the breach and were walking, self-satisfied, over the cribs, adjusting them. Suddenly the plugs heaved upward, the men ran, and the cribs were sucked into the earth. They now knew that they would have to build dams to protect the breach from the water. That project took several weeks. The threat to the livelihoods of both Minneapolis and St. Anthony was enormous. It finally took an appropriation by the U.S. Congress to preserve the falls and upper river navigation. And it was not until eight years later, in 1876, that the U.S. Army Corps of Engineers finally succeeded in securing the breach and safeguarding the falls with a concrete dike. Four years later a wooden apron was completed.[12]

As could be expected, W.W. Eastman, the face of the four partners in the endeavor, was roundly criticized, and in response he published a two-page explanation in the *St. Anthony Falls Democrat*, explaining what the Tunnel Company was doing and why. The essence of his defense was that this sort of tunneling had been successfully performed before and was essential for the economic growth of St. Anthony. The disaster that struck the project could not have been anticipated. Of his critics he wrote, "Frank fair and manly criticism on my acts and motives, I do not object to and will always be received in the manner in which it is given; but I do not desire to reason with low abuse, and malicious slander. I will not stoop to do it, against false reports, I will place facts. Those are what the public now desire, and none but cowards add fuel to popular clamor. My motive for digging the Tunnel, was of course to benefit myself and partners, but incident to such benefit, had the Tunnel been a success, there would have been added, in course of time, taxable property to the city of St. Anthony of at least $1,000,000 in value, besides greatly benefiting the St. Anthony Water Power Company."[13]

With the failure of the tunnel, it was 1879 before Eastman and Merriam got reliable power on Nicollet Island. They were able to accomplish this by brokering a $400,000 deal between Mr. Butterfield of New York and James J. Hill of St. Paul, and, as a commission, Eastman received a sawmill at the falls and three mill sites with power.[14] Eastman now had turbines on Hennepin Island that drove a continuous rope cable through an interchannel tower across the river carrying power to the southern tip of the island. The mechanism worked, and the Island Power Building was

The Loring/King mansion was built on the west side of the island by the Father of the Minneapolis Park System, Charles M. Loring. Entrepreneur and U.S. Congressman William S. King and his family later lived in the home.

built on what is now Merriam Street near the east channel to house the businesses that wanted to make use of the power. And businesses came: the William Bros Boiler Works, the Cedar Lake Ice Company, the McDonald and Delamater sash, door, and blind factory (later renamed the Island Sash and Door Company), a carriage works, and several stair and box manufactories.[15]

While they worked through the problem of getting power to Nicollet Island, Eastman and his partners set about developing the northern end for residential use. Eastman built his own mansion there and encouraged family members such as his brothers Haskett and George

and his sisters Mrs. Clara DeLaittre and Mrs. Charlotte Secombe to join him there. He also invited friends and other prominent businessmen to do the same. [16]

A VERY FASHIONABLE ADDRESS

In 1869 Charles M. Loring built what became known as the King mansion. Loring recounts, "I saw a statement recently that King built that old house. I built it myself in 1869 and lived there about eight years before I sold it to Mr. King. Nicollet Island was a dreamland in those days. We had a delightful little community there. W.W. Eastman, the

Delaittre family, our house, and a few others. The island was really a park as it stood. It was thickly grown up to a grove of as beautiful native maples as one would care to see. I think of it many, many times."[17]

Loring was one of the great publicly-minded men of early St. Anthony and Minneapolis. His young life was spent in Maine as mate on his father Captain Horace Loring's ship. Loring went on voyages to the West Indies, but was drawn to the Midwest, first Chicago and then St. Anthony. In 1862, he came to St. Anthony and fell in love with it. In St. Anthony he prospered as a businessman, but he truly made his mark as a progressive civic builder. He was a Republican and in 1864 he was elected road supervisor, a position of which he said, "I guess they chose me because they knew how little I knew about roads."[18]

That same year Loring arranged the first flower show in the city's history. In 1866 he was elected secretary of the Atheneum Library; that same year, he, Franklin Steele, and others planted trees along Minnehaha Avenue. In his long public career, he held numerous commercial and public positions, but his mark was made because of his love of trees. In 1883, the Minneapolis Park system was formed, and Loring served on the board for twelve years, nine as president of the Park Board. Loring Park in Minneapolis is named

after him, though when the land for that park was purchased it ran into criticism. Nicollet Island resident Joel B. Bassett remarked, "You young fellows will ruin the town. Why, it's all park beyond Seventh Street, anyway." Loring personally donated trees for parks and as Park Board president helped to secure the legislative action to structure the park system. He is considered the Father of the Park System, and it is in no small measure due to his efforts that Minneapolis to this day has one of the finest park systems in the United States.[19]

Along with encouraging detached homes, Eastman developed the Eastman Flats, a double row of fifty town houses, thirty on the north side of Eastman Avenue and twenty on the south side. The eight-unit Grove Street Flats (which still stands) was built in 1877 and was similarly constructed. Built between 1877 and 1882 in the French Second Empire style, the first flats were built from limestone quarried on the island; the latter ones had brick fronts. Eastman had made a study of similar constructions out East and had improved on their design, aiming at "comfort, convenience, elegance, good taste, commodity" and one observer remarked "it is no bold assertion that he has been preeminently successful in attaining to his aim." As the *Minneapolis Tribune* put it, "We think it safe to say that the scheme of W.W. Eastman to build a row of houses the width of Nicollet Island is the largest building enterprise of the city or state. Without exaggeration this is the star block of tenement houses."[20] Eastman Flats set a new standard of style and elegance for the town, and affluent young couples considered it a highly desirable address.

Another man who became involved with the Eastman Flats and W.W. Eastman himself was E.T. Abbott. He had arrived in Minnesota in August of 1871 and quickly found work in an abstract office, and this position introduced him to several property line disputes on Nicollet Island, one between W.W. Eastman and Samuel Hill, the son-in-law of James J. Hill.

The Eastman Flats, built between 1877 and 1882, were a double row of town houses which spanned the width of the island. Designed for high class tenants, they were considered the preeminent block of housing of this type in Minneapolis.

Another case concerned the width of an alley. Abbott arrived at the conclusion that W.W. Eastman's lawyer, a man named David Secombe and W.W. Eastman's brother-in-law, preferred to deal in lawsuits. Many years later, in 1937, only a few months shy of ninety years of age, Abbott penned some of his recollections. "Mr Secombe rather peculiar attorney I opined if He could [get] a thing by asking for it He would institute a Law suit in preference, which is what He did in this Alley Case."

Abbott also assisted in clearing out the Eastman Flats sewer system, which consisted of a tunnel that ran the width of the island under a limestone ledge. Shale had fallen into the tunnel and Abbott assigned several men with wheelbarrows to clear out the tunnel. A few days into the project, Abbott's foreman ran into his office and said, "THE RATS have driven us all out, Three big rats jumped into My face at once—." Abbott had his foreman set a couple of big rat traps, and the next day the traps were full. A year after the incident, Abbott was walking in San Francisco with his wife when a car went by and someone stood up in it, "waved his Handkerchief and Shouted *RATS* to the Mystification of My Wife and other Pedestrians—"[21]

As the island developed, people moved into the residential area in the northern two thirds, and an interesting group it proved to be. A survey of the island's residents reads as a veritable Who's Who of early Minneapolis. Several men associated with the newspaper business were Islanders. Newspapers in this period were entertainment, advertisement, news, information, moral instruction, and political bloodsport. They tended to align with political parties with no pretense of nonpartisanship. Names such as the *St. Anthony Falls Democrat* or the *Minnesota Republican* were commonplace, and wealthy men purchased or started newspapers to fight their political battles and develop political capital for government appointments.

In 1859, Colonel King boldly started the weekly *Minneapolis Atlas* newspaper, following the collapse of several other publications. It stayed afloat for eight years until, in 1867, another weekly, the *Chronicle*, appeared. After several months of competition, the two papers decided to combine, becoming the *Minneapolis Tribune*. Colonel King remained a stockholder in the *Minneapolis Tribune*, which after some years was taken over by the *St. Paul Pioneer Press*. The new newspaper was dubbed the *St. Paul and Minneapolis Pioneer Press and Tribune*, but Minneapoli-

tans didn't like it and pushed for a newspaper of their own called the *Evening Tribune*. In 1879, David Blakely, another Islander, became an owner of the *Evening Tribune* for several years. His neighbor Joel B. Bassett purchased the *Minnesota Democrat* and turned it into a Republican paper. [22]

Yet another Islander newspaperman was Charles Nimocks. A Michigan native, Nimocks had fought in the Civil War as Captain of Company C, Seventh Regiment, Michigan Infantry. He was wounded at the Battle of Gettysburg defending Cemetery Ridge against Pickett's Charge. In 1871 he came to Minnesota and became involved in the newspaper business. In 1880, for $2,000, he and a partner bought out the name and circulation of the *Minneapolis Evening Journal* whose plant had just burned down, whereupon he became the editor. He later spent two years in Detroit as the business manager of the *Tribune* and returned to Minneapolis to start the *Evening Star*. In 1889 he founded the *Minneapolis Daily Times*. Nimocks made use of both personal connections and his newspaper's pages to encourage the establishment of the Minneapolis Park Board. He later served on the board, and in 1908 he was appointed a deputy U.S. Marshal, a position he held for four years. His home was at 30 Grove Street. It later became the Bassett residence.[23]

Among the stories readers followed in the various local newspapers was that of W. W. Eastman's son Fred. No sooner had memories of the collapse of the Eastman tunnel begun to fade than Fred Eastman's collapse began to draw notice. Fred was a person of local infamy, a drunkard who was no doubt an embarrassment to his prominent parents and a burden to his wife, Jeanette Hale Eastman. His appearances in newspapers chart his decline, starting with his wife's attempt to get a divorce in a court appearance on June 18, 1895.[24] The grounds for divorce were unfaithfulness with drinking as a contributing factor. A month later the couple reconciled for the sake of their five-year-old son. On April 2, 1896, Fred Eastman was arrested and fined for drunkenness. Drinking continued to be a chronic problem as on April 21, 1896 the *Minneapolis Journal* reported:

FRED EASTMAN TAKES FRENCH LEAVE FROM ROCHESTER HOSPITAL

Fred Eastman who was committed to Rochester Hospital a few days ago, charged by his father with being an inibriate, escaped from the asylum Friday and returned to the city yesterday. He claims to have been assisted in making his escape by an inmate named Martin, who brought him a rope, down which he slid, together with two companions, one of whom he claims was Wallace W. Harrison. They stayed in Rochester at a hotel till last Sunday evening, when they took a private rig to Spring Valley, taking the train to St. Paul and thence home by the Interurban. Eastman claims to have been well treated there, although he is not pleased with the asylum as a place of retreat.

Apparently Fred Eastman's escape did not please his wife; on May 22, 1896, Jeanette Hale Eastman received her divorce from Fred Eastman after a judge heard from witnesses of Fred Eastman's cruelty and mistreatment. Fred Eastman offered no defense, and when the divorce was granted he approached Jeanette and said, "Well I suppose we may as well shake hands?" "We might as well, Fred," said his wife, "I'll bid you good-by," and the two chatted cordially. Fred Eastman soon after found himself in a workhouse from which his father won his release by telling a judge that his son would take the Keeley cure. Whatever the efficaciousness of the Keeley cure, Fred Eastman's prospects do not appear to have altered materially. On October 11, 1898, the *Minneapolis Journal* ran an article entitled:

AN AWFUL THRASHING
FRED EASTMAN PUNISHED
BUT WON'T TELL WHO DID IT

The gay and debonair Fred Eastman, of more or less local fame, fell into the hands of someone last night that treated him far from gently. He was a sorry-looking object as a policeman led him to John DeLaittre's residence at 2 a.m. His clothes were torn and ragged and his features bore the marks of the most brutal treatment. The policeman summoned the occupants of the house and Eastman was taken in. The officer could not give any particulars of the fray other than that he found Eastman in the street unable to take care of himself.

Every effort was made to get particulars from the wretched young man, but between groans he piteously protested that there was nothing to tell.

Fred Eastman's family was part of the elite of Minneapolis and St. Anthony, as were many of the other families on Nicollet Island. Many of those families had servants whose lives inevitably intertwined with their own. Some of these stories were quite sensational and came to the attention of the public. Such was the case with the Secombe family who shared a double house with the Reas. J.P. Rea and his wife Emma lived at 23 Grove Street. J.P. Rea was a probate judge affiliated with the firm of Rea, Hooker, and Wooley. David Adam Secombe and Charlotte A. Secombe, the sister of W.W. Eastman, lived in the other half of the house at 25 Grove Street.[25]

One of Secombe's servants was Kate Noonan, a young woman who worked for the Secombes for four years and then for their neighbors, the DeLaittres, until 1873.[26] Four years after leaving the service of the DeLaittres, Kate Noonan made headlines for the murder of an estranged lover named William H. Sidle. Sidle, twenty-one at the time of his death, was the nephew of the president of the First National Bank, and, according to Noonan, something of a blackguard. Noonan had been a virtuous girl, admired and pursued by many young men, and Sidle determined to seduce her to settle a bet. One evening he plied her with drink and had his way with her; she became his mistress, but he soon tired of her, and Noonan attempted to extort money from him to allow her to leave the city until she was able to get honest employment. Sidle said, "How much?" Noonan replied, "Eight hundred dollars," to which he said, "Make it eight and I'll talk with you."

Unsatisfied with the offer, Noonan began to stalk Sidle, and on Friday, February 16, 1877, she approached him in front of the Nicollet House and importuned him once again for money to leave the city. Sidle declined and said, "I wish you was in hell, roasting." Noonan replied that they might as well roast together and shot him. Sidle died several hours later and Noonan was arrested. In jail she related to Mayor Ames that she had planned to kill herself, but was unable to follow through with her plan. She was put on trial and her former employers, the Secombes, came to her defense.

Mr. David A. Secombe represented her for some of her legal proceedings. Mrs. Charlotte Secombe was a character witness for her trial: "...she was one of the best dispositioned girls I have ever known, her reputation for good character was, so far as I know, very good." Noonan's first trial offered a defense of *insanitas transitoria*, temporary insanity, and a hung jury was the result. The trial was followed avidly by the public and press.

The press was largely unsympathetic toward Sidle. One newspaper published the opinion that the law of homicide should be modified to permit seduced women to kill their seducers: "Such so-called murders are nothing more than a species of a higher law which a wronged woman takes into her own hands, and awards a speedy justice in many cases in which a corrupt jury might overlook in their lack of appreciation of a distinction between virtue and lust...why not so amend the law as to give the woman whose innocence is murdered and whose honor is robbed, the sacred right to shoot down her betrayer like a dog." Another paper concluded, "We are informed that the more that this case is understood, the more general is

The Queen Ann style Griswold house at 107/109 W. Island Avenue was built in 1890. The picture above appears to show the Griswold family with some of the fifteen Griswold children, most of whom grew up in the house.

the feeling becoming that Kate Noonan, in shooting Will Sidle, did a most righteous act and rid the world of a monster—of one who made other hearts bleed besides those of Kate Noonan and her relatives."

A second trial was held and Noonan's defense again offered a theory of *insanitas transitoria* and suggested, rather speciously, that poor medical treatment more than the bullet in Sidle's body was a factor in his death. On December 24, 1877, the second trial gave Noonan an acquittal, likely reasoning that Sidle was a cad who had recklessly ignored the timeless injunction concerning a woman scorned.

IN THE EYES OF CHILDREN

As the neighborhood formed at the north end of the island, families with children began to move in. Franklin C. Griswold, Dakota war veteran, rented the house at 163 Nicollet Street in 1883 and moved into 99 Nicollet Street the following year. He then moved his family to the Lake Calhoun area, but moved back to the island and built and lived in a house at 11/13 (now 15/17) Maple Place in 1886. In 1890 he built and moved into another house at 107/109 West Island Ave. He raised most of his fifteen children in the latter house and became a major landlord on the island, build-

ing 27 Maple Place in 1888.[27] The Griswold children were among the many that grew up on Nicollet Island during this era.

Recollections by the children who lived on Nicollet Island during this period provide a glimpse into what must have been a charmed Gilded Age childhood environment. In 1974 Miss Mildred Schlener provided a written account of life on the island which she ably recalled from her childhood there. Her father owned the John A. Schlener stationery company, had been a deputy toll collector for the suspension bridge, and was a prominent Mason.[28]

During her childhood years, Miss Schlener lived with her parents and brother in a ten-room gray clapboard house that her father built opposite Eastman's house on East River Avenue and Grove Place. Schlener provides a firsthand account of her neighbors, and one of the most noteworthy was W. W. Eastman himself, who at the time owned Nicollet Island and had developed most of it.

Eastman had arrived in St. Anthony in 1854 and became involved in flour milling with one of his brothers (see page 26). He sold out his interest in that project and, with a new partner, Paris Gibson, built the Cataract Mill, the first flour mill on the west side of the Mississippi. A few years later, Eastman and his partner built the North Star Woolen Mills nearby. He was also responsible for building the first paper mill on the east bank with Charles C. Secombe. In short, W. W. Eastman had a hand in diverse economic interests, from lumber and wheat to brewing, railroads, and real estate development. Eastman and his wife Susan raised three children, the infamous Fred, Ida May, and Josie Belle. They were members of the Church of the Redeemer congregation.[29] Miss Schlener had the following to say of her next door neighbors, the entrepreneurial Eastmans:

I was very fond of Mrs. Eastman, a very portly woman, always dressed in elegant black silk, many strings of jet beads, and both hands covered with many diamond rings. She also had a red wig which fascinated me. I wonder why those early wigs were always red! She went driving in a Victoria every day with a coachman, certainly not a chauffeur, carrying a little fringed sunshade as ladies did at that time to keep the sun out of their eyes. I loved the klip-klop of the horses hooves…

The Eastmans traveled to Italy and returned with a sculpture that Mildred Schlener particularly admired:

When they returned from Italy they brought a beautiful statue named "The Lost Pleiad"…One evidently got lost and the statue was a life-sized woman leaning over at a precarious angle balanced on one foot, one hand shading her eyes but not touching her brow. I was so impressed by the balance. It was on a swivel on a marble base.[30]

Colonel William Smith King, another prominent neighbor, was a native New Yorker who arrived in 1858. The son of an itinerant Methodist minister, he had been involved in politics and the newspaper business before moving west to Minnesota. He was appointed to the staff of General S.S. Burnside in the state militia where he acquired the title "Colonel," which stuck with him for the rest of his life. He was a Republican and an abolitionist when those beliefs and principles were unpopular, as was shown by his role in the Eliza Winston affair (see pp 38-39). Colonel King was president of the Minnesota State Agricultural Society, and under his direction, it ran an unusually large Minnesota State Fair in 1877. The following year Colonel King resigned from the Minnesota State Agricultural Society and started a rival agricultural exposition. The Bill King Fairs ran from 1878 until 1882 and they were popular affairs.[31] They were held somewhere along Minnehaha Avenue and around

Colonel William S. King helped establish the Park Board and Lakewood Cemetery, built a pavilion at Lake Calhoun and owned several newspapers. He served as a U.S. Congressional Representative and ran the famous "Bill King Fairs."

30th Avenue South. One of the popular attractions at the Bill King Fair was the hot air balloon launch, and the launch of 1881 was especially notable. The balloon was named The Great Northwest, the destination was New York, and the occupants were reporters from Minneapolis and St. Paul. The professor who was to lead the voyage wrote, "I have every confidence that we shall reach New York in perfect safety. I imagine now that I hear the wild shouts of the multitude as we sail away, the music of bands and the whistling of the winds. In a moment we shall have jumped far beyond earth and its cares and will go whirling miles and miles upward and onward. The greatest interest is being manifested in our airship in the east and it will prove to be a pioneer in aerial navigation." Sadly the balloon did not quite make it to New York. As it ascended, it dropped sandbags onto the spectators below who scrambled out of the way and the balloon itself promptly descended into a German farmer's cow pasture in the Midway area between Minneapolis and St. Paul. The farmer immediately threatened a lawsuit, saying that his cows had been frightened and their milk strained. The reporters, for their part, clambered out of the basket and arrived back at their offices somewhat earlier than expected to write about their adventure.[32]

Colonel King played a pivotal role establishing the Minneapolis Park Board and donated land for Lyndale Park, a portion of the Lake Harriet frontage, most of King's Highway, and a large portion of the Minnehaha Parkway land. Colonel King was also interested in the newspaper business and started the weekly *State Atlas* in 1859. He was also a stockholder and city editor for the Minneapolis department of the *Pioneer Press* newspaper. He was involved in agriculture, railroads, the establishment of the Lakewood Cemetery, and building a pavilion at Lake Calhoun. He attempted to start a street railcar system in Minneapolis. He was selected to be the postmaster of the United States House of Representatives in 1861 and ran for Congress as a Republican in 1874, serving from 1875 to 1877. After his term as a United States Representative he gradually acquired 1,400 acres of farmlands adjacent to Lakes Harriet and Calhoun. He named it the Lyndale Farm and raised a famous breed of Shorthorns on it. He was twice married, first to Mary Elizabeth Stevens and later to Caroline M. Arnold, both of Ilion, New York. Colonel King, like the Eastmans, was a member of the Church of the Redeemer congregation.[33]

Years after Colonel King's death in 1900, his widow, Caroline King, was taken advantage of by a confidence man named Carleton Hudson, who sought to defraud her of her wealth. The scheme was brought to light in a court trial in which federal Judge Amidon said of Hudson, "this minister of darkness was to betray her into the loss of everything that she had in the world." The judge ordered the cancellation of the deeds which Hudson had maneuvered King into. The case was settled on December 24, 1914, and a local paper quoted the widow King as saying, "I will have a quiet Christmas, a very quiet Christmas."[34]

Of the Kings Miss Schlener recalled:

The King house was a large, yellow clapboard house. King's Highway out near Lake Calhoun, after you passed Lakewood Cemetery and near the rose gardens, was named for him. He had a large farm there with enormous barns. It is probably all gone now. I will omit all the bits of scandal I collected as a child. He had one daughter. (I think that was all). She married a man named Hefflefinger, another old Minneapolis family. Their son named King didn't turn out too well. He was a teamster and kept his horses or someone else's, and the wagons, in the King barn which opened onto the alley. I don't know what happened to Mr. Hefflefinger, whether he died or was divorced. Mrs. Hefflefinger was very handsome. She went to Italy and returned with a new husband named Mastinelli and a small daughter named Helen Mastinelli who was a friend of mine.

Another family in the neighborhood, the Bassetts, were descendents of French Huguenots who had left France after the St. Bartholomew's Day Massacre in 1572. The Bassetts had come to America via the British Isles and settled in Massachusetts as early as

1640. Joel Bean Bassett had been raised as a Quaker by his father, Daniel Bassett, Sr., who believed so strongly in freedom that he had manumitted a slave. Joel left his father's farm, engaged in lumbering in Maine and, after marrying, came to St. Anthony in 1850. In 1852, he homesteaded the land at the mouth of Bassett's Creek on the west bank of the Mississippi, north of and almost opposite Nicollet Island, and involved himself in lumbering and milling enterprises. He built a house north of the creek on a small knoll near its mouth and farmed there for four years before selling the land. Politically, Bassett was a Republican and a strong anti-slavery advocate like his father. He and another Islander, John Wesley North, helped to organize the Republican Party in Minnesota in 1856. To further the interests of the party, Bassett purchased the *Minnesota Democrat* and turned it into a Republican paper. He eventually became a probate judge and a well-regarded Government Indian Agent to the Ojibwe. In this capacity he arranged the treaty in which the White Earth Indian reservation was established.[35]

Mrs. Bassett was also accomplished: in 1858 she won the best display of cheese competition at a Minnesota Territorial Fair, one of the precursors to the Minnesota State Fair. Miss Schlener recalled:

...Next door was a very dark-colored clapboard house built by Will Basset. His father started the Basset Mills on Bassett Creek and lived with them, a very dignified gentleman who always walked with a cane. I remember him best dressed in light grey with a "Prince Albert" coat and a hat to match, high but rounded, in the Victorian style. The Bassetts had two sons, Jay and Norman, both much older than we were but Norman occasionally condescended to play with us. Mrs. Bassett was very good looking, always smartly dressed and had to have the first of everything. She had the first cocktails served in the neighborhood, the first dyed hair, the first electric coupe, and the first divorce.

Another prominent island family was the DeLaittres. In John DeLaittre's autobiography he wrote that his grandfather and grandmother had fled the French Revolution and, according to his grandmother, had watched the mob break into the Bastille. The DeLaittre family settled in Maine and John grew up on a farm. The farmer's life didn't appeal to him, however, and DeLaittre became a commercial fisherman on a schooner. Hearing of gold in California, he jumped on a steamer which got him to Panama where he and some young companions walked across the isthmus. At the time, Panama was teeming with cholera and yellow fever, and John was happy to catch a mail steamer to San Francisco within three weeks of arriving on the Pacific. Back on the east coast after some prospecting in the Sierra Mountains, DeLaittre married Clara Eastman and they came to St. Anthony at the behest of her brother William. DeLaittre's joint ventures in flour and wool with his brother-in-law have previously been covered. He also became a partner in the Bovey-DeLaittre Lumber Company and trustee and president of Farmers and Mechanics Savings Bank. Running as the Republican candidate for mayor in 1877, he defeated the corrupt incumbent Dr. Ames, and once in office, tried to untangle some of the frauds and chicanery of his predecessor with regard to liquor licenses. This cleaner government approach was not popular with the German population of the city. After one term as mayor he accepted an appointment as the state's Stillwater prison inspector and was on the committee that developed the Minneapolis city hall and courthouse, and another committee that planned the current state capitol.[36]

In his autobiography, which he wrote for his children and grandchildren, DeLaittre advised:

I cannot close this chapter of my life without saying to you, my grandchildren, and to other young people who may chance to read these pages, that during all these years of my young life,—whether on the ocean, among rough sailors—on the crowded steamers—or in Panama with its cholera, fevers, sickness and death—or in the mining camps of the Sierras, I never forgot the teachings of my sainted mother. Her image was always with me, and thoughts of her and the grief I knew it would be to her feelings should I become careless and indulge in vicious practices, kept me free from many of the pitfalls and vices so alluring to the young. She always advised the selection of good, pure-minded companions. And to you, my young people, I cannot impress too strongly on your minds the importance of this: evil and vicious companions, like extinct coals of fire, "blacken, if do not burn."

DeLaittre's son Karl likely benefited from this advice. Karl DeLaittre was a lumberman, part owner of the Green and DeLaittre Warehouse Grocery Business, a state legislator, and President of the Minneapolis City Council.[37]

Of the DeLaittres Miss Schlener remembered:

Next door was the de Laittre family. I believe she was an Eastman. Mr. W.W. [Eastman] sold the lots to family and friends. They had two children, Karl and Corinne (later Mrs. Horace Ropes). Corinne had an ordinary ugly white bulldog named Borgia and drove a single seated carriage with a high rein check and cropped tail, —a very smart turnout and she was a very good driver. She was a very handsome woman, smartly dressed, hatted, veiled, and gloved.

Schlener also had a word to say about the Howard Upton family. Howard was the son of Rufus P. Upton, one of the builders of the Minnesota Mill, a grocer, planter of a commercial garden on Nicollet Island, and a booster of steamboat navigation above the falls. Rufus P. Upton was married three times, and one of his sons, Howard, was a ticket agent at the Union Station in Minneapolis.

Next to that was the road leading to the bridge over the railroad. It was a good sliding place in the winter. The other side was a duplex where Howard and Sadie Upton lived. Howard was in the ticket office at the old original Union Station across the river. Sadie was plump and jolly and made wonderful doughnuts. I must have

smelled them from my house as I always managed to arrive at the right time for the first batch.

Clarence Eastman (the son of William Eastman's brother Haskett) and his wife Amelia had moved to the island with William's encouragement. Clarence was involved in the manufacture of electrical lights.

Next door lived a darling diminutive white-haired couple, Mr. and Mrs. Clarence Eastman and his mother Mrs. Haskett Eastman. Their house was cream colored clapboard with gables and curlecues. Everything about them, even their maids and home, were tiny and perfect. They rode in a small closed carriage, beautifully dressed always. Mr. Eastman, like most of the men, usually dressed in pale gray, and the ever present Prince Albert coat. No weeds in the lawn, always perfectly kept. The whole thing, including the occupants, was right out of Pride and Prejudice. The house was filled with treasures which would be worth a million now.

Schlener also knew Fraulein Schoen, one in the long line of island musicians that had started with Ann North giving lessons on her piano and continues to this day:

Next was another clapboard house, very dull color, owned by Mr. Moffat and rented to Fraulein Schoen. Renee, who aspired to grand opera but didn't quite make the grade, gave voice lessons. From there to the corner were the limestone Eastman Flats. I laugh to hear them called town houses. That word was not invented then. They contained a "higher class" of tenants. Some very fine families lived there. Many were my playmates and family friends. There was a Mrs. Hull with two daughters, Minnie was a clerk in Thomas Drygoods Store. Bell was a traveling sales woman for a salt company. I thought that was quite wonderful. They were definitely "ladies," a term which would not be understood now.

Across the tracks is the Alexander house…The third floor was removed. It had "turrets" at the corners. Also removed [were] the porches which were at the sides and front. The children were all older than we, but Danda played with us. The oldest daughter Margaret, whom we called Greta was the first bride in the pro-cathedral built on the "Fish Jones" property on Hennepin Avenue. He later moved his exotic birds and fish to Minnehaha Falls where he built a replica of Longfellow's home and started the Longfellow Gar-

dens. The pro-cathedral was not finished but Greta was determined to have the first wedding there.

Schlener mentions the old beer caves of Nicollet Island which had since been converted into a mushroom-growing operation. She also attended Nicollet Island elementary school, located at the north tip. The lot for the school had been purchased by the Minneapolis Board of Education in 1899 and the school opened in 1900. The school was a two-story frame building with clapboard siding. Central stairs divided the two classrooms on each floor. The school was established for the many children living on the island; it closed around 1920.[38]

There were a number of other clapboard houses on East Island Avenue up to the end where there was a large mushroom cave. I believe there were a number of caves in the rock under the island. The mushrooms were grown by a little gnome-like man. I never saw him go in or emerge from the cave, but every day he carried at least 12 boxes to the street-car to take to the best Clubs and Hotels. Beyond the cave was a small 4-room yellow clapboard school. My father was President of the School Board about the time my brother was ready to go to school, so they built this school so the little children wouldn't have so far to go. The janitor was good to all the little children. He rang a hand bell to get us in at nine o' clock. The principal, who also taught, was Mrs. Mather, a very wonderful teacher. When we reached the 4th grade we had to go to the Holmes School on Fifth Street and Third Avenue Southeast. We walked that distance every day in spite of the bitter cold wind from the north as we crossed the bridge. No school buses to pick us up, no car pools to get us there. We even walked home to lunch. Four trips a day didn't hurt us any.

Schlener also writes about her neighbors the Smiths, who owned a liquor store in downtown Minneapolis and a wine cellar on Nicollet Island, and she notes the cold storage facilities which were a relatively new technology at the time, far more efficient than the local caves.

Beyond the Eastman flats to the north was the A.M. Smith house. A.M. Smith had a large liquor store with fine imported cheeses and sausages. My father went there often and sent home large orders and important delicacies... Mr. and Mrs. Smith were a portly and pleasant couple. Mrs. Smith always drove what I suppose was called a buckboard, and filled the seat comfortably. She wore very mannish clothes and a fedora hat tied with a veil. She drove a pair of handsome horses and drove very, very fast. Beyond their house was the railroad then a large cold storage with wide loading docks. I don't know what they stored. To me it was simply the "cold storage."

Well-to-do attorney Franklin C. Griswold owned many of the houses on the island. Griswold was married twice and had fifteen children. Putnam, one of his sons by his first wife, was a Metropolitan opera singer, a friend of the great Enrico Caruso, and favorite of Kaiser Wilhelm in Germany, who twice decorated him. Putnam sang at the Kaiser's daughter's wedding. He died young of surgical complications. Another of Griswold's sons (by his second wife), Franklin W. Griswold, grew up on the island and became a business owner, inventor, real estate developer, and philanthropist. In the early 1920s he invented the collapsible "bobby signal," a traffic signal mounted in the middle of an intersection that folded if it was hit by a vehicle. He may have been inspired by the railroad tracks near his home which he had to cross over to get to the central and southern part of the island. He sold the device to many municipalities and later developed the traffic controlling concept into Griswold Signal Co., which manufactured the flashing railroad crossing signs and gates used throughout the United States and Canada. He owned a number of businesses and enjoyed speedboat racing on Lake Minnetonka and bred world champion Holstein cattle in Eden Prairie.[39]

Of the Griswolds Schlener wrote:

Beyond that was a large brown clapboard Griswold house. There were 2 or 4 children by the first wife and 10 by the second. A very fine family, Emily was my first music teacher, Mildred married my brother's best friend, Leland Madland. The two youngest were Frank and Leslie. I think the youngest was my age. I have heard that the house is being restored, by whom? Probably Frank as I have heard he made a great deal of money. He was very, very, shy, but he must have recovered from that as I have been told he married several times.

Complementing Schlener's detailed and arch observations are the recollections of a host of other Nicollet Island children who were interviewed by Barbara Flanagan in 1974. Flanagan, then a columnist for the *Minneapolis Star* newspaper and a Nicollet Island afficionado, interviewed Leslie Griswold, Mrs. Ella Griswold Guilford, Mrs. Ruth

Ziemer Leubner, Leon McKinney, Ethel Helbach Kummer, siblings Genevieve, James, and Clarence Smith, Edith A.C. Johnson, Katherine Anderson Koelfgen, Ellen Greenwall Nelson, Alice Carriebelle Heffelfinger Redding, and Josephine Brown Altman.

The interviewees recalled lamplighters coming around at dusk to light the streetlights and the city shoveling the sidewalks in winter. Mothers washed on Mondays, ironed on Tuesdays, baked on Wednesdays, mended Thursdays, and cleaned Fridays, occasionally helped by a maid or hired girl. Leslie Griswold recalled that "on Saturdays, all the boys were stuck with hauling manure out of the barns and over to the mushroom caves at the north tip of the island." The mushroom man then sold his mushrooms to the fancy hotels.

The environment generated friendships and adventurous play. Leslie Griswold said, "Back then he'd (Frank Griswold) hitch a horse to a bobsled and we'd all ride." Leon McKenney recalled how as boys, he and Leslie Griswold would go to Boom Island, just north of Nicollet Island. The two straddled logs in the east channel and floated down the river. If they got their clothes wet or otherwise irritated their mothers, they would hide in the sewer tunnels under the island. Edith Johnson remembered rolling down the long hill on the Eastman's lawn. Ruth Ziemer Leubner added, "We'd roll down in summer and ski there in winter, or the boys skied and the Eastman's coachman would chase us away." Frank W. Griswold, the inventor of the railroad signal, also constructed a merry-go-round in their yard, Leubner recalled. She also noted that Fred Eastman, Mrs. Eastman's son, had the first "electric" car on the island. Leubner's mother scolded him for driving on the sidewalks when the streets were muddy. Perhaps this was the first indication of his wayward behavior.

Ellen Greenwall Nelson, daughter of the Eastman's coachman, said, "All I remember well is Mrs. Eastman's parrot. When the phone rang, it would say, 'Hello, fourth floor, St. Paul.'" Another of the children, Alice Carriebelle Heffelfinger Redding, grew up with her great-grandmother, Mrs. William S. King, in the King mansion. Redding's aunt was Helen Mastinelli, a ballerina and protégé of Sarah Bernhardt. Helen died tragically when her costume caught fire as she danced on stage at a benefit in St. Paul.

Those who were interviewed recalled that the hobos who visited the island were always well fed, but that the Gypsies who camped on the island every summer were only tolerated. Early residents recalled the beauty of the island's wild flowers, gooseberry and elderberry bushes, and a walkway that was a lover's lane.[40]

Another child of the island, Augusta Starr, lived during the 1880s in the south row of the Eastman Flats. The daughter of a Minneapolis china store owner, Starr grew up to be a staff member at the Minneapolis Library and her memory was undimmed when she reminisced about her childhood in 1963.[41] Starr vividly recalled childhood island adventures but also noted the elite environment she was in. Many of the island's residents were wealthy and Starr draws a vivid picture of the social atmosphere which is worth quoting at length:

...Mr. Eastman had, with others, built a flour mill, a woolen mill and a paper mill. He opened stone quarries, from which he constructed among other buildings, his own home on the Island. A mansion finished in mahogany and marble. Nearby was the handsome home of his brother-in-law, Mr. John DeLaittre while Col. Wm. King's house rose from a high plat of land, with a tower rising even higher. Across the upper end of the Island were pleasant houses set in a grove of maple trees, whence the name of Maple Place. At the north end of the Island down at the foot of the river bank was a settlement of small cabins, painted pink or blue, occupied by the so-called "Frenchies," the lumbermen who worked on the river. Through the center of the Island ran the one business street then called Central Avenue but now East Hennepin. South of the street were a lumber yard, an ornamental iron factory and a shop of bee-keeper's supplies.

If the Island satisfied the social and artistic cravings of our parents, what did it mean to us children? There was no limit to our joys.

Perhaps the first thing that we remember is the Kindergarten opened by Mrs. E.R. Holbrook in her home at 29 Eastman Ave. This was the first such institution in Minneapolis. Opened by a student of the German teacher, Froebel, it appealed to parents seeking advanced educational ideas. But the children loved it.

Then there was a hill down which we could ride our velocipedes in summer and coast on our sleds in winter. One year, there was a coasting slide down the east bank onto the ice, but after an accident, that was closed.

But always there was the River, so near and ever entrancing. On Sunday afternoon walks with our parents, we circled the north end of the Island, and hung over the fence to watch the logs tumbling and rolling as they floated toward the East Channel. One child of tender kindergarten age remembers stealing away from paren-tal supervision, climbing down the rocky bank, and trying to walk on the logs. It is a wonder that she survived to be a grand-mother. But the height of excitement was to stand on the east side of the Island to watch those mettlesom[e] logs climb meekly up the flume to the saw mill across the river on Main Street, and to hear the scream of the saw. Many a time, I hung over the fence watching that never-ending procession of logs. I do not remember but another child does, the dramatic fires at that mill, with roaring flames, crashing of timbers, shouts of men, and galloping horses of the fire-engines.

On rare occasions, we children accom-panied our elders on trips by horse car to the East Side, a quiet college town where professors and their wives still spoke with the accents of their native New England. If we rode over the new Suspension Bridge, we reached Bridge Square, then paved with cobble stones. Here we faced a wide vista, with farmers' horses hitched at the drinking fountain in the center, the rail-road station on our left, Mr. Gale's market on our right, and in the background, the limestone towers of Center Block.

However, there was little need to go far afield in search of pleasure if one lived on Eastman Avenue. There were two gangs *of children, those who lived on the north side of the street, and those who lived on the south side. Sometimes, they jeered and taunted each other, and sometimes, they joined in royal games of Run Sheep-Run, and Andy-Over. The ladies living in neighboring houses made sedate afternoon calls, or accompanied their husbands to correct evening parties.*

But the high tide of social activity came on New Year's Day. Joys and excitements of Christmas were put aside, houses were swept, lamp[s] were burnished and punchbowls polished. The ladies were ready with elegantly bustled gowns of satin or velvet but it was the gentlemen who shone resplendent, for New Year's Day was a man's day. They wore long Prince Albert Coats, patent-leather buttoned shoes, over coats of broadcloth, and sealskin caps. Young bloods who owned fast horses, filled their cutters with selected friends, while those who had no horses, hired snappy livery turnouts. In groups they drove from house to house during the afternoon, bursting in at the door with cries of "Happy New Year." Decorous or otherwise, mostly otherwise as the day wore on. They piled their coats on the hall hatrack, greeted the ladies, and made for the punch bowl and the loaded dining-

table. Then, dropping their cards on the silver card-tray and resuming their coats, they were off to the house next door or across the street. Many a child was posted at the front window to report the progress of the callers from door to door.

I shall never forget my New Year's Day on the Island. I wore a white wool dress, adorned with a tiny silver bell, tied with a bow of red baby ribbon. My duty was to guard the card tray, and to empty it when it overflowed. To me, our young uncle was the best-dressed caller because he wore, not only a cap of sealskin but a long coat of that soft fur, trimmed with beaver. But the grandest caller was a Russian nobleman come from Odessa to sell wheat to the Washburn Crosby mill. He may not have had a title but there was no doubt of his nationality. To me, he looked like Goliath as he towered above the other men, with a black curly beard that exactly matched his tall cap and the band of black astrakhan that trimmed his coat from top to hem.

Do you wonder that those of us who are left treasure our recollections of life on Nicollet Island![42]

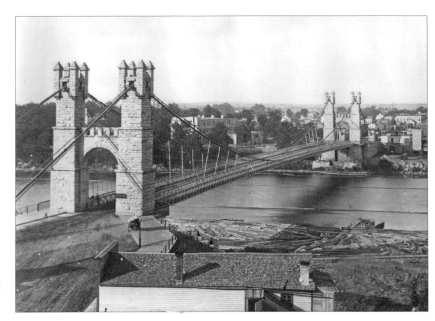

The second suspension bridge was built in 1876 to accommodate Minneapolis's growth. The new bridge had design flaws, however, and soon proved to be inadequate for the needs of the city. Construction on a new steel-arch bridge was began in 1888.

ANNEXATION

While the island's children were at play in their neighborhood, political and technological change was occurring all around them. On February 28, 1872, the Minnesota State Legislature approved the incorporation of St. Anthony and Minneapolis into one city. Minneapolis had outstripped its neighbor across the river in both economic vigor and population, having about 13,000 residents compared with St. Anthony's 5,000. Both cities voted on the proposition, and great majorities in both cities favored unification. In 1873, the first city hall was erected in Bridge Square on the west bank where the Hennepin Avenue Bridge provided a gateway from old St. Anthony and Nicollet Island to old Minneapolis proper.

The now-unified city sorely needed a new bridge. The old one had been heralded in its day as the first suspension bridge spanning the Mississippi, but it was fast becoming obsolete, and in 1874 the architect Thomas Griffith was called back to furnish a replacement. Controversy erupted when another great bridge builder, James J. Eads, urged the Minneapolis City Council not to approve Griffith's plan for another suspension bridge, which he regarded as weaker, more expensive, and less

Panoramic view of Minneapolis, 1874
This view of Minneapolis in 1874 looks out over the cupola of the Winslow House Hotel on the east bank of the Mississippi River. Milling activity can be seen on both banks of the river and on Nicollet Island to the right, and Hennepin Island to the left. The first suspension bridge crosses Nicollet Island joining the recently united cities of Minneapolis and St. Anthony. Mansions and more humble homes can be seen in Nicollet Island's central and northern portions. To the left is the Stone Arch Bridge with Spirit Island below it.

durable than an arch or truss bridge. Griffith weathered the uproar and completed a new suspension bridge just north of the old bridge in 1876. It was much bigger than the old one and had medieval parapets and turrets in its towers. No sooner was the new bridge opened than, as Eads had predicted, it proved maintenance-intensive, inadequate, and expensive.[43] Twelve years later work commenced on a new steel-arch bridge that was completed in 1891.

As Minneapolis continued to grow, civic leaders recognized the need for institutions to guide its development. One of these was the Minneapolis Park Board, established in 1883 by residents of Nicollet Island and other prominent Minneapolitans to serve as a body to acquire and regulate park land for the city. The loss of Nicollet Island as a city park to private development in 1866 had not been forgotten. As Charles Nimocks's *Evening Journal* put it, "The hesitancy of the [City] Council and regularly constituted authorities, combined with the illiberal and unsettled state of public opinion at the time, lost the city Nicollet Island which could have been secured years ago and made into one of the prettiest little parks in creation. Had we then had a park commission like the one now proposed, empowered to go ahead and take the responsibility and arrange the details, Nicollet Island would not have gotten away from the city."[44]

A forum for park advocacy gained momentum when Colonel William S. King reorganized the Board of Trade and got it involved in the park movement. On January 29, 1883, Charles A. Nimocks presented a resolution to secure a legislative Park Act to the Board of Trade. The proposal passed unanimously and the Board of Trade established a committee on Parks and Public Grounds. It was appointed by the President of the Board of Trade, George A. Pillsbury, and consisted of S.C. Gale, W.D. Hale, O.C. Merriman, C.M. Loring, John DeLaittre, W.S. King, C.A. Nimocks, R.C. Benton, and W.W. McNair.[45]

The committee soon drafted a park bill and public meetings were held. The park proposal was opposed by the City Council, who thought that too much power was vested in an unasked for and unaccountable entity, and the bill was amended to answer some of these concerns.

Although the bill had not yet been approved, the Park Board of Commissioners formed on March 14, 1883 and included many familiar and prominent residents. The officers were Charles M. Loring as the president, Albert A. Ames (sometime mayor of Minneapolis) as the vice-president, and Rufus J. Baldwin as the secretary. The commissioners by appointment were Charles M. Loring, Eugene M. Wilson, Dorilus Morrison, John

H. Pillsbury, Samuel H. Chute, Benjamin F. Nelson, John C. Oswald, William W. Eastman, George A. Brackett, Judson N. Cross, Daniel Bassett, Adin C. Austin, and Andrew C. Haugen.

The bill was proposed and the state legislature passed it, with the provision that it had to be voted on by the citizens of Minneapolis. On April 3, 1883, the citizens voted on the park act. The opposition was organized by W.W. McNair, Judge Atwater, and H.G. Sidle (father of the slain William H. Sidle). Nonetheless, the act was ratified by a vote of 5,327 to 3,922.

At a meeting of the Board of Trade on April 9, 1883, Colonel King exulted, "Mr. President: the efforts and struggles of 25 years to endow the city of Minneapolis with such a system of public parks as nature seems to have provided for the special happiness and glory of her people, has, at last, thank God, culminated in victory. The intelligence, the pride, the public spirit and the humanity of our people have at last been vindicated. That mean, wicked and cruel spirit of selfishness and greed which for so many years has obstructed and defeated every effort to endow our city with public parks, has at length, been overcome by the uprising and better sentiment and nobler spirit of our citizens."

The Park Board had been born with the best efforts of several prominent Nicollet Islanders, and the Park Board, in turn, would have decisive influence on the future of Nicollet Island. Yet though the creation of the board was a sign that Minneapolis was maturing as a city, the promotion of commerce continued to be the city's chief concern. In 1886, the Industrial Exposition Building was built on the east bank of the Mississippi opposite Nicollet Island, at the site of the old Winslow House hotel. It was the largest public building to be built in the Twin Cities before the turn of the century—and since the unification of St. Anthony and Minneapolis, "the Twin Cities" meant Minneapolis and St. Paul. The massive structure, which was designed to promote Minneapolis's commercial enterprises, was 356 feet long, 336 feet wide, 80 feet high, and featured a 260-foot corner tower overlooking the river. The style was an eclectic mix of Renaissance, Gothic, and French classical elements. It opened with great fanfare on August 23, 1886. A procession departed the West Hotel from the west bank of Minneapolis and crossed the bridge over Nicollet Island to an opening gala that featured products ranging from barbed wire to flour. First Lady Mrs. Grover Cleveland started the machinery remotely by the touch of a telegraph key in New York. She had been invited to attend but decided to go fishing instead, which then, as now, was probably a legitimate excuse only in Minnesota. The exposition ran for six weeks. A Mexican cavalry band performed regularly in the building's art and sculpture garden, and other events were held such as a visit by Johann Strauss and his orchestra.

The building was the site of even more excitement in 1892, when the Republican Party held its national convention there, nominating Benjamin Harrison for a second term as president. Six telephones were made available for this event. The exposition building failed financially in 1895 and a futile attempt was made to get it used as the state capitol.[46] A few years later it was purchased by Marion Savage, the owner of the famous pacer Dan Patch, to house his International Stock Food Company. It was finally torn down in 1940.

Mrs. Cleveland's remote start up of the machinery of the Industrial Exposition Building was a sign of the technological innovation of the era. During the 1880s, electric streetcars powered by a hydroelectric power plant on Upton Island (the first in the country) began to run on the city's streets, allowing Minneapolis to spread outward. Railroads had overtaken water transportation a decade earlier. (One prominent set of tracks cut across Nicollet Island.) In 1883, James J. Hill, a St. Paul entrepreneur, had built the beautiful Stone Arch Bridge about half a mile south of the island to bring trains from St. Paul and places east directly into downtown Minneapolis's milling district.

On Nicollet Island land disputes continued to erupt from time to time. One of the fiercest involved the exact location of the outside line of Island Avenue. W.W. Eastman claimed title to a strip of land between Island Avenue and the river. The claim was contested by Franklin C. Griswold who feared loss of shore rights by other island property owners. In 1891 District Court Judge Lochren heard the case and decided that the outside line of the avenue was the margin of the bluff by the river. A variation of the same dispute reappeared in 1899 at the roads and bridges committee of the city council, with Eastman expressing his intention to fix the width of Island Avenue at forty-six feet all around the island, and both Franklin C. Griswold and Roman Alexander arguing against this proposal. Franklin C. Griswold argued that, "the city should not yield any claims it might have to territory facing the bluff line, for by so doing it would give Mr. Eastman the desired title to the shore line, and cut lot owners off from any show of ever realizing their shore rights." Those Islanders who were going to receive the benefit of a wider street were in favor of the plan, while those who, like Roman Alexander, stood to lose some width in the street in front of their property were against it. As an account in the *Minneapolis Journal* put it, "The committee grew more mystified the further the argument went at yesterday's meeting, and finally put the matter over two weeks for further argument."[47]

THE RISE OF FLOUR MILLING AND THE GREAT FIRE

All around the island, flour milling, which had taken a back seat to lumber milling since 1851, was coming into its own, due to both the expansion of rail connections (which brought the grain into the city for milling) and the depletion of the northern forests. On the west bank, a milling district had been created in 1857 when the first segment of a canal was constructed along First Street South to improve distribution of water to the milling industry. The mouth of the canal opened above the falls, flowed through underground headraces, then dropped into deep turbine pits connected to machinery in the mills above. Once the water had dropped through the turbines it flowed out to the river again beneath the falls.

In 1878 the Washburn A Mill was the site of a flour-dust explosion that leveled several mills and killed 18 men, but it did nothing to slow the burgeoning industry. By the 1880s, Minneapolis had become the Mill City, and it was the flour milling capital of the world. The names of mill owners and grain traders of the era—Washburn, Pillsbury, Peavey, Cargill—are well known in the industry even today.

Milling was a dangerous industry in those days, and the risk of fires, explosions, and severed limbs was ever present. But the danger that most threatened the residents of Nicollet Island was the Minneapolis Conflagration of 1893. It had been a dry summer and August 13 was a hot, windy day. That afternoon, some boys were smoking near the Lenhart Wagon Works on the southwest side of Nicollet Island and set fire to it. The Minneapolis Fire Department arrived to find the Lenhart plant fully engulfed, with fire spreading to the Cedar Lake Ice House and approaching the Clark Box Factory. The firemen fought the blaze, but it jumped to another ice house and a brick boiler factory, and firebrands carried on the wind eventually spread the fire to the residential area at the northern end of the island. From there the fire leapt to Boom Island, and the Backus Lumber Company was soon engulfed in flames. The fire then spread into Northeast (Nordeast) Minneapolis, where recent immigrants made their homes. Five sawmills along the river, more than a hundred dwellings, sheds, dry kilns, and block after block of lumber and wood yards burned.

The St. Paul Fire Department was summoned and a defensive line was made at

The Great Fire of 1893 marked the end of the Gilded Age on Nicollet Island. The fire began at the southern tip of the island and spread to Boom Island and Northeast Minneapolis. The fire was the costliest in Minneapolis for the next fifty years.

Marshall Street. A fire storm developed and a thermal column of flame 300 feet high and gale force winds swept toward Marshall Street. Crews on Marshall faced this onslaught as they sought to protect the residential district. Crews halted the flames at the Grain Belt brewhouse after its stables, bottling houses, and malt house had burned. By 4:30 p.m., the east flank of the fire was secure. Spark fires still shot throughout the city and spread to the west bank. People had to be evacuated by police and boatmen on the river using skiffs or logs to rescue them. The fire was so intense in the heart of the conflagration that a fire hydrant caught in the middle spouted steam instead of water.

Gradually the fire was brought under control, and at 11:41 p.m. it was officially declared out. About 200 people were burned out of their homes and sought shelter in churches and lodge halls. Only one resident died, and that was of an apparent heart attack. Firemen were scorched but none were killed in the conflagration. In sum, the fire destroyed twenty-three square blocks containing four factories, five saw mills, a planing mill, a brewery bottling house, malt house, and stables, four ice houses, two stables, a workers' dormitory, 103 houses, more than 50 dry kilns, sheds, barns, and outbuildings, 50 million feet of stacked lumber, and several blocks of wood and slab yards. The fire caused $975,582 in damages (more than twenty times that figure in modern dollars) a figure that would not be exceeded for the next 50 years. The sawmilling plants were never rebuilt; the west bank mills took up the extra work. The biggest fire in Minneapolis history had started on Nicollet Island.[48]

Although the fire did not spell the end of the Gilded Age of Nicollet Island, that time was near. The era that had started with a park proposal and the collapse of the Eastman tunnel had approached its nadir in fire. Economics and technology were creating a new world and the old way of life was soon to pass. The children who had grown up on the island were about to face World War I and the lingering romance of the old world would soon be gone forever.

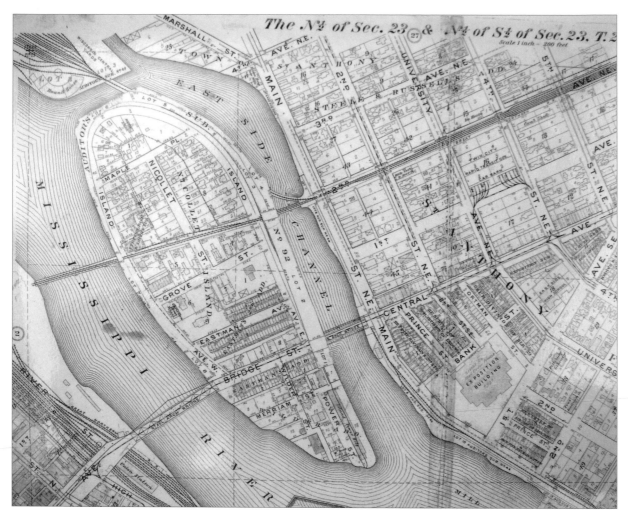

This 1914 map of Nicollet Island shows how prominent railroad development has become on the west bank with the Union Station at the western end of the Steel Arch Bridge. It also shows the railway switchyard that was built on Boom Island after the fire of 1893 had swept through it. On the east bank of the river the massive Exposition Building can be seen. On the northern tip of Nicollet Island the residential neighborhood remains but in the center some of the mansions have begun to disappear. The DeLaSalle Institute (DeLaSalle High School) C building has been built at the intersection of Island Avenue West and Eastman Avenue. Along Bridge Street commercial development continues and on the southern tip are industrial buildings.

4

Christian Brothers, Hippies, and a Donkey Named Sheba

It reeked of alcohol, but the rents were cheap, even for those days.

In the years after the Civil War, steel rails were expanded across the country. In 1867 the St. Paul and Pacific Railroad built a bridge through Nicollet Island. (It's now the Burlington Northern Santa Fe (BNSF) bridge.) It was the first railroad bridge across the Mississippi River in the Twin Cities, and it cut across the island, separating the northern residential neighborhood district from the remainder of the island.

James J. Hill, the St. Paul railroad tycoon and entrepreneur, built the Stone Arch Bridge across the Mississippi River in 1883 at the request of Minneapolis flour millers to facilitate train travel across the river, and at the height of the railroad era a dozen railroad companies moved freight and passengers in and out of Minneapolis. The Manitoba Line brought wheat from the Red River Valley and the Canadian prairie, and the Great Northern's Empire Builder brought passengers to Hill's Union Depot on the west bank.

The Milwaukee Road Depot, also on the west bank, served other railroad lines.

The trains that brought wheat to the mills on both banks of the river for processing also carried off the flour to be sold throughout the country. One of the lines was the Soo Line, also known as the Miller's Line. This railway line was established by mill owners to provide a more affordable alternative to the Chicago-owned railroads. The line carried flour from Minneapolis to the east via Sault Ste. Marie, Michigan—hence the name.

Immigrants and local workers crowded on and off the trains that coursed into the Union Depot at Bridge Square in the heart of the city, along with freight of every size and description, and Minneapolis began to see itself, like St. Louis, as a Gateway to the West. The name was soon applied to the entire area around Bridge Square, which became known as the Gateway District or Lower Loop. The Gateway District had been the great labor market center for the upper Midwest where seasonal labor could be rented at "slave markets." The businesses in the Gateway District catered to these men and the area was populated by bars, missions, flophouses, a red light district, and accompanying crime and public drunkenness.

By 1890, sawmills powered by steam were spread up and down the Mississippi in Minneapolis. The industry peaked in 1899, though the mills continued to run for several decades before Minnesota's forest resources were exhausted. Minneapolis was the largest saw-milling city in the nation for six years, but by 1910 the timber was largely gone and steam-powered mills in Virginia, Bemidji, Crookston and International Falls—much closer to the remaining forests—were drawing most of the business. The last Minneapolis lumber mill closed in 1920.

By the time the Gilded Age on Nicollet Island drew to the close, the once-pristine air of Nicollet Island had become fouled with soot as prevailing winds blew in industrial pollutants, making the island a less prestigious residential address. By 1930, due to freight rates and tariffs, Buffalo, New York, had replaced Minneapolis as a wheat-milling center, and many of the local mills were torn down.[1] By that time the Nicollet Island aristocrats had long since moved to more pristine and fashionable parts of the city, and worn-out men

from the old milling economy began to congregate in the Gateway District to the west of the island. As a result, the neighborhood gradually became rundown and dirty, lined with flop houses and gin joints and crowded with unemployed day-laborers.

PLANS FOR REVIVAL

In time this district and its extension down East Hennepin Avenue onto Nicollet Island became an embarrassment to the city, and in the early decades of the twentieth century various schemes were developed to improve the area. In 1906, A Civic Plan for Minneapolis was drafted by John N. Jager and three other architects, B. Straus, C.E. Edwins, and F.E. Halden. Known as the Jager Plan, its outlines were published in the *Minneapolis Journal* on December 2, 1906. It envisioned a remaking of Minneapolis along modern lines: "The modern city is a business corporation and should be managed on the same principles as a great railway or other large business organization. Its civic development should follow well studied and definite lines, based on natural laws of growth."[2] The plan proposed a permanent industrial art exposition for Nicollet Island, asserting that Nicollet Island's easy accessibility and spaciousness made it perfect for both large exhibition buildings and smaller pavilions. Though both beautiful and functional, the Jager Plan was never adopted, and the question of Nicollet Island's role in the redevelopment of downtown Minneapolis remained unanswered.

In 1909, the Committee of Civic Improvements of the Minneapolis Commercial Club reconsidered the question of a city plan. It formed a Civic Commission of Minneapolis which developed a plan in cooperation with civic-minded clubs and organizations. The commission's work (which had no legal authority or sanction) was guided by the architect Edward H. Bennett, who, early in his career, had worked with Daniel Burnham, pioneer of the City Beautiful movement. When he took on the Minneapolis project, Bennett himself had already drafted similar plans for the cities of San Francisco, Chicago, and Manila. Nicollet Island resident John DeLaittre worked on the plan but died before it was published in 1917.

In the published plan Nicollet Island rated a section of its own. The section began, "The manifest destiny of Nicollet Island is to be a park."[3] It suggested that Nicollet Island was ideally suited to be a park due to its history, proximity to the business district, and the fact that it would not interfere with transportation. The plan proposed that the island be encircled with a drive tied to existing avenues and deco-

rated with water-gardens, aquaria, and similar features. Ambitiously, the plan also proposed an airfield and a stadium:

The central portion is splendidly suited for a great stadium, large enough indeed for an aeroplane field. Areas for aeroplanes to alight in must ultimately be provided. The familiarity which is being gained with this form of transportation by the European War, will have unforeseen results when the brains now wasted on destruction are turned to construction. A centrally located aeroplane field will be of importance, and Nicollet Island could not be better placed for this purpose, with a natural means of approach for flying machines formed by the River valley in either direction.

But irrespective of its use for aeroplanes, its availability as the greatest of all playgrounds cannot be over-emphasized. The quadrennial Olympic Games, last held at Stockholm, could well be held here, when they come to America in happier days. All sorts of outdoor sports could be provided for. The River on both sides invites river-swimming pools in summer, and inundated skating ponds in winter. Its possibilities for sports of all kinds are unsurpassed.

The parking [sic] of Nicollet Island

will be a splendid advertisement for Minneapolis. Belle Island is the boast, —and a well-founded boast—of Detroit. But it is by no means so accessible as Nicollet Island will be.

The unbuilt upon and the dilapidated portion of the Island should be acquired at once, the acquisition of the rest to be prosecuted with vigor.[4]

This plan, like many others, was never implemented. However, one aspect of the earlier Jager Plan inspired an early Gateway clearing project. In 1915 two blocks of historic buildings were demolished to build a park, though the results were not what the city fathers intended. The new Gateway Pavilion and Park, located in the center of skid row, simply filled up with unemployed workers and vagrants.

Other slum-clearing projects were initiated from time to time. Many of the district's former inhabitants fled to the last vestige of skid row, East Hennepin Avenue on Nicollet Island.

Meanwhile, light industry was creeping into the residential portion of Nicollet Island, further changing its character. The Minneapolis Cold Storage Warehouse building, with portions dating from 1886, was built next to the railroad tracks, and the Roman Alexander store fixture building was built in 1908 (or possibly earlier). The stone quarries of Henry Down and the wine cellars of A.M. Smith further eroded the residential character of the central and northern portion on the island.[5] At the southern tip, the inter-channel tower was removed in 1916 to make way for the Third Avenue Bridge. The Island Power Building, which it powered, was razed in 1937.[6] The island's gracious homes began to lose their luster as well. Houses and flats were subdivided and rents fell. And some of the old buildings were demolished to make way for a new presence—the Christian Brothers.

THE CHRISTIAN BROTHERS ARRIVE

The Christian Brothers are a Roman Catholic teaching order founded by Saint Jean-Baptiste DeLaSalle in 1680. DeLaSalle organized the lay brothers to teach Christian principles—and reading, writing, and arithmetic—to working class and poor children. The DeLaSalle Brothers, absent clergy, a first for a Roman Catholic order, were to live in community and conduct schools in which the good of the student was emphasized. Corporal punishment was banned and the course of religious and educational instruction aimed at the formation of good Christian citizens.

The Christian Brothers had arrived in

St. Paul in 1871 to open a school which eventually became Cretin-Derham High School. Minnesota's Archbishop, John Ireland, was pleased with the Christian Brothers's efforts in St. Paul. Evidently so was Anthony Kelly, a businessman who died in 1899 and willed $10,000 to Archbishop Ireland for the founding of a Minneapolis school for boys run by the Christian Brothers.[7] Anthony Kelly was born in Ireland, one of six brothers. When, his father died, his mother remarried and came to America, living on the U.S. side of the border near Canada. When Kelly reached adulthood he moved to Savannah, Georgia, and worked as a planter. In 1859 he moved to Minneapolis where he and his brother Patrick started the Kelly Bros. grocery store. Their grocery enterprises grew but their family was divided by the Civil War. Anthony and his brother John were ardent Southern sympathizers. John fought in the Confederate Army and was killed. Another brother, Dudley, fought in the Union Army. During the war the Kelly Bros. grocery store sold ammunition to the Dakota Indians that was later used in the uprising in 1862, an act that later weighed on Kelly's conscience, though neither he nor anyone else had prior knowledge that a war with the Dakota was imminent.[8]

With Kelly's bequest, Archbishop Ireland called a meeting of clergy and laity and raised another $15,000. And with this $25,000, in the year 1900 (the year in which Jean-Baptiste DeLaSalle was canonized) the DeLaSalle Institute, later to be known as DeLaSalle High School, was founded.

Brothers Athanasius, Lewis, and Benedict were the first Christian Brothers of the DeLaSalle Institute. Fifty boys comprised the initial DeLaSalle class. They studied in the C building on the west side of the island. The C stood for "commercial," which was the focus of the course of instruction at DeLaSalle at the time. This class graduated 13 students in 1903, all of whom secured jobs before graduation in leading Minneapolis business firms. By 1907, an addition to the school was built, and by 1914 the Loring/King property had been acquired to expand for the school further. Its enrollment now stood at 352. By the 1920s, there was a desire for a college preparatory school, and building B was built on the grounds of the Loring/King mansion in 1922. The Christian Brothers themselves lived in the mansion until the 1950s when they moved into a new Brothers' residence. The Loring/King mansion, Blakely house, and the William W. Eastman carriage house were demolished for various expansions of the school. By the 1930s, the school had earned a dual reputation for excellent education and athletic prowess. By the 1950s DeLaSalle dominated

Minnesota Catholic high school athletics.

DeLaSalle has always taken pride in its mission of educating the young regardless of means. A signature story illustrates this aspect of the school. A mother came to the director, Brother Cassian, seeking to withdraw her son from the school because her husband had lost his plumbing business during the Great Depression. Brother Cassian arranged for the son to continue his education for $40, half the normal tuition, as that was what the family could afford. Years later, the boy who had benefited from this largesse became a donor to the institution.

Another noteworthy DeLaSalle student, Charlie Brown, graduated from DeLaSalle High School in 1944 and went on to art school where he became friends with Charles Schulz. When Schulz began drawing his famous Peanuts comic strip, he named the main character after his friend Charlie Brown.

In 1942, controversy erupted when DeLaSalle purchased the Eastman Flats and the area bounded by Grove Street, East Island Avenue, Eastman Avenue, and most of the current school grounds. This area included the grounds of the old Eastman mansion, which had burned down, and the Flats themselves, which were home to between 250 and 300 residents at the time. DeLaSalle sought the area for an expansion to build a football

The entrance to DeLaSalle High School building B, built in 1922 to accommodate a growing student body.

field, baseball diamond, and other athletic facilities.[9] The residents, many of them pensioners or on public assistance who enjoyed their inexpensive accommodations due to rent controls, were given 60 days to vacate before the scheduled October 1 demolition. They were not happy with the situation. One of the residents, Mrs. Anna Peterson, began circulating a petition. The residents argued that DeLaSalle should wait until after World War

II was over, as it was difficult for the residents, many of them elderly, to find new housing they could afford. Brother Jerome, principal of the school, countered that he had received a number of letters from real estate agencies saying that there were suitable living quarters available for the displaced.[10] Mrs. Peterson's petition with 215 signatures, urging a delay of the project until after the war, was presented to Brother Jerome, and in reply he said that he had been informed that the Minneapolis office of the war production board had given permission to go ahead with the project.[11] The flats were eventually demolished over the next several years.

With the arrival of the baby-boomer generation following World War II, DeLaSalle needed to expand, and in 1959 building A was opened. By 1964 DeLaSalle had reached its peak enrollment—1651 boys.

In a 2008 interview Kenneth Gieske recalled his days at DeLaSalle, first as a Christian Brother and later as a lay teacher. In 1968, Kenneth Gieske was assigned to DeLaSalle. Gieske had graduated from Sauk Centre High School and in 1963 became a novitiate for the Order of Christian Brothers. For a year Brother Gieske learned the fundamentals of the order at St. Yon Valley adjacent to St. Mary's College in Winona, Minnesota. As a novitiate he

Most of the Eastman Flats were demolished in the early 1940s to make way for an expanding DeLaSalle High School.

took vows of poverty, chastity, stability in the order, and a life dedicated to teaching the poor, which in practice meant teaching youth. Following his noviatiate, Brother Gieske attended St. Mary's College where he majored in history. Upon graduation Gieske was assigned to DeLaSalle High School. Prior to assignment Brother Gieske thought that he would have been better suited to a rural setting, but once at DeLaSalle, he found that the city suited him well. The Brothers lived in a residence hall with its own chapel. They would occasionally wear a black habit with a white collar for celebrations, but in public they typically wore a black suit with vest and white collar. Morning and evening prayer services were held daily, though Brother Gieske would often miss the latter as he drove the DeLaSalle bus for the sports teams.

Prior to Brother Gieske's arrival, DeLaSalle had more applicants than space, and tests were administered to determine whom to admit. This demographic surfeit of Catholic schoolboys was a factor in the establishment of Benilde-St. Margaret's and Totino-Grace schools. However, Brother Gieske's arrival roughly coincided with the end of the baby boom bulge. That year the school population was about 800. Gieske later recalled that logs were still stuck in the east channel when he arrived and a skid row of businesses lay directly in front of DeLaSalle. He also recalled a car falling partially into a crater in the parking lot where the old Eastman Flats had stood. It seems there were underground gaps left by the demolition of the building. He suggested that the tradition of DeLaSalle schoolboys throwing their books into the Mississippi may still have been observed occasionally but was infrequent due to the fact that books could be resold if they were going to be used again.

In several ways, the year 1971 was a watershed for DeLaSalle. The original C building burned down that year and a statue of Jean Baptiste DeLaSalle was moved to the location. That same year the all-girls school of St. Anthony of Padua in Northeast Minneapolis closed down. In response DeLaSalle opened its doors to girls for the first time.

By the 1970s the enrollment at DeLaSalle had dropped to 475 and like the island around it, the school had lost some of its former vigor. In the late 1960s DeLaSalle, in an attempt to be progressive, had introduced a modular class system and an open campus, but as it turned out, the combination of free periods and the ability to leave campus proved too tempting for many DeLaSalle students, who took advantage of the enticements of the city. Competition from other Roman Catholic high schools such as Benilde-St. Margaret's and Totino-Grace was also a factor in the decline. Many families who had moved to the suburbs no longer found DeLaSalle's inner-city location convenient, and it was forced to cut programs further. Deficits grew and some were convinced that DeLaSalle would have to close.

While the students at DeLaSalle were studying their lessons, other young men were hard at work in the factories and businesses that had grown up on the island, particularly at the southern tip. Frank M. Schneider, for example, worked in his father's small machine shop, Twin City Machine

Company. The business was housed in the Island Power Building, the old grey structure built of limestone and large wood beams by W.W. Eastman. The shop was kept warm by several large hand-fed coal stoves; it lacked even the most rudimentary plumbing facilities, and water had to be brought up by hand from the Mississippi. As for a lavatory, Schneider wrote, "Our sanitary facility was a narrow small enclosure in the back of the shop toward the river and it would be called an 8 holer; but this had no holes and the men had to balance themselves on a ledge. At 10 or 20 degrees below, this was a breezy operation and the men did not linger or rest."[12] The Twin City Machine Company specialized in grinding and corrugating the rolls that were used to grind flour, feed, linseed oil, and soybeans at the nearby mills. Schneider's recollections, written down in 1975, provide us with vivid picture of the business section of Nicollet Island as it was in the early twentieth century:

In the Teens, Twenties, and early thirties, if you wished to go to Nicollet Island from the Minneapolis loop, you would go North on Hennepin or Nicollet Avenues (Nicollet joined Hennepin at about 2ⁿᵈ St.) past the Great Northern Depot and across the bridge to the island. On your left was an old red brick hotel called the Commer-

cial and on that side of East Hennepin were several smaller hotels including the Old French Hotel. Across the street was the Boustead Electric and Manufacturing Co. who are now located at Madison Ave., West. Then you came to Wilder St., which had a pattern shop on one side and a brick building which housed a saloon was across Wilder St. When prohibition came in, this saloon was run as a restaurant. At different times, it was reported that you could purchase drink there with hard liquor in it. This was only an unconfirmed report. Further along that side of East Hennepin was a fruit store and a Salvation Army outlet or second hand store.

Wilder St. was the only one going to the East Side of the Island. As you go down the hill on that street a pattern works was on your left and on your right was the Kunz Oil Co. who now are in Edina. The founder of that concern fa[s]cinated me when I was about 5 years old at the time I first met him. He had had all his teeth washed with yellow gold and to me that was a sign of great wealth. His brother, Jake Kunz, was president of the Minneapolis Brewing Co., for years. Some of the 3ʳᵈ generation of the Kunz family are still living.

As you get to the bottom of the hill on Wilder street, the Durkee Atwood Co. is

The southern tip of Nicollet Island was occupied by industry from the late 1800s through the mid 1900s. The location provided ready access to waterpower, railways, and Minneapolis itself.

in a brick building. Turning to the left and in a half block turning to the right were two gray stone buildings owned by the Salvation Army. At one time, one of the buildings housed men who were down on their luck. Then on your left was the old 3 story Power Building. Besides Twin City Machine Co. the Coffin Box and Lumber Co., was in it as well as a rug clean-

ing outfit and a pattern shop. The Wm. Bros Boiler and Manufacturing Co., was directly across the street from Twin City Machine Co. This was their original building and it had their office there rather than in the larger plant they constructed on Johnson and East Hennepin. They closed their Nicollet Island Plant in the thirties and sold it to Durkee Atwood Co., and moved their offices to their newer larger plant, where they were for many years....

Further West ... was the Steel De Sota Ice Cream and Dairy Company/ Mr. Steel was the name of the man who owned and managed the company. In the twenties, they bought the family-owned Milton Dairy of St. Paul.

While education and light industry dominated the central and south end of the island, the north end remained a close-knit residential community. One woman, Carrie Almos, lived on Nicollet Island for 63 of her 95 years. In 1971, she was interviewed for the *Minneapolis Star* by Barbara Flanagan. Almos had been born in 1876 in a village near Trondheim, Norway, and she emigrated to the United States with her parents, Mr. and Mrs. Peter Almos. Before coming to Minnesota, the Almos family spent a year in the Dakotas. In 1881 they moved to Minneapolis where Peter Almos found work as a lumberman.

In 1908 Carrie and her sister moved to the island: "The island has always been an isolated and pleasant place to be, and so convenient. My sister, Emma, and I found this place with a newspaper ad. We liked it because we could walk over town to work." Miss Almos worked as a tailor for the Brown Brothers and later made fur coats for Jans Furs until her retirement in 1951. Thus her life on Nicollet Island spanned the last vestiges of the Gilded Age. She spoke of the Eastman Flats and how lovely they were, and of Mrs. Eastman and their mansion. She also remembered the groves of maple, oak, and elm trees that once covered the island: "I don't think there's a maple tree left. There were some along the river when we moved in, but they cut them down for oil tanks. My, that upset father."[13] Miss Almos's reminiscences offer telling details of how the island changed in the first half of the twentieth century as the aristocrats departed and a new type of resident began to make its mark.

Along with this shift in status, rents on the island declined, which in turn encouraged the subdivision of existing buildings. Many signature pieces of architecture were lost to development, as the June 9, 1929 *Minneapolis Journal* reported: "The Joel B. Bassett and John De Laittre homes built on Nicollet Island approximately 60 years ago and at one time show places of Minneapolis will be wrecked this week to make way for industrial progress."[14]

In 1940, the most recognizable landmark on Nicollet Island, the neon Grain Belt Beer sign, was constructed. It displayed the firm's new logo—a red diamond with a bottle cap behind it—which it had adopted two years

The iconic Grain Belt Beer sign is the best known landmark on Nicollet Island. Constructed around 1940, and measuring 50 feet wide by 60 feet tall, when built this neon sign was one of the largest in the United States.

earlier. The brewery itself was located just north of Nicollet Island on the east bank of the Mississippi in Northeast Minneapolis.

Grain Belt Beer, originally called Golden Grain Belt Beer, had been introduced in 1893 by the Minneapolis Brewing Company, a descendant of the old John Orth Brewery which stored its beer in the caves under Nicollet Island. In the earliest days beer was delivered in horse-drawn wagons in glass bottles with labels that said, "Properly sterilized – Does not cause biliousness." When Prohibition arrived, breweries shifted production from beer to near beer, soft drinks, ointments, and rubbing alcohol. Once Prohibition had been

repealed, Grain Belt returned to the product it knew best, using a new slogan: The Friendly Beer with the Friendly Flavor. On the neon Grain Belt sign each letter of "Grain Belt Beer" flashed sequentially over the red diamond and bottle cap. When it was built it was one of the largest neon signs in the United States, measuring 50 feet wide and 60 feet high.

By this time the mills had all but disappeared from the riverfront. A few nineteenth-century homes remained on the northern end, both humble and grand, decayed in their old-world charm, and down-and-out workers from the nearby Gateway District found refuge on Nicollet Island's East Hennepin Avenue in increasing numbers. The portion of Hennepin Bridge that crossed the island became populated by cheap hotels, bars and missions, including the Salvation Army Men's lodge, which had taken over the Island Sash and Door Factory. The building now houses the elegant Nicollet Island Inn, but in the late 1960s and into the 1970s it housed 180 men a night, most of them on welfare or pensions, along with some transients.

Alice Lyke operated the mission in those days and offered shelter, counsel, and compassion to the elderly men, many of whom were alcoholics. Upon her arrival, Lyke organized a major cleaning of the lodge, which had been filthy. Although Lyke was an officer in the

Women's Christian Temperance Union and no drinking was allowed in the lodge, she did not refuse shelter to the drunken: "Many of these men have been drinking for a good part of their lives. You can't expect them to just stop their drinking. We try to teach them to control their drinking." Of the men, she said, "I don't want them to lose confidence in me."[15]

HIPPIES, AND A DONKEY NAMED SHEBA

A 1961 census showed a total population of 581 living on Nicollet Island—340 alone, 82 in families, with 74 children among them. Only three of the houses were owned by their occupants. Landlord David Lerner owned many of the houses on Nicollet Island and had an adversarial relationship with some of his tenants. Those tenants withheld their minimal rent and in return Lerner withheld repairs on his properties. In one of his properties a divorcee with nine children and a pregnant dog paid $125 a month and lived huddled around a space heater. She had lived there for five years and some of her children never left the island. "The kids don't care to go to school. Their schoolmates call them island trash," she said. Instead the children spent their days chasing each other over cold grimy floors. Lerner remarked, "You should give me credit for taking her, I'm the only

landlord who would. It's your own individual house-cleaning. Some people live nice, others just live dirty. I will fix the place when she moves out."[16]

At the time, many considered David Lerner a slumlord, and some of them picketed the Lerner family home, which made a lasting impression on David and Ethel Lerner's then-ten-year-old, Mark Lerner. He recalled that the bad press was caused by people who did not want to pay their minimal rents and hid behind the state of disrepair of the houses, which was the reason they were inexpensive in the first place.

To those who knew David Lerner best, he was an honest man in a difficult situation. Harry Lerner, founder of Lerner Publishing and David's younger brother, said that their father Morris Lerner got his family started on Nicollet Island. Around 1921, Morris and his wife Lena rented the storefront at 7 East Hennepin from the three Johnson brothers who owned and operated the Island Cycle Shop next door. "Our family knew the Johnson brothers well. They were good landlords and decent people, except for Art Johnson's wife, who often made anti-Semitic comments. Her nasty words made an impression on me as a ten-year-old," Harry recalled. Art Johnson managed the bicycle shop, Ed handled the retail side of the business, and George did

Pictured above is Morris Lerner, owner of the Morris Island Grocery on Nicollet Island. The Lerner family owned a number of properties on Nicollet Island including several houses and the Grove Street Flats.

the repairs. George was blind but nonetheless could make any repair on a bicycle.[17]

The store that the Lerners opened was initially called Morris Island Grocery and was open seven days a week. Morris Lerner took the bus to work every day. He and his wife worked long hours and in the winter were kept warm by a small cast-iron furnace.

Harry Lerner remembered delivering groceries from the shop on his bike to customers at the Grove Street Flats and to the neighborhood at the northern tip. After Prohibition the Lerners got a liquor license, one of only two grocery stores in Minneapolis to get one. The store was renamed Morris Island Grocery and Liquor. Harry Lerner recalls, "The most popular beverage, other than beer, was muscatel, a wine with 20 percent alcohol content. The customers called it 'mustn't tell.' No one drinks it today."

During the 1940s Morris Lerner bought the Grove Street Flats. The Grove Street Flats were rent controlled during World War II but the tenants could sublet their properties and make a profit. Morris Lerner, as the owner of the property, could not increase rents, and lost money on the proposition. As for the Island Grocery, it was no more profitable than the Flats. When customers had money in hand, they would often go to a different grocery store in town, but when they wanted to put it on their tab they would come to the Island Grocery.

Morris Lerner was not a great businessman; he would often ignore customers in the front of the store while he was in back, and his kindness allowed people to run up large tabs. He kept a daily journal, and, more often than not, the journal showed greater expenses than income. Lena Lerner would remark that her husband should have been a teacher or professor. When Morris died from a heart attack on February 13, 1948, he left the store in debt and it fell to his son David to take over the island businesses. Harry was too young to take over, and the other brother, Aaron, was at Michigan University at the time. Aaron went on to medical school at Yale, and was involved

in the discovery of the substance Melatonin. The last child was their sister Mariam who graduated from the University of Minnesota, married a psychology professor, and moved to Pennsylvania.

David Lerner was working in California at the time of his father's death. He returned to Minneapolis to manage the Morris Island Grocery and Liquor Store, and began buying up some of the houses at the northern tip of Nicollet Island, hiring his younger brother Harry to mow some of the lawns. Harry recalled that one of the Islanders, Doris Park, asked his brother's permission to graze her two donkeys in front of the Grove Street Flats where the grass was long. David agreed. Harry recalled David as being kind, perhaps overly so, to some of his renters who simply did not pay their rent, although he was not without influence on them. On one occasion he rented a bus to take island residents to a precinct meeting where they voted along with him *en masse* on the issues. Though he sometimes indulged his tenants, David's business acumen put the family businesses on a profitable basis and he was able to get out of debt.[18]

One of the Islanders who rented from David Lerner was Clague Hodgson, who lived on the north end of the island from the summer of 1967 to the spring of 1968, and in a different home from the spring of 1969 through 1971, with the interim devoted to world travel. During Hodgson's first stay he worked as a handyman for Lerner. Lerner ran his domain from a perch in the Island Grocery where many of his tenants had their social security checks sent. Lerner would cash them, take the rent due off the top, and then supply the residents who desired it with Thunderbird or some other alcoholic beverage with their groceries.

On one occasion, a man was getting shaken down for his money by some winos and Hodgson, observing this from his car, moved to intervene. Lerner yelled, "Clague, get back in your car!"—perhaps the lesson being that the skid row jungle had a natural order. Hodgson recalled that Lerner did not throw anyone out for being two or three months late on rent, and sometimes accepted work for payment in lieu of money. He treated people as well as they treated him.[19]

Hodgson remembered that the Harvest Field Mission was near Lerner's Island Grocery and Liquor. The down-and-out could get a free meal there if they listened to hymns and prayers during the meal. The Island Café was also nearby; it served the best roast beef Hodgson had ever eaten. At Stanley's Bar the locals hung out and could get a beer for 5 cents. Hodgson heard old stories of counterfeiters and bootleggers practicing their clandestine arts in the old caves under the island.

During his second stay on the island, Hodgson, a man of some artistic talent, made jewelry by placing metal on the railroad tracks. Once it had been shaped by a passing train he would use it to make his popular snake bracelets. Hodgson also made charcoal sketches or watercolors of some of the homeless denizens of the island, and discovered that many were not currently winos, but rather *had been* winos.

One of Hodgson's sketch subjects was Cap'n Jack, who stood at the Hennepin Avenue Bridge and saluted traffic. He was reputed to be the nephew of Gabby Hayes, the cowboy film star. Cap'n Jack had been a drunk who used to suck the ethanol out of radiators, but somehow had managed to escape becoming blind. Another such character was the Wolf Man of the Pracna. Hodgson encountered the Wolf Man on a cold November day and observed him picking up frozen bananas from the ground to eat; wolf-like, he shied away when he detected Hodgson's interest. Hodgson learned that the Wolf Man's real name was Sam Valen and that he reportedly lived in the abandoned Pracna warehouse on St. Anthony Main, which ran along the east bank of the river. It was rumored that prior to hitting the skids and earning for himself the moniker of Wolf Man, Valen had been an attorney and an occasional stock trader. The IRS was supposedly on the lookout for him but couldn't find him because he didn't have a real address. When Hodgson met him he was said to be purifying alcohol from hair tonic in the Pracna ware-house. Valen met a sad end when some boys fired a .22 rifle at a box by the railroad tracks. The box moved and the boys found Valen dead inside.

Sam Valen, the Wolf-Man of the Pracna. Apparently a vagrant, he haunted Nicollet Island and came to a sad end accidentally shot with a .22 rifle.

One memory of the era stuck in Hodgson's mind with special clarity. On a snowy winter night in 1967, he was driving across the island on the Hennepin Avenue Bridge when he saw a man in one of the rooms on East Hennepin Street. A light bulb was suspended from the ceiling on a wire, and he could see the man's head bowed in prayer with his hands clasped in front of a loaf of bread, just like the old man in Enstrom's painting, *Grace*. He seemed solitary and bereaved, and Hodgson wondered what his life was like. Years later, Hodgson saw the same man standing outside Minneapolis's Old Soldier's Home wearing a soiled jacket with military medals on it. Hodgson offered him dinner and they ate at Gray's Drug in Dinky-town. The man's name was Charlie Johnson. He had been a Rough Rider and had fought at Teddy Roosevelt's side during the Spanish American War. He survived San Juan Hill only to lose his wife and eleven children to the Spanish Influenza outbreak in 1918. Somehow he had retained his faith, as he was seen praying years later by Hodgson on Nicollet Island.

Hodgson recalled smelling Mulligan stew cooking at night and hobos' fires crackling along the riverbanks at night. Bodies were occasionally dumped on Nicollet Island. Hodgson had a particularly disturbing story related to him by a man who claimed to be a retired Minneapolis cop. The man said that he once had a partner who particularly hated winos, so much so that he suspected him of mistreating them or worse. On his off hours, the retired cop said, he followed his partner and one night trailed him to Nicollet Island where he saw him about to kill a wino. He reported the incident to then-Chief Charles Stenvig (later Mayor Stenvig) who sent his partner to the state hospital in St. Peter, Minnesota. Whether this story is true or not is impossible to say, but at that time the death of transients was common and not scrutinized.

Hodgson also recalled one of the tragedies of Nicollet Island. Reed Diamond had been raised in a Jewish family and fell in love with Evelyn Pankratz. (Hodgson had gone to high school with Evelyn and been on the debate team with her, describing her as a beautiful girl.) The couple was married and moved to Nicollet Island. They then spent some time on a kibbutz in Israel before moving back to Nicollet Island, where, on the night of August 4, 1973, Evelyn stabbed Reed through the chest and killed him. The case went to trial and Evelyn was found guilty of first degree manslaughter. It was appealed to the Minnesota Supreme Court and the details of that night were included in that ruling.

On that fateful night, Evelyn was with her husband in his home on 163 East Island Ave. (Even though they were recently married, the home was not Evelyn's regular residence.) She, Reed, and a male friend of Reed's were partaking in a night of beer, whiskey, marijuana, and television. Another woman stopped in and later departed after Evelyn made sexual advances towards her. At 2:30 a.m. two more friends came to the house and saw an ambulance waiting outside. The ambulance driver said he was unable to gain entry and left. The friends peered in the window and saw Reed on the floor with a knife wound in his chest. They called the police who arrived immediately and took charge of the crime scene.

Evelyn had departed by that time, but the next day she turned herself in, accompanied by her attorney. She showed the police injuries consisting of a torn fingernail, small lumps on her head, a small red mark on her arm, and similar marks around her throat. She also made a written statement describing a convoluted chain of events.

Unfortunately for Evelyn's case, her version differed from that of the friend. Evelyn contended the Reed had struck her in the stomach, hit her in the head and throttled her. She picked up what she thought was a bread knife for her protection and Reed impaled himself on it. The forensic evidence and the testimony of their friend did not support Evelyn's version of events. The friend said that he did not hear an altercation; rather, all he heard Reed say was, "Time for bed, Eva." Her case was further weakened by the fact that previously she had stabbed the friend in the hip with a five-inch knife. On other occasions she had threatened her husband at least eight times with an array of weapons including a knife, an axe, a meat cleaver, and a .22 caliber rifle. The jury found that Evelyn Diamond had caused the death of her husband.[20]

ARTISTS AND MUSICIANS

Nicollet Island's unusual setting and low rents made it a haven for counter-culture types during the 60s and 70s, and many artists and musicians found a home there at one time or another. The "head" hippy, according to Hodgson, was a man named Arhelger whom women held in high esteem due to his Vikingesque good looks. Another former Islander (and high school friend of Hodgson's) was Ellen Stewart. Stewart lived on the island with her husband between 1966 and 1969, by which time Arhelger, or Arg, as he was known, had left. Years later, after a divorce, Stewart dated Arhelger, and she remembers him as creative, funny, and brilliant, which jibes with Arhelger's opinion of himself as the smartest man in the world. Steward remarked that he had a "large overwhelming personality, he was charismatic and in the thick of things. Everyone liked him." At one point he said he had lived with Jessica Lange and her husband Paco Grande.[21]

Arhelger lived in 107/109 West Island Avenue, the old Griswold house, and was always accompanied by a black dog named Boroavia. Once, on a lark, he shot out the lights of a sign for a roofing company located on Boom Island to the north of Nicollet Island. On another occasion, when Stewart had a problem with a prowler, he drew a picture of a dog with laser eyes and advised her to post it on her door to ward off the danger. He liked to sketch and he liked totems, owls in particular. He was also a tinkerer, collecting and fixing up old radios. He and a friend had a garage shop for tinkering down in the Bohemian Flats, and he made money by fixing up Mercedes, Volvos, and motorcycles. He loved motorcycles and got Stewart interested in Vespas. He was one of the founders of the Blind Lizard motorcycle rally, an event which is still held on Nicollet Island every year. The rally began as an antique bicycle rally in 1976 but quickly grew to incorporate motorcycles. During the rally, motorcycle aficionados bring their motorcycles—classic or new, iconoclastic, personalized, American—and park them around the island. Arhelger owned a lizard costume which he sometimes wore in honor of the rally.[22]

John Chaffee, another Islander, recalled that the Blind Lizard rally also had a kids component, with children parading on their bicycles in front of an appreciative crowd.

Paul McLeete recalled that the idea for the rally was hatched by Arhelger, Bob Meisch, and himself. Inspiration was fueled, in McLeete's words, by "a gallon of wine and a few other things." According to McLeete, the name "Blind Lizard" is open to interpretation but was intended as a reference to the reptilian part of the human brain which controls involuntary responses—an explanation which itself is open to interpretation. McLeete missed the first year of the rally, which was 1976 , but heard that five to seven people had showed up. By the second year it had grown to thirty to forty people and featured both bicycles and motorcycles.

McLeete's connection with the island went well beyond the motorcycle rally. He moved there

Steve Arhelger and Ellen Stewart his girlfriend are pictured in front of 107/109 West Island Avenue. Arhelger was the head hippie on Nicollet Island and was one of the founders of the Blind Lizard motorcycle rally.

in the summer of 1972 and stayed for twenty-five years, first living in 31 Maple Place. McLeete's upstairs neighbor was a Vietnam veteran who listened to Frank Zappa and kept a cockroach farm in his residence. McLeete remembers long battles with the Minneapolis Community Development Agency (MCDA), which hatched various stratagems to induce people to leave the island. McLeete and other Islanders resisted. His experience resisting the MCDA and his recollection of his upstairs neighbor prompted him to take the cockroach as a personal totem. The cockroaches' capacity to survive against adversity inspired this choice.

The city eventually demolished 31 Maple

Place, but by then McLeete had moved into 27 Maple Place. He worked as a locomotive mechanic, switchman, flagman, and pilot for the Chicago and Northwestern Railroad, and in his free time he rebuilt Volkswagen and Porsche engines downstairs in 27 Maple Place. He recalled a cottage industry of drug use on the island, with one man making LSD in the upper level of 17 Maple Place and others distributing it. There were some "serious fruit punch parties" on the part of the northern tip called "Central Park." Even Owsley, a man who bankrolled the Grateful Dead and traveled with the affiliated rock band The Merry Pranksters, once had a summit with the island chemist, the Pranksters having parked their tour bus on the island.[23]

McLeete also remembered Steve Arhelger as a creative guy who could make diabolical contraptions. Arhelger died two days after a Blind Lizard rally of a gunshot wound. Arhelger was manic-depressive, and when he was in a manic stage, or as he called it, "on the run" he would pick up an odd assortment of companions. He was in such a state when he died and had been hanging out with a transient who (according to Ellen Stewart) vanished immediately afterward with Arhelger's TV. Arhelger had died from a gunshot wound, but when his body was found the handgun was in his non-dominant hand and his wallet was empty. The police deemed it a suicide.[24]

Before her time with Arhelger, Stewart lived on the island with her husband in 31 Maple Place, which no longer exists, and rented from David Lerner. Her husband was a student at the University of Minnesota and he also worked at an American Fruit Cold Storage facility on the east side of Nicollet Street just north of the railroad tracks. Stewart studied archeology at the University and also worked there as a secretary and as a waitress at a bar called The Huddle located on the east bank of the Mississippi across from Nye's Polonaise Room. She recalled that the Grove Street Flats were called the "Wino Flats" and

the houses were so decrepit that 111/113 West Island Avenue had two dead birds poking out of the filigree. The island was dangerous in those days, at least for women, with all the transients going through on the railroad, and a visit to Lerner's Island Grocery was a bit intimidating: "It reeked of alcohol, but the rents were cheap, even for those days." A goat was often pastured on the island's northern tip and fossils could be found in the limestone on the banks of the island.[25]

The community was divided into the natives, who were poor, and the newcomers, who were hippies who had arrived in a couple of waves. Arhelger led the first wave and Stewart was in the second. The natives and the hippies occupied the same space in parallel worlds but didn't have much interaction or conflict, aside from disputes arising when children of the natives were accused of stealing things or being unruly.

The hippies embraced a countercultural lifestyle, indulging in marijuana and LSD, and grooving to the sounds of Jimi Hendrix, Country Joe and the Fish, Janis Joplin, Jefferson Airplane, John Mayal, and Cream. The hippie colony shared a sense of comraderie and individuals dressed with imagination and flair. They were mostly left alone by the larger society, though the drug dealing of some of the Islanders, naturally attracted the attention of the police. On one occasion officers raided the house at 163 East Island Avenue and found, scrawled on a wall, the slogan Get Bent—a double entendre, in that "Bent" was not only one of countless synonyms for "stoned" but also the name of one of the supervisors of Minneapolis police narcotics at the time.[26]

Cindy Gentling, a friend of both Hodgson and Stewart (with whom she had gone to high school) was another island resident. She and Hodgson had also gone to Northwestern University together before enrolling at the University of Minnesota. Gentling's grades at Northwestern had been poor and when enrolling at the University of Minnesota they told her that they were not sure if she was a screw-up or if she was dumb and that she had a single quarter to prove she belonged there. She worked hard all quarter and had a 4.0 GPA going into her humanities final with John Berryman, the Pulitzer-Prize winning poet. But as she studied late into the night for her final, Hodgson showed up and charmingly repeated, "You don't want to be doing this." By 3:00 a.m. she was convinced that Hodgson was right; she skipped the final and the two of them went to Nicollet Island and hung out for two weeks.[27]

Gentling lived in 109 West Island Ave from 1967 to 1969 with a boyfriend and another unmarried couple, renting from David Lerner. Lerner, unlike many landlords, was not overly concerned about the marital status of his tenants. He found eccentric people interesting. The residence was heated only by a space heater and was extremely cold in winter. Lerner showed Gentling where she could find another space heater abandoned in a snow bank, and with two it was tolerable. Gentling remembers Lerner as being kind, offering a little snifter of wine when she had a cold and inquiring after her life. Gentling recalls that visits to Lerner's "shady, dirty, store where he held court were always interesting because of the bizarre people there. Inelegant people could always be found in that inelegant store talking with Lerner."

Gentling's descriptions of the hippie culture reinforces the image of individuals living on the margins of society with little money but plenty of mind-altering substances, which were often considered a spiritual resource as well as a social activity. Nicollet Island hippies would walk through Minneapolis on Sundays, high on LSD, for seven or eight hours. They walked to the University's West Bank to wash their clothes and hang out at the Triangle Bar. On at least one occasion young men from the suburbs came down and threw rocks at one of the houses looking to roust them, and white men cruised the island in cars assuming that the hippie women would engage in prostitution. They were rather disappointed and embarrassed when they were turned down, finding the hippies to not be quite as marginal as they had hoped.

In an ironic echo of the Gilded Age, when many of the city's aristocrats lived on Nicollet Island, the island's hippie colony was thought to have more caché than similar colonies at the MCAD art school, the West Bank, and Macalester College.

John Heiman, who lived on the island from 1972 to 2003, first in 20 Maple Place and later at 184 E. Island Avenue, also recalled a class of people who worked just enough to get by and pay their minimal rent. "There were some great parties, a lot of pot, LSD, peyote, and no little amount of alcohol was drunk. We used to have a good 4th of July party and a Christmas party that was characterized by debauchery—to quote another island resident 'lewd and licentious behavior was prevalent among everyone.' Local politicians and park board members were invited to one of these parties. Wedding punch was served in which everyone dumped in what they had, people got loaded and I am not sure if it was the demise of anyone's political career or not."[28]

While the hippies lived on the island by choice, Gentling said others lived there because they were "alcoholic, mentally ill, alcoholic and mentally ill, or barely functional." Many of them were veterans. She remembers a man who made hobo art from little objects he would find, and another man named Jack who wore a black knitted cap and perched on the bridge. "Good morning little hippie," he would say when she went by. This "Jack" may have been the same man as Hodgson's "Captain Jack," but in Gentling's recollection, Jack claimed repeatedly to be the brother of Helen Hayes, the New York stage actress, and further asserted that she would be coming for him in a limo to take him to a ranch in Montana. Gentling reported that some of her friends did see Helen Hayes finally come and whisk Jack away.

Gentling observed another island denizen growing his beard out, and she remarked that it was getting kind of long. He explained that he was the Santa at Power's department store. His fake beard had once been detected by a girl so he decided to grow his own, and steered clear of alcohol from September on to prepare for his role. Gentling described her hippie days on Nicollet Island as "a great adventure."

SHEBA THE DONKEY

In 1971, John Chaffee and his sister Doris Park moved into 15 Maple Place; John got his own place at 17 Maple Place a few months later. In an interview in 2008, he observed, with the eyes of a surveyor and carpenter, that the houses on the island were in pretty bad shape in those days, and 17 Maple Place had sparrows living in the walls when he moved in. He had found out about the island through friends who recommended him informally to David Lerner. That was about the only way to find a place there.

Chaffee's sister, Doris Park, was an animal lover who had taken an eclectic sampling of animal husbandry courses at the University of Minnesota. One day in 1975 she purchased two donkeys, Pearl and her daughter Sheba, from a farmer in Lakeville for $75 and stabled them behind her home. Sheba became known as the "Nicollet Island lawnmower."

It wasn't long, however, before animal control officers appeared to inform Doris that hoofed animals were not permitted in Minneapolis. She then obtained a permit for the donkeys from skeptical city officials under an obscure provision which allowed residency for "animals kept for display." Legalized, the donkeys lived happily, and Pearl died several years later of natural causes. Sheba became a fixture on Nicollet Island, receiving many visitors from whom she accepted carrots, apples, pop (which she could drink from the can) and occasionally beer, which Park did not encourage. She appeared on publicity posters issued by the city promoting the "Mississippi Mile."

Sheba the donkey (right), also known as the lawnmower of Nicollet Island, moved to the island with her mother Pearl (left) in the early 1970s. They are shown here with their owner Doris Park.

As a public figure, she appeared on *A Prairie Home Companion* when it was broadcast from the Nicollet Island amphitheater. She also marched in a parade down Hennepin Avenue under the sponsorship of a local political group. Sheba made an appearance at DeLaSalle High School for a program in which a teacher, selected by a vote of the students, received a kiss from her.

Sheba disappeared a couple of times. On one occasion she was found in a DeLaSalle High School classroom (no doubt a crowning achievement for some pranksters), and on another occasion she was found on Washington Avenue being led by an 11-year-old boy who wanted to surprise his mother.

Sheba's public appearances were not always successful, however. She auditioned for the movie *That was Then, This is Now*, which was filmed on the island, but was found in one of the movie trailers with her nose buried in a can of face powder; whether she was eating it or preparing for an appearance, she never divulged.[29]

Interesting people were the norm for Islanders. Frank Allen lived at 163 East Island Avenue. He and his wife Mary were heavy drinkers; Frank, for his part, perhaps to silence some of the things he had seen in the Pacific as a soldier during World War II. He had also been a prizefighter, and Chaffee recalled seeing him dancing on Nicollet Street with Molly Mason, a well-known country musician. "Molly's brother was fiddling on a hay bale, which was for some reason on the street. Young Molly was dancing with Frank, who was wearing a torn white shirt. You could see that he had been a prize fighter because he moved so well and was a very good dancer," Chaffee said. Paul McLeete remembered Frank and Mary too, recalling their heavy drinking and the fact that Mary was half Indian. When Frank died of emphysema, Mary got a new boyfriend who was going door to door for Alcoholics Anonymous. "She won the argument," as the boyfriend starting drinking soon after. Mary died in her sleep.

Bikers lived at 93 Nicollet Street and some time later it was occupied by "Garbage John." Garbage John claimed to be some sort of artist who at night would scavenge the city looking for material to build a house. He eventually filled up the whole back of the house and the yard with the material, at which point local authorities told him he had to get rid of it. Garbage John was eventually evicted.

Musicians both lived on and visited the island in those days. Islander Dick Reese could play ten or twelve instruments. Peter Ostroushko, one of the original musicians on Garrison Keillor's *A Prairie Home Companion*, lived upstairs in 107/109 West Island Avenue. Chaffee himself played the mandolin family and participated in some of the jam sessions held on the island. One of the best musicians he ever jammed with was George McNiff, a transient who often spent the night on his stoop or in the back of his pickup. McNiff was of Scotch-Irish and Native American descent; he worked occasionally as a steeplejack, water tower painter, and cement mason, and had done time for robbing Red Owl grocery stores. But when he had just enough to drink he was a remarkable guitarist. McNiff had perfect pitch—the ability to identify a note without context unerringly—and he taught Chaffee a few tunes. McNiff jammed with Stephane Grappelli, jazz's most venerated fiddle player, when he was in Minneapolis.

The house at 101 West Island was destroyed under suspicious circumstances. It belonged to the owner of a garbage hauling company on the adjacent lot, located at the corner of West Island Avenue and Maple Street. He was a rough looking fellow and was reputed to be an ex-con, as were several of his employees. Passersby often noticed an abundance of freshly painted cars and stacks of televisions on the premises. The owner sought to expand his lot onto the 101 West Island lot but was denied a permit by city authorities. A few weeks later the house on that lot conveniently burned down and the business was able to expand.

A June 1, 1983, article in the *City Pages* newspaper provided a thumbnail sketch of life on the island and what tourists driving through might see:

(Julie) Carswell is the island's community gardener. The tourists she dismisses will see her handiwork in the beds of tulips she's planted on every street. They'll miss the patchwork glass and plastic-paned greenhouse where she cultivated her neighbors' tomato and herb plants. That's hidden behind a row of houses, near where Sheba and Pearl, a neighbor's two burros, are tethered.

They'll see the turreted, sienna-colored Griswold mansion where Carswell and her husband live with a band of cats, but they'll miss Michael Latimore, a hospital aide who spends days in a third-floor alcove, painting vibrant oil canvasses of airplanes, oranges, balloons and friends' faces. To get to Latimore's studio, you must climb a stairwell redolent of cat piss, navigate a hallway stuffed with debris and mattresses, and knock on a far door.

Sightseers with architectural guidebooks in hand will recognize the Italianate style of the house on West Island Avenue with all its windows boarded up. What they won't know is that the house's last occupants were a fence and a thief, and that the windows were smashed by neighbors one bitter cold night after the pair stole someone's stereo.

Ken Armburst sees all these things when he circles the island, wearing an amorphous khaki cap, walking a raffish dog named Rip. Armburst has lived on the island for 34 years, ever since he moved to the cities from Leech Lake and rented a white clapboard house on East Island Avenue that was built five years after the Civil War ended. His neighbors include a member of the Wallets [an accordion-based rock band of the time] a graphic artist, an antique radio collector and a doctor. All are nearly 30 years his junior. "Kenny is, in a most affectionate way, a sort of supervisor to us," says one neighbor.

Amburst's wife, Doris, was even more of a lynch pin in the small Nicollet Island community. A capable cook who single-handedly prepared the Fourth of July picnic every year, she was also the island social worker, cashing social security checks and running errands for the older neighbors. She was a strong-jawed woman with black hair and a weathered face, who learned to cook, when she worked for a railroad crew in northern Minnesota. 'She had a firm sense of what's right,' recalls a neighbor. 'She wouldn't take any bullshit from anybody—not the mayor or any public official—if she thought they were threatening the island.' Doris Armburst died this spring [1983], a few months before the agreement that would have brought her closer to owning the home she and Ken rented for 34 years.[30]

As the buildings on Nicollet Island continued to decay, even the Grain Belt Beer sign, whose towers had tempted many a DeLaSalle schoolboy, lost its light. It was a symptom of the decline of the island itself, which had turned its back on the changing world. Nonetheless, the island remained a true neighborhood. According to Islander Fred Markus:

The atmosphere of the Island itself helps generate this sense of community. The pace of life slows and there is always time to stop and say hello to one's neighbors, to enjoy the tranquility of a summer's evening, to look across the river at the city as if it were a distant land, inhabited by strangers who have lost their sense of community and sharing, who have lost their sense of identity with the past and with the land and live in the country of the blind. The buildings that have stood for many generations and live on in quiet old age, looking upon the affairs of young and old alike with the impassive dignity of eyes that once looked upon the city in its infancy. And the river, the Father of Waters, flows beyond the pale of human concern.[31]

But though the island seemed to float in a timeless backwater, detached from the hurried pace of the city that surrounded it, change, as always, was afoot. In fact, Nicollet Island was soon to become a focal point for the grandiose schemes of city planners who cared little for the local residents.

This 2008 orthophotographic map shows how the Minneapolis riverfront and Nicollet Island have de-industrialized. A neighborhood still remains at the northern tip but there are fewer houses. In the central portion the Eastman Flats and all detached houses have disappeared with only the Grove Street Flats remaining. DeLaSalle High School has grown and all that remains of the industrial buildings at the southern tip are the buildings housing the Nicollet Island Inn and the Nicollet Island Pavilion. At the southeastern part of the island is a newer addition, the Merriam Street Bridge.

5

The Rebirth

To find five 100-year-old houses, all located within a single block, is unusual in itself, especially in view of the extensive demolition that has taken place in what were the older areas of the city.

In the early decades of the twentieth century various schemes had been devised to rearrange and revitalize Nicollet Island, often as part of larger proposals to turn the riverfront into parkland, but these efforts had been more successful at removing buildings than finding a viable plan for Nicollet Island's renewal. Between 1957 and 1965, an even more ambitious plan for the Gateway District, put into effect under the post-war rubric of "urban renewal," led to the destruction of more than 180 buildings, with businesses relocated and residents displaced. In a few short years one-third of downtown Minneapolis was obliterated, the historic Gateway District became a thing of the past, and much of Minneapolis's architectural heritage was lost.[1]

Nicollet Island was the next part of the city to interest urban planners, and it became a keystone in the growing movement to restore the riverfront. In a 1957 interview, a noted consultant from Chicago, Frederick Aschman, echoing the words of previous generations of city planners, said, "The place has enough historical significance so that the state would be justified in buying it…DeLaSalle High School could be left where it is, but the rest of the island could be cleared. A private concessionaire forbidden to introduce honky-tonk attractions, could make it a delightful amusement park, unique in America, and equal to the wonderful places in Europe, such as Tivoli park in Copenhagen."[2]

In 1961, Aschman was chosen by the Downtown Council to make a report determining the island's potential for redevelopment. It was his conclusion that Nicollet Island and the St. Anthony Falls area could be turned into a 12-acre nineteenth century period park with exhibits, working replicas of items such as a saw or flour mill, a ferry, and period hotels, print shops, and entertainment

The Gateway Urban Renewal Plan was an attempt by city officials to transform downtown Minneapolis and the skid row area along Hennepin Avenue by demolishing the rundown buildings that had become havens for the homeless and destitute. Between 1957 and 1965 more than 180 buildings were torn down.

venues. The report recommended purchasing the area, and estimated the cost of development from $1.5 million to $2.5 million.[3] The proposal was not adopted but elements of it made an impression on civic leaders, in particular the notion of making the island into a park.

In 1964 a plan to build an interstate, 335,

over the northern tip of Nicollet Island, was proposed, and later abandoned.[4] The following year the Citizens' Committee for Nicollet Island, a group of Minneapolis businessmen and civic leaders, proposed a $10 million North American Conservation Hall of Fame and Museum to be built on fifteen acres of the island. This proposal had backing from the International Association of Game, Fish, and Conservation Commissioners; it had originally been proposed by Governor Karl Rolvaag in 1963. It was thought to harmonize with a proposal by the Minneapolis Chamber of Commerce to have a historical park at the southern end, complete with replica lumber and flour mills and early island bridges. This plan also failed to win the necessary support.[5]

In 1968, a plan to replace the Hennepin Avenue Bridge was put to the city council. The old bridge, built in 1891, was the third major bridge on Nicollet Island. According to Kenneth Gieske, a teacher at DeLaSalle High School in the late 1960s, the third bridge was higher than the previous suspension bridge, and some of the businesses that fronted it had to build new doors since the previous doors were too low for the third bridge. Growing traffic needs necessitated a fourth bridge. The plan was opposed by business owners and mission operators on old East Hennepin Avenue. But it was exactly these operations that some planners were aiming at, and the new bridge was seen as an opportunity to demolish the businesses and missions which lined the old bridge.

The wrecking ball came and the last vestige of the Gateway District's skid row was demolished. In 1990, in its place, a concrete twin suspension bridge was erected, which contains one span from Nicollet Island to the west bank and splits into two spans from Nicollet Island to the east bank. It has separated sections for one-way traffic on each of the spans.[6] Originally a flat freeway slab bridge had been proposed by county engineers, but opposition to losing the historical bridge resulted in a design compromise to honor the historic bridges. Lit by accent lighting at night, the new bridge design is reminiscent of the first two suspension bridges on the site. Footings and cable anchors from the 1855 and 1876 bridges were uncovered during the new bridge's construction. The Park Board later used these historic remains as the centerpiece of First Bridge Park on the west bank of the river.

RESIDENTS VS. RENEWALISTS

In 1971, another push was made to remake Nicollet Island. The first plan presented to the City Planning Department contained a park, festival gardens, ponds, and a

historical village on the island. The second proposal was an appraisal of the Salvation Army building, formerly the Island Sash and Door factory, on the southern tip. This appraisal, by the John G. Alexander Company, said that the "highest and best" use for the site would be a marina and service station, though this appraisal recognized that there was value in the site for a historical park. These proposals went nowhere.

In 1972, a report, "Mississippi/ Minneapolis –A Plan and Program for Riverfront Development," concluded that "Nicollet Island should function as the center of attraction for Riverfront revitalization. As a usable island with a significant historic past located in the midst of a metropolitan area, it presents a clearly outstanding potential for becoming one of the major identifying elements, not only of the city, but of the entire region." This plan went on to detail a vision of the island dedicated to public use: green space cut through with manmade canals for skating in the winter, a learning center in the Grove Street Flats and/or in the older DeLaSalle High School buildings, and a historic village in the southern portion, perhaps made from transplanted houses from the northern tip and elsewhere near an amphitheater built for outdoor events.[7] Also in 1972, a proposal was made to build a Riverfront Learning Center

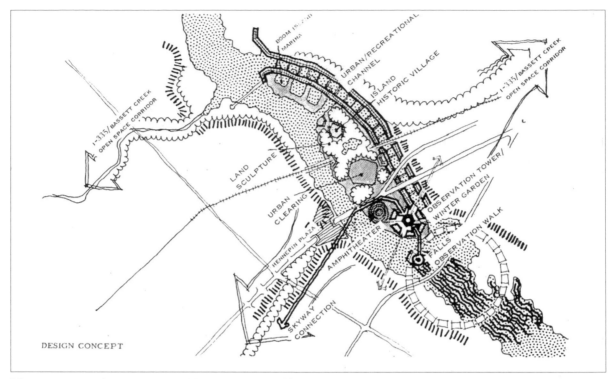

DESIGN CONCEPT

Many imaginative plans were proposed for Nicollet Island. The plan pictured here included an historic village, a catwalk on the southern tip to observe the Falls of St. Anthony, and a winter garden.

which would include an urban observation and urban affairs library along with a learning center for children.[8]

Several proposals were put forth by three teams of architects commissioned by Minneapolis and the Art Center. The first proposal's centerpiece was to be a Museum of the Mississippi. It envisioned a 2,558-foot by 25-foot granite strip running the length of the island. It was to be accompanied by a list of cities, wildlife, people, events, and inventions related

to the Mississippi River. Alongside were to be monuments of Mississippi icons such as "Tom Sawyer's white fence, the Spirit of St. Louis, a riverside plantation mansion, Elvis's guitar, an obelisk at Cairo and a cannon at Vicksburg."[9] This proposal also included a Nicollet Island hotel which was to incorporate elements of the Island Sash and Door Company and the Durkee-Atwood buildings. The second proposal imagined Nicollet Island as a park, having a pyramidal labyrinth at the southern tip, gardens with pools in the center, and a fountain and Embarcadero in the north. The third proposal imagined housing and commercial development on the eastern length of the island and a winter garden/conservatory at the south end, with the central portion cleared for public gatherings, the preservation of the historic houses at the northern tip of the island as a historic village, limited automobile access, a connection to the mainland with a sky bridge, land sculptures, and a Falls Observation Walk, a catwalk at the southern tip overlooking St. Anthony Falls.

Yet another plan was developed by the Nicollet Island-East Bank Project Area Committee, a group of local residents. It envisioned a neighborhood with communal gardens, bee hives, a petting farm, sauna baths, grist mill, a methane plant and a solar energy plant.[10]

These plans, and ideas for a heliport, a space needle, condominiums and many others, did underscore one fact. Nicollet Island was considered to have great potential for development by many groups of people who unfortunately differed in their ideas of what would be most appropriate. The major contenders among advocates for development were the Park and Recreation Board, the Minneapolis Housing and Redevelopment Authority (MHRA), the Metropolitan Council, and the residents, most particularly the residents of

the neighborhood at the island's northern tip.

A *Minneapolis Tribune* article from December 6, 1980, stated that, "the Park Board has jealously eyed Nicollet Island as the missing link in the city's park system for almost a century." The MHRA had come to own most of the houses on the island through condemnations of property owned by David Lerner and other landlords. The Metropolitan Council had the power of funding and final approval of plans that would inevitably affect the residents who lived on the island, loved it, feared eviction, and mostly wanted to be left alone. The differing goals of these factions were not easily reconciled and the standoff continued for years.

The MHRA initially tore some houses down, just as they'd done in the Gateway District, and the residents fought an ongoing battle to stop them. Mark Lerner recalled that his father David was particularly angered by the faction which advocated urban renewal, seeing himself as a Gary Cooper character arrayed against evil forces. Although a Humphrey Democrat, Lerner frequently found himself at odds with, using a term of the day, "goo goo liberals" —do gooders who wanted to use the power of government to compel behavior and perfect human society in their vision. He felt that "liberals who lived in places like Linden Hills wanted bike paths and didn't want to be exposed to people with messy lifestyles." Lerner catered to a population that mostly wanted to be left alone, and he was particularly irritated by the concept of "blight" being used by the government to characterize their lifestyles, assert eminent domain, and seize private property. As a result, he was involved repeatedly in legal battles to prevent the city from condemning his properties. His son Mark later observed that the people who were dislocated to apartment living during this process seldom lived long or happily in their new environs.[11]

Also fighting the urban renewalists were island residents, Fred Markus and John Chaffee prominent among them, who sometimes appeared *en masse* at political caucuses to elect delegates sympathetic to their cause. After no little effort of persuasion, some of the MHRA members came around to the Islanders' position that having people living on the island's northern tip made it a safer place, and that the island was one of Minneapolis's oldest neighborhoods whose houses were part of Minnesota's heritage. The Islanders gained further support when, in 1971, Nicollet Island was included in the Falls of St. Anthony National Registry of Historic Places. Further succor came from the formation of the Heritage Preservation Commission (HPC) in 1972, an advisory committee to the city council whose purpose was to act as a watchdog of inappropriate uses of historical places.

Though some of the members of the MHRA were sympathetic to the Islander's claims, the Minneapolis Park Board was determined to demolish the neighborhood, which they saw as vagrant housing, and they worked to acquire the land and incorporate it into a massive 150-acre riverfront park with funding through the Metropolitan Council.[12]

As momentum gathered to include Nicollet Island in an urban renewal project, the Nicollet Island-East Bank Project Area Committee (NIEBPAC) was formed in 1972. According to John Chaffee, the formation of this Project Area Committee was a federal requirement when federal urban-renewal funds from the Department of Housing and Urban Development were going to be used in a specific project area. The aim was to give local citizens affected by prospective projects input into the process.

The NIEBPAC influenced city officials to change the original 1969 urban-renewal plan that called for demolition of all the existing buildings on Nicollet Island. That change was officially made in 1973. The NIEBPAC also urged officials to commission a historic study of the houses on the island.

The issue of what to do with the island houses reached a turning point when the

MHRA commissioned a study by Miller-Dunwiddie Architects, Inc., to analyze the historical significance of Nicollet Island and a portion of the east bank. The study, published in 1974, concluded that "an unusually high percentage of buildings in the neighborhood have some architectural significance," and that the group of dwellings remaining on the north tip of the island constituted an important collection of related elements forming a neighborhood group. "To find *five 100-year old houses*, all located within a single block, is unusual in itself, especially in view of the extensive demolition that has taken place in what were the older areas of the city. When one considers that much of their original fabric remains intact, it is even more unusual! There may be other examples to be found in the city, but they certainly are not present in abundance."[13] This study curtailed efforts to destroy the houses, though a viable solution to the issue of what to do with them remained elusive.

Meanwhile, the growing recognition of the historic value of the houses on Nicollet Island led the MHRA in 1976 to undertake a stabilization effort of some of them. They contracted with the Kraus-Anderson Building Company. Three of the houses were the Queen Anne duplex at 107-109 W. Island Ave, a small French Second Empire house at 27 Maple Place, and an Italianate fourplex at 111-113 W. Island Ave. Florent Heiman led the crew in unraveling the mysteries of the restoration. A *Minneapolis Tribune* article from 1976 reported, "Board by board, his carpenters searched for rotted lumber. Counting layers of paint and scrutinizing the type of paint in each layer they dated modifications to the original buildings. Old fashioned square nails were also clues to what was original construction." For the Queen Anne, an old woodcarver had to be contracted to craft replacements for some of the rotting details. Some of the details were copied right off the building. "We laid 'em out and sawed the patterns right here," said Heiman. Full restoration was neither financially nor architecturally possible and modern materials were sometimes used. The Queen Anne, which cost $5,000 to build in 1890, ended up costing $48,000 to restore, though to do it to the highest standards would have cost as much as $83,000, according to an estimate.[14]

That year also saw the construction of an outdoor amphitheater at the southern tip of the island for the national bicentennial. Former Vice President and U.S. Senator Hubert Humphrey gave the dedication speech on July 2, 1976.

In 1980, the MHRA and the Park Board tangled over the old Island Sash and Door

Company building, which had most recently been a Salvation Army outpost. The MHRA was in the process of negotiating a plan with a private developer to develop an inn and restaurant there. This brought them into conflict with the Park Board. As it then stood, the Park Board had come into possession of the southern tip of the island and land around the rim for park property. Many of the northern houses, the Island Sash and Door Company Building, and DeLaSalle High School were considered outparcel land (excluded from the park). If use of outparcel land was discontinued, then these areas would come into the Park Board's possession. This was the Metropolitan-Council-approved status quo in 1978. What precipitated the conflict in 1980 was the fact that the first plan to restore the Island Sash and Door building by Carl Eller, a former Vikings football player, had fallen through. When the MHRA sought a second candidate, the Park Board claimed that the property use had been discontinued. A settlement on this issue and the larger issue of use of the entire island was needed.[15]

In 1981, the City of Minneapolis proposed such a settlement to the Metropolitan Council. The central theme for the island in this proposal was "leisure activities." The elements of the proposed settlement were:

- The Island Sash and Door Company should be leased to a private developer.

- DeLaSalle should not be forced to move, but neither should it expand on the island with athletic fields or otherwise.

- The seventeen houses on the upper end of the island should be supplemented by bringing in buildings of the same general character and period from other parts of the city, the houses should be repaired and redecorated with emphasis on their historical appearance outside and livability inside.

- Some homes should probably be turned into commercial establishments.

- The Grove Street Flats, restored to something approaching their original form, should be a civic asset, but the job will require someone with extraordinary imagination, knowledge, dedication, and financial resources.

- Park development, so far as practical, should accommodate to the fact that the island will become a front yard for future intensive housing developments on the opposite shores.

- The Metropolitan Council, as dispenser of taxpayers' funds, and the Minneapolis Park Board, as operator of the island, should both adopt standards that are unique to this project, Capital funds for acquisition, restoration, and development have been provided by the Legislature through the Metropolitan Council, but the existing law provides that the City will keep things going…Therefore private occupancy and operation of many of the facilities to be provided on the Island is an absolute necessity.

• Of all the various agencies available to initiate and interpret the theme of leisure activities, the Minneapolis Park Board is the most appropriate.[16]

THE FLATS AND THE INN

One aspect of this proposal was, in fact, already under way, and that was the restoration of the Grove Street Flats, the last remaining flats built by the entrepreneur W.W. Eastman. On October 31, 1980, the city council met to approve the demolition of the Grove Street Flats. They had grown extremely decrepit and had been condemned after a reporter walked through them and found them to be inhabited by transients living in squalor. At the eleventh hour a developer, John Kerwin, appeared with a purchase agreement he had signed hours before. According to Kerwin, the city council wisely decided to honor his purchase agreement. Kerwin approvingly said,

"the city council was run by the DeLaSalle mafia who made long-term decisions, which had a profound impact on the future success of the city." Kerwin had some credibility with the council because he was involved in the restoration of the Lumber Exchange Building at the time, and had done projects such as the Bellevue Hotel rehabilitation. The demolition was delayed and Kerwin set to work.[17]

Like many, Kerwin was amazed when he discovered Nicollet Island. He was working on a restoration project in the Minneapolis warehouse district when he looked across the river toward the east bank and saw mansions. Kerwin was familiar with Northeast Minneapolis, and knew there were no mansions there, so he headed over the bridge to get a closer look. What Kerwin discovered was the decaying grandeur of the architecture on Nicollet Island, and no building's grandeur was in greater decay than the Grove Street Flats with its front façade collapsing and its roof caving in.

Kerwin had developed an appreciation for architecture while growing up in the historic Crocus Hill area of St. Paul. A hands-on restoration of the Flats appealed to him. His involvement in the Lumber Exchange Building restoration had been as an executive, and he wanted to do the "nuts and bolts of restoration," something which appealed to him

In 1980 the Grove Street Flats were restored by John Kerwin, who saved them from demolition at the last minute. The restoration of the eighteen flats was an important step in the revitalization of Nicollet Island.

not another plan, but rather action. With that thought in mind, Kerwin went to the Lumber Exchange and asked his foreman if he could work the following day, which was a Saturday. The foreman agreed and the next day Kerwin, the foreman, and a few men showed up at the Flats with steel I-beams to secure the front wall. Neighbors gathered, wondering who the non-Islanders were and what they were up to. John Chaffee and his sister Doris Park were among those present, and Chaffee pointed out to Kerwin that the walls of the Flats were bowed. A survey was needed, and Kerwin hired Chaffee, a surveyor, to perform the task, and also to produce a more general survey which proved instrumental during the restoration.

as a former Navy Seabee. It took two years of importunity with the owner of the Grove Street Flats, Harry Lerner, and the threat from the city to demolish them and make Lerner pay for it, but, at the last minute, Lerner agreed to sell the Flats to Kerwin for $100,000.

After leaving the city council meeting, Kerwin headed for the Minneapolis library and asked for everything they had on Nicollet Island. He was presented with a stack of plan after plan and proposal after proposal. As he sifted through the sea of unrealized proposals, it occurred to him that what was needed was

Kerwin's task precipitated the formation of the Nicollet Island Restoration and Development Company or NIRDs. It was a loose confederacy of contractors, many of them Islanders, and they had a keen interest in restoring the Flats to historical standards. The founders of the NIRDs were John Drucker and Doris Park, who told her brother John

Chaffee about cutting pipes out of the Flats's walls with an acetylene torch and cleaning the mansard roof with a concoction she made out of lye and corn starch. The construction crew during restoration insisted on rebuilding the original slate roof with hexagonal shingles that had to be hand cut, and Kerwin said "they made me build wooden wells rather than using the galvanized ones I'd bought. Know anyone who wants to buy 12 metal window wells?" In all, eighteen Grove Street Flats were restored and sold for $138,000 to $225,000. In spite of hopes, there was no profit for Kerwin in the restoration: it was a nearly break-even proposition. The restoration was an act of love.

Kerwin, no stranger to controversy, stirred up some conflict when he cut down 93 sapling trees on the riverbank west of the Flats to build a stairs and boat launch. Some island residents and the Park Board cried foul, and, according to Kerwin, dispatched personnel with tape measures to measure the diameter of the trees. Kerwin had a permit to cut saplings so much hinged on the definition of "sapling." Kerwin prevailed and exulted in the little boat landing.

While Kerwin was restoring the Flats, the restoration of the old Island Sash and Door Company building at the southern tip of the island had also gotten under way.

One of the oldest commercial buildings on the island, the Island Sash and Door Company was built in 1893 and survived the great fire that swept through the island later that year. It continued operations until 1899 and later served as storage for several milling companies. It eventually fell into disrepair, was fixed up by the Salvation Army in 1913, and was a men's shelter for the next 60 years. In the 1970s the Park Board bought the building and it fell into neglect once again. In 1980, plans for restoring the building brought the MHRA and the Park Board into conflict. By 1981, suitable developers had been found. The financial investors were Ron Jacob and Alan Fishlowitz. They hired architect David Shea to design a plan for a restored restaurant and inn. Restoration commenced in the spring of 1982, and during the process an old limestone quarry was discovered under the inn. It is likely that stone from this quarry contributed to such landmarks as the Eastman Flats, Grove Street Flats, and Our Lady of Lourdes Church.[18]

When the inn opened in July 1982, it was a beauty to behold. It featured a glass elevator, twenty-four Victorian-style rooms, and fine dining in a newly added glassed-in porch restaurant. With a nod to history, the inn featured the Captain John Tapper Pub, the Franklin Steele executive board room, and two banquet rooms named after Kenneth McDonald and Fred Delamater, the men who had built the Sash and Door Company building in 1893. However, after a hopeful start, the original owners of the Nicollet Island Inn filed chapter 11 bankruptcy in September 1986 and the inn was taken over by the developers Howard Bergerud and Craig Christenson. A few years later operations were assumed by yet another set of owners, Larry and Caryl Abdo. With each new owner, there was a change in cuisine and style but the old-world atmosphere remained. Wedding parties, anniversaries, and special occasions continue to be celebrated there to this day, and horse-drawn carriages can frequently be seen lining up outside the inn, awaiting passengers for tours of the island and beyond.

The year 1983 found the tireless John Kerwin working on another project adjacent to his successful Grove Street Flats. It was the West Island Avenue condominiums. Built in the Second Empire Style and facing westward toward the Mississippi River, the nine condominiums were completed in the summer of 1984. For an additional fee, buyers could have the nine-foot interiors done with oak trim and doors, a Second Empire stylistic element. As with any development on the island, this one was full of controversy concerning whether the

land that the condos were to be built on was outparcel or not. If it was outparcel than it was not part of the park and could be developed. Kerwin argued that a 1978 agreement signed by the Park Board allowed housing next to the Grove Street Flats, a fact which was confirmed by former city council President Lou

The Island Sash and Door Company fell into disrepair and in 1913 was taken over by the Salvation Army and used as a shelter for the next 60 years. In 1982 it was restored as the Nicollet Island Inn.

Demars: "I do feel the Park Board went back on its word." He further said the city council never signed the agreement. Kerwin also had an advocate in state Representative Phyllis Kahn. The Park Board and the Minneapolis Community Development Agency (MCDA), the successor to the MHRA, made an agreement to designate the parcel as park land. However, before the MCDA could approve the agreement, Rep. Kahn wrote a letter to the executive director of the MCDA stating that a 1982 state law had already designated the boundaries of park land and what parts were outparcel. She pointed out that the new agreement was not in accord with the state law and could jeopardize the flow of funds to the park. This was no idle threat as Rep. Kahn was the chairman of the subcommittee that handled park and open space money.

City officials cried foul and accused Rep. Kahn of improper legislative interference in local affairs and even blackmail. Rep. Kahn defended herself, saying that she was affirming prior agreements, and pointed out the poor record of the Park Board, saying it "wants a monstrous acquisition dream with no plan for what to do with it. They have destroyed use of the land all along the river. The developers of the Grove Street Flats and Nicollet Island Inn have done more to enhance the city than all the park planners."[19] In the end Kerwin and

Kahn prevailed and the new condominiums were built on the outparcel lot, an area which extended to the northwest side of the Grove Street Flats.

On the east side of the Grove Street Flats stood a Hertz truck rental garage. The building was designed by Harry Garrish in the 1950s and built in 1960 on a site formerly occupied by the R.P. Upton house.[20] This was on outparcel land and Kerwin initially planned to build a Second Empire Style building similar to the West Island condos there, a plan which pleased the Heritage Preservation Commission (HPC). However, many Islanders wanted the rental garage to be saved.

One Islander in particular, Olie Foran, convinced Kerwin that the building was something special. The two had first met when Foran drove by the Grove Street Flats in a bread truck while Kerwin was working on the Flats. Foran told Kerwin that the truck garage had a signature architectural element used by Frank Lloyd Wright—the hyperbolic paraboloid, which was the shape of the roof of the building. Foran argued that this modern stylistic element was far rarer than a reproduction Second Empire or Victorian style building. With this information, Kerwin attempted to contact Frank Lloyd Wright, not knowing he was deceased. When that failed, he contacted Taliesen West where he learned that a man named John Howe had worked with Wright for four years and had carried on his legacy. Howe happened to be conveniently living in semi-retirement in Burnsville, Minnesota. Kerwin contacted Howe and Howe sketched out some condo possibilities retaining the distinctive roofs. Accompanied by Howe, Kerwin went to the HPC expecting a warm reception with a disciple of Frank Lloyd Wright at his side: "The HPC laughed me out of the room. They didn't believe modernism was historical, for them, at the time, historical architecture ended with the Queen Anne style." Not easily dissuaded, Kerwin arranged a meeting with Mayor Fraser, which he assumed would be private. When he arrived, he found one wall flanked with his opponents at the HPC and the other flanked with some of the Grove Street Flats tenants with whom he had disputes. The odds were clearly stacked against him, and development never took place. Temporarily defeated, Kerwin retained Intercity Truck Service as a tenant, although they ran their garage late into the night and played country music at all hours. He also rented some of the odd corners of the building to artists who began to live there in violation of city code. Eventually the truck company moved out and more artists filtered in. Kerwin was cited for violations of health and safety codes. "This was at the height of white flight from the city,"

he later recalled, "and I was getting cited for housing artists…an artistic class is important for the life of the city."

Kerwin went to visit Merwin Larson, the Minneapolis head of codes. He spread a floor plan of his building out and said, "We want these people here. If you want me to kick them out I have KSTP news waiting to put their skycam trucks in. The building isn't unsafe." Larson looked at the plan, drew a cross through it, and said, "Let's call it a four-plex. Have fun." He then gave Kerwin a few stipulations to fulfill for improving the health and safety of the building. Kerwin implemented the requirements, but also allowed the tenants themselves to improve their spaces in the property. In the final equation, "the tenants did 70 percent of the improvement and I did 30 percent."[21]

NEW BUILDINGS (AND A BRIDGE) ARRIVE

With the restoration of the Grove Street Flats and the Nicollet Island Inn, and the basic framework for Nicollet Island's future outlined, it took a few more years and one more intervening proposal to establish what direction Nicollet Island would take.

In 1984, the Hennepin County Historical Society made a bid to transform the old Durkee-Atwood complex, a collection of buildings built between 1893 and 1923 which had come into the possession of the Park Board. From its perch at the southern tip of the island, the complex had a vantage point on old St. Anthony, old Minneapolis, the mills on either bank, St. Anthony Falls, and the Stone Arch Bridge—in short, the heart of the birthplace of the city. The Board of Directors of the Hennepin County Historical Society sought to rehabilitate the buildings and build a new glass interpretive center with a reception area, exhibit space, offices, and storage. The theme of the interpretive center was to be the urbanization of Hennepin County, from Indian days to the modern era. The site was also to include a trolley station, a refectory for the Park Board, bicycle rental, public toilets, and a picnic shelter area. This proposal, as had so many before it, came to naught.[22]

In the mid 1980s, the Park Board demolished the Durkee-Atwood complex. At the time Bob Roscoe, a historical preservation consultant, was in the Preservation Alliance, an organization dedicated to the preservation and restoration of historically significant buildings. Roscoe recalled a series of meetings the Preservation Alliance held called "Breakfast with a Preservationist." One of these meetings was held at the Nicollet Island Inn and Mayor Don Fraser was the invited guest speaker. Roscoe said, "Fraser was starting to

catch the fever of preservation and as he made his speech about the importance of it, wreckers demolished the Durkee-Atwood building through the window behind him. Mayor Fraser turned and looked and said, 'Maybe this shouldn't have happened.'"[23] The entire complex was not lost, however. The William Bros Boiler Works, which had been repaired after the Great Fire of 1893, was kept and restored as the Nicollet Island Pavilion. It overlooks the upriver end of St. Anthony Falls and has beautiful views of downtown Minneapolis, the falls, and historic St. Anthony. It is available for private rental with a catering option and is frequently in use. A scene from Arnold Schwarzenneger's 1996 film *Jingle All the Way* was filmed there. The pavilion is surrounded by a park and small outdoor amphitheater, across the street from the Nicollet Island Inn.

By 1986, a compromise regarding the future of Nicollet Island had been reached with input from Mayor Fraser. The MCDA was to restore a historic village at the northern tip, transferring its land to the Park Board. The Park Board was to own and develop the parkland on which the houses sat, and most of the residents would get to stay.[24] Private citizens screened for the financial means were permitted to enter a lottery in which a primary and alternate were picked. The winners would have one year to restore the house they won using professional contractors. Island residents with the financial means would be grandfathered into their homes in accordance with federal law. Two Islanders were qualified and took advantage of the opportunity. The land under the houses would belong to the Park Board, and the lottery winner would hold a 99-year lease on the land for one dollar. Property taxes per se would not be paid by the property owner because he would not own the land under his house; rather an alternate and equivalent personal tax would be levied upon the property owner.

Six of the largest of the original seventeen houses were to be restored by the HRA and set aside for low-income housing. In proposals prior to the 1986 agreement, funding was sought to restore all of the houses on the island for residents, but the estimated cost of $4 million for 36 living units caused Minneapolis councilmen to balk and the lottery scheme was developed for all but six of the properties. These six were restored by the HRA under plans, contracts, and financing obtained by the Mid-River Residences, a cooperative housing corporation organized by Islanders for low-income individuals. A limited number of additional historically appropriate homes were permitted to be moved onto five vacant lots on the island to fill out the neighborhood. After years of acrimonious wrangling, a com-

promise had finally been reached that was satisfactory to most of the parties involved.

Because the seventeen homes on the island were separated by gaps due to fires and demolition, five historically and architecturally significant houses were moved onto the island. The first to arrive was moved by Jeffrey Siegel, his then wife Dorothy Sams, and John Kerwin, to 105 W. Island Drive. Siegel had worked with the HPC to make a list of houses suitable for inclusion on Nicollet Island, and right at the top was the Meader-Farnham house at 913 S. Fifth Ave. Although it was scheduled for demolition by its owner, it was being pursued by another renovator. When that renovator's plans fell through, the Siegels and John Kerwin acquired the property. Kerwin recalled, "Jeff came to me and said we can buy a house for a dollar, but we have to move it today." Siegel and Kerwin each put in 50 cents and Kerwin arranged for Doepke Movers to move the house. The house was cut into three parts and transported by truck in the middle of a summer night. Utility lines were moved and city employees were paid overtime to accommodate the special arrangements.

John Chaffee recalled his sister Doris Park saying that when a portion of the house arrived on Nicollet Island one of the truck tires collapsed through a sidewalk. The house swayed precariously. Unperturbed, the hired house mover jumped out of his truck and determined that the house needed a jacking, and soon the operation was underway. Some time later Siegel and Kerwin found a dollar and some change in a sofa in the house and made a profit on their one-dollar purchase.

The house was not immediately emplaced in its new location; rather, it spent a winter sitting vacant while final approval for the site was given. The Siegels and Kerwin felt that a near *fait accompli* was needed to get slow city bureaucrats to approve the move, so they had transported the house in the winter of 1985, even though the compromise plan wasn't approved until the next year. While waiting for final approval, the house became more damaged and suffered vandalism, but it was finally reassembled in its current location and lovingly restored by Siegel, Sams, and the NIRDs. The original plan had been to divide the house into two units, one for Kerwin and the other for Siegels, but as the restoration progressed it became apparent that such engineering was unwise and Kerwin bowed out. Some time later the Siegels purchased and moved a second house onto 101 West Island Avenue.[25]

Two of the five houses that were moved onto the island to fill in gaps were the Loberg homes from the Cedar-Riverside neighborhood of Minneapolis. These houses were built by Norwegian carpenter brothers and are mirror images of each other.

The Siegels' two homes were the first two of five that were moved onto the island.

The Siegels found the costs of moving buildings to be prohibitive and the MCDA moved two houses from the Cedar-Riverside neighborhood to 171 and 175 East Island Avenue in June of 1990. Unlike the customary $1 offering, these houses were offered for around $22,000 to cover the costs of moving and installing them in their new lots. Bob Roscoe was hired by the MCDA to mastermind the move, and he worked with the HPC and the MCDA to emplace the houses 20 feet apart, side by side, as they had been in their previous setting. Roscoe was no novice to Nicollet

Island architecture and politics, having had experience restoring the Milwaukee Railroad Company neighborhood and having been a member of the HPC. He also had consulted on the limited redesign and restoration of 105 West Island Avenue—the Meader-Farnham home, 18/20 Maple Place, and 163 East Island Avenue. The move of 171 and 175 East Island Avenue was not without difficulty, however. The houses were uprooted from their 1814 and 1812 Cedar Avenue addresses and put on blocks for about six months while a ramp off the newly rebuilt Hennepin Bridge was being completed. Once in place, Roscoe was hired by the owners to outline the houses' redesign as well. Like all the other homes on the island, they would be costly to restore.

The house at 167/169 East Island Avenue was also moved in 1988 from its original location of 716 Twenty-First Avenue South, across from Augsburg College. The home owners both moved and restored the property.

The final house new to the island was 97 Nicollet Street, built in 1996 on a lot won by a Park Board lottery winner. This was the only empty lot offered in the lottery, and it was done to fill a gap created with the demolition of a house previously on the lot which had no architectural merit. Roscoe designed the replacement house and it was his judgment that condemned the previous house, as he had

The houses at 93 and 91 Nicollet Street are shown here undergoing restoration in the early 1990s.

been called in as a consultant to determine if the house as worth saving.

While houses were being moved onto the island, restoration on the native ones also got under way. The lottery winners were able to hire their own restorers and the HRA completed the restoration of the six largest homes, which had been kept out of the lottery.

The lottery houses were also being restored and the Nicollet Island Restoration and Development Company (NIRDs) had a big hand in the process. The NIRDs, which came into existence for the restoration of the Grove Street Flats, had continued with varying membership to have a hand in island restorations. They had developed some political clout along the way, but as contractors they were still required to get approval from local political authorities. Bob Roscoe recalls that when NIRDs met with 9th Ward council member Tony Scallon he told them he wouldn't sign off on any of their contracts if they "didn't get all their goddamned broken down vehicles off the island by Monday." Scallon told Roscoe that as he drove by the following Sunday he saw a parade of derelict vehicles caravanning off the island.

With such appeasements to conventional decorum made, the summer of 1991 found the NIRDs in full force, working on 93 Nicollet Street with Bob Harwood as one of the primary NIRDs. Harwood's sister, Christine Keirn, had entered the lottery at the encouragement of her brother and won the house. When work began, the house was gutted, the floors straightened, the basement excavated, the foundation shored up, and the house itself jacked up and put on a pair of I-beams. Traces of the first roofline could still be seen on the upstairs wall. A crumbling summer kitchen on the back end of the house was demolished and an addition built. Original elements were refurbished such as a little curved staircase, which might have been added after the original construction.[26]

Both the cooperative homes and the lottery proved beneficial to the island community. Most of the old residents who had lived on, fought for, and loved the island were able to stay, either in lottery houses which they had been given a preferential opportunity to buy, or in the restored cooperative houses. Yet the lottery also brought in new blood, some with young children. A love of the island was almost assured with the newcomers because the cost of restoring a home was likely to be higher than its value upon restoration. And in the unlikely event that a house later increased significantly in value, the lottery winner who sold it would have to split any capital gains on the home—minus the average rate of home appreciation in Minneapolis—with the Park Board and the city of Minneapolis. Restoration was more an act of love than an investment.

In 1986, while spindles were being turned and foundations shored up, another piece of history was preserved and found a permanent home on Nicollet Island—the Broadway Bridge. This bridge spanned the Mississippi a mile upstream from Nicollet Island and was slated for replacement. It had been designed by the engineer Andrew Rinker and built between 1887 and 1889 by the King Iron Bridge Company of Cleveland, Ohio. One architectural historian later described it as a decorated bridge, designed with a studied sense of proportion and a richness of detail. "The elegance and lightness of its four 'Pratt' truss spans made it appear to leap across the river.

An exact contemporary of the Eiffel Tower, the Broadway Bridge expressed the exuberance of its time and the seemingly endless possibilities of designing with steel." In 1966 it was deemed eligible for inclusion on the National Register of Historic Places but never added, and because federal funds were involved in its replacement, a study of the historic impact of its demolition was necessitated. The study's rather underwhelming conclusion was that the bridge had significance because of its many years of usage. This study was strengthened by a June 11, 1981, letter from Russell Fridley of the Minnesota Historical Society in which he drew attention to the aesthetic value of the bridge and recommended that at least one of the spans or portals should be reused if the bridge were demolished. A year and a half later, the Federal Highway Administration and Minnesota Historic Preservation Office agreed that one of the four spans would be reused, and that the builder of the new bridge would be responsible for relocating it.

Thus on Tuesday, September 2, 1986, one of the 200-foot trusses found a new home on Nicollet Island. The plan was to celebrate the relocation by christening the bridge as it floated downstream, and city, county, state, and federal officials were all present, cruising on the Mississippi River on a houseboat rented for the event. However, the downriver odyssey of the bridge met with a series of mishaps. First, the county official who was going to christen the bridge with a $2.89 bottle of pink champagne cracked the bottle open on one of the barges transporting the bridge rather than the bridge itself. A more serious problem arose when the bridge had trouble getting underneath the Plymouth Avenue Bridge due to mechanical problems in lowering it. The government officials celebrating the event circled the bridge aimlessly while chatting with reporters and eating clam dip. The ever-watchful residents of Nicollet Island and other onlookers surveyed the happenings with binoculars from the shore.

The bridge segment finally made its way underneath the Plymouth Bridge the following day, but was found to be too tall to get under the Burlington Northern railroad bridge that crosses from the island to the east bank. Larry Granley, foreman of the Lunda Construction Company crew that had been handling the project said, "We thought we'd sneak through by a couple of inches, but we missed by an inch." On Friday, his crew dredged the bottom of the Mississippi River to create the necessary clearance and by Saturday the bridge segment was safely lodged on the southeast shore of Nicollet Island where it spent the winter. In the spring of 1987, the truss was hauled up the bank, renamed the Merriam Street Bridge,

In the fall of 1986 a section of the Broadway Bridge was floated downriver and emplaced, refurbished, and renamed the Merriam Street Bridge the following year. It links the lower end of Nicollet Island to the east bank, St. Anthony Main area. Our Lady of Lourdes Church is in the background.

and set in its current location, linking Nicollet Island in the vicinity of the Nicollet Island Inn with the old St. Anthony Main east bank area, which had recently been revitalized.[27]

The year 1987 found another bridge on Nicollet Island being refurbished, the Wisconsin Central Railroad Bridge at the northern tip. Boom Island, to the north of Nicollet Island, had been the site of extensive lumberyards that were destroyed in the Great Fire of 1893. After the fire, the Wisconsin Central Railroad built railyards on Boom Island and an access bridge was built in 1901 by the Butler-Ryan Company of St. Paul. It

was W.W. Eastman's intention to have the Wisconsin Central railway run a line down to his Island Power Building, which had some vacancies, and which he hoped to convert to a manufacturing center. Eastman arranged to have dirt transferred from the Wisconsin Central's main terminal in Bridge Square to fill in part of the east channel and create a path for the railroad below the bluffs on the east side of the island. The dirt was transferred and the line was built, but never as far as the Island Power Building—yet another unrealized plan of Eastman's. Rather, the line connected with a switch in the rail line that separates the northern third of the island from the central portion and was used by trains to change over to the Great Northern Railroad line.[28]

Over time Boom Island's east channel had become filled, joining it with the east bank and making it an island in name only. The real estate was acquired by the Park Board in 1982 and turned into a park complete with boat landing and miniature lighthouse. The old railroad bridge was then refurbished as a pedestrian and bike bridge linking the paths on Boom and Nicollet Islands.[29]

Many island residents took part in the revitalization process through their neighborhood association, the Nicollet Island East Bank Political Action Committee (NIEB-PAC). John Heiman remembered that John Chaffee and Fred Markus got money for projects and neighborhood cleanups, while Heiman himself helped build the stairs down to the trestle bridge that crosses over to Boom Island at the northern tip and cleared a walking path around the island, cleaning up the garbage that people had strewn on the bluffs.

According to John Chaffee, through NIEB-PAC they organized neighborhood cleanups and planted community gardens, trees, flowers, and shrubs throughout the 1970s and 1980s. One NIEBPAC member obtained a state nursery license and bought wholesale trees and shrubs. The maple trees in the boule-

vards at Maple Place and West Island Avenue were bought and planted by NIEBPAC members to replace elms killed by Dutch elm disease, and an apple orchard was planted where 103/105 West Island Avenue is now. The apple trees were later relocated to other places on the island. The group also planted the 40-foot catalpa in front of 167-169 Nicollet Street and the rose garden to the south of the house on 95 West Island. It also made improvements to the neighborhood park known by Islanders as "Central Park" at the intersection of Nicollet Street and Maple Place.

By the 1990s, NIEBPAC had largely fulfilled its purpose of saving historic homes on the island against deterioration, fires, and demolition by city officials. It was then reorganized as the Nicollet Island-East Bank Neighborhood Association (NIEBNA), with a board containing roughly equal numbers of Nicollet Island and east bank residents. NIEBNA took part in a community planning process for the development of park land on the island and surrounding areas, and a park master plan based generally on that process was issued in 1996.

In the late 1990s, NIEBNA provided resident input into the spending of Neighborhood Revitalization Program (NRP) funds provided by the city. NRP was a unique Minneapolis program, now largely phased out, which gave citizen groups money to spend on their neighborhoods, subject to general guidelines. NIEBNA still serves as a forum for neighborhood issues such as traffic, parking, and crime, and reviews development proposals which are being presented to the city. NIEBNA and the other Minneapolis neighborhood organizations have no legal power to regulate development, but city officials tend to give their opinions careful consideration, especially in cases where a developer wants an exemption from zoning requirements.[30]

Gentrification came hard to some of the Islanders, most particularly the four-hooved kind. The donkey Sheba, it seems, was at odds with the changing climate of the island, and on July 27, 1988, Doris Park was issued a citation to remove Sheba or get special permission from the city council for her to stay. Park said that she had such a permit issued to her by City Council President Lou DeMars years ago, but Animal Control Officers could find no record of it and Park admitted that it had lapsed.[31]

Spurred by the citation, Park requested a special permit but before it could be obtained, a complaint about Doris Park's cats in 95 W. Island Avenue led the Humane Society and Animal Control Officers to her doorstep on August 23. The report of Assistant Animal Control Supervisor Steven Putnam reads,

"Upon arrival at 95 W. Island Ave. at 1149 hours, I pulled into an empty lot next to the above address. At that time, I saw the above mule staked out on the south side of the house…At that time I got out of my truck and started to walk to where the above mule was. Two people who were working on the nearby house then ran to the above mule, unhooked it and fled with the above mule toward Maple Pl. between the houses. I then ordered them to stop and gave chase on foot. At that time I called for police assistance."

As the animal control officer pursued the escaping Sheba, one of the workers obstructed his path, for which he was cited for interfering with an animal control officer. Police arrived to assist in the pursuit and Sheba was apprehended and tied to the animal control truck. Putnam then followed up on the initial cat complaint and entered 95 West Island Avenue to see numerous cats in cages. Putnam departed the house and returned with Humane Society Officer Streff. When they re-entered the home, the cats had disappeared, and Robert Harwood was standing in the house. He said he did not know where the cats were. Officer Streff said that he had seen Harwood, pussycat in hand, earlier, and that was suspicion enough for Harwood to be considered an accomplice in the cat escape. Harwood was cited for interfering with an animal control officer. Park was restrained as Sheba was put into a trailer and deported. The donkey days of Nicollet Island were over.

Sheba was later returned to Park who took her to Clear Lake, Iowa, a territory more hospitable to donkeys.[32] She died in 2002 from a tragic drowning in a pond, having just recovered from a bout with the West Nile virus. She was 34-years-old, or 102 in human years, when she died. She is fondly remembered as one of Nicollet Island's unique residents.

The year 1989 witnessed another sign of island revitalization—the relighting of the Grain Belt Beer sign. Winthrop Eastman and William Eastman III, great grand-nephew and great grandson of W.W. Eastman, respectively, owned the sign and Winthrop Eastman organized a group of preservationists to restore it. Sign Crafters Outdoor Display, Inc., of Fridley worked on the restoration which required 3,000 feet of wiring, 1,100 incandescent lamps, 800 feet of neon tubes, 50 gallons of black paint, and forty rewired transformers. It took seven months and cost $125,000. On May 24, 1989, a private party was held at the Lumber Exchange by G. Heileman Brewing, which had bought out the Grain Belt brand. The party proceeded in a convoy of Grain Belt Beer trucks to Nicollet Island and ceremonially relit the sign.

One year after the lighting, the G. Heileman Brewing Company went bankrupt and the sign darkened again. In 1992 it was relit by Minnesota Brewing, who had bought the rights to the Grain Belt label, and Mayor Don Fraser threw the switch.

Sadly, the sign has once again gone dark. In an interview, trustee owner Winthrop Eastman, great grandnephew of W.W. Eastman, said he has considered relighting it, trying to build a townhome in its frame in the form of an old mill, building a concessionary, or building a restaurant with water access to it. In 2009 it was offered for outright sale. Several months later Schell Brewery, the current owner of the Grain Belt brand, expressed an interest in relighting it.[33]

In 1996, Nicollet Island received a new railroad crossing bridge. The previous bridge had been a wood-and-steel construction. The new one was made of concrete. But because the tracks ran just south of the island's residential zone, some residents feared that such improvements would eventually destroy the neighborhood's small-town feel, but they fought a rearguard battle. The new concrete bridge was built high enough and wide enough to comply with federal standards and to allow future light rail transit.[34] That same year, with $60,000 worth of the funding funneled from NRP funds through NIEBNA, the streets on the island's northern tip, which had been oiled dirt, were paved with cobblestones; overhead wires were placed underground; and antique-looking streetlamps were added to the neighborhood.[35]

TEEPEE-DWELLERS, PEACE BELLS, AND AN ATHLETIC FIELD

Although the island had become gentrified in many respects, it had not lost its ability to attract unique people. In 1996 or 1997, Sanders Marvin, who lived at 18/20 Maple Place, near the island's northern tip, pitched a teepee in his back yard. He had befriended a Frenchman named François Medion who worked as a chef in the Loring Café in Minneapolis. Medion needed a place to live and Marvin proposed the idea of the teepee, and Medion, who had an adventurous personality, was happy to give it a try.

Medion was born in Champagnolles and raised in Rochefort sur Mer, in the Cognac region of France. He dropped out of high school and was a social worker until the funding for that job evaporated. He then joined his brother as a stunt man in an itinerant circus. "I could do a handstand on the car when it was up on two wheels." He did this for four years but by 1983 had become disenchanted with circus life. He then connected with a traveling troupe of American ex-convicts called The Family who were performing in French prisons and needed a sound engineer. Medion spoke no English and the troupe spoke no French, but Medion could speak a little Spanish and most of the troupe was Puerto Rican.

When the group had completed its run in France, the Family asked Medion to join them in Newark. He was happy to go, having previously applied unsuccessfully for entrance to the United States. (Evidently, affiliation with ex-cons was precisely the ticket required to get legal entry into the United States.) But Medion was appalled by Newark: "I couldn't believe there was such a place in America." Medion lived with the troupe for a while but felt exploited because they wanted him as a "house slave" receiving no pay; rather, they wanted him to pay them. In addition, they stole from him, and Medion, finding no honor among thieves, parted ways and worked in New York City for David Bouley in his restaurant.

Medion later married and came to Minneapolis. After an expensive divorce he thought the teepee idea would be a money-saver, and Medion also shared the enthusiasm of many Europeans for Native American culture. He had been enthralled by *Black Elk Speaks*, and found the simplicity of Native American religion appealing. "Animals would visit me in my teepee on Nicollet Island, I was close to nature," he said.

At first Medion kept a storage unit for those of his possessions that a teepee couldn't accommodate, but later had a teepee garage sale in an effort to simplify his life further, and then gave his remaining books to the Fond du Luc Indian Reservation library. After delivering the books he was looking around for some teepee poles for a second traveling teepee when he met Jim Northrup Jr., son of the Ojibwe author and humorist Jim Northrup. Jim helped Medion cut some poles, and in exchange Medion provided some food and medicine for a Native American Church ceremony.

By 2000, Medion had paid off his debt, and he took a trip to the Grand Canyon with his brother and his brother's children, and spent a month at the bottom on the canyon among the Walapi Indians who live there. Not long after his return, Jim Northrup Jr. invited Medion to live on the Fond du Lac reservation, and he lives there today while studying plant biology at nearby Superior campus of the University of Wisconsin.[36]

But it is not only itinerant Frenchmen who draw religious meaning from Nicollet Island. In 1996, Alameda Rocha, a Dakota tribeswoman, was dispatched by her tribe from Fort Peck, Montana, to make tobacco offerings to ancestors and spirits on Nicollet Island, to the falls, and in the sacred area. The Fort Peck Dakota are descendants of the Dakota who initiated the war of 1862 and were later driven from Minnesota. Alameda Rocha performed her mission aided by National Park Service Ranger Dave Wiggins.

By the late 1990s, the revitalization of Nicollet Island was nearly complete. The Nicollet Inn and Nicollet Island Pavilion were fully and beautifully restored and were doing brisk business. DeLaSalle High School's student body was growing again. The Grove Street Flats, the West Island Condos, the Truck Building, and the houses at the northern tip had all been beautifully restored, and the island itself was ringed with bike paths, walking trails, and trees and shrubs flourishing amid the ruins of demolished businesses.

On July 22, 2001, a sculpture entitled the Bell of Two Friends was dedicated in the Nicollet Island Pavilion park area by Minneapolis Mayor Sharon Sayles Belton and Japanese dignitary Mitoji Yabunaka. The 12-foot sculpture, crafted by Minneapolis sculptor Karen Sontag-Sattel, was based on the design and shape of a 2,000-year-old terra cotta mold of a bronze bell discovered in Ibaraki, Japan. The sculpture itself was presented by Minneapolis's sister city, Ibaraki City, Japan, honoring the then 20-year friendship between

The Bell of Two Friends

president was Brother Michael Collins, who had joined the order two weeks after graduating from DeLaSalle in 1955. He returned to DeLaSalle in 1959 as a teacher, teaching religion, English, and music. He spent nine years at DeLaSalle, the last two and a half as an assistant principal and dean of students.

As dean, Brother Collins had disciplinary responsibilities. "Times have changed since then," he now recalls. "Disciplinary problems used to be about hair length, smoking cigarettes, and the occasional fight over a girl at a dance. The island was rough in those days, fathers would drop their daughters off for a dance and pick them up immediately afterward with strict instructions not to venture beyond the doors of DeLaSalle."

After receiving a master's degree in secondary school administration, Brother Collins was assigned to Shanley High School in Bismark, North Dakota, in 1967. As a black man in a very white North Dakota, his reception, unbeknownst to him at the time, was not welcoming, with parents circulating a petition to have his assignment rescinded. (The parents who did so were told by the bishop that their children would not be allowed in any schools in the diocese if they did not stop what they were doing.) It was an experience he likened to the arrival of the black sheriff in the movie *Blazing Saddles*. Despite the chilly recep-

the cities. Visitors who pass through the sculpture can ring a bronze bell hanging inside as a prayer for world peace and continued friendship between the two cities.[37]

Such prayers for peace had little effect, however, on the controversy that engulfed the island when DeLaSalle High School expressed the desire to expand its athletic facilities.

Like the rest of the island, DeLaSalle High School had experienced a rebirth, and in 1991 it also came under new stewardship. The new

tion, Brother Collins went on to a successful twelve-year assignment there and left in 1978 to pursue doctoral studies in San Francisco.

In 1987 Brother Collins was lured back to Minnesota for a job he didn't want, effecting the merger of two Catholic high schools. He was made co-principal along with a sister of St. Joseph of Carondelet, guiding the merger of Cretin High School and Derham Hall in St. Paul. Cretin was a Catholic all-boys military school and Derham was an all-girls school which was heavily invested in the peace movement. This marriage of Mars and Venus was not without its difficulties. When taking actions he was sometimes told that "this isn't Minneapolis, it's St. Paul." At one point Brother Collins reached an impasse with his co-principal and took the opportunity to resign and finish his doctoral dissertation.

In 1991, Brother Collins became president of DeLaSalle High School. At that time student enrollment was about 300. The school's endowment was approximately $80,000, it had $80,000 in debt, and got frequent notice of impending bankruptcy. Under his watch enrollment doubled and the financial outlook stabilized.[38]

Other DeLaSallians had returned to the school as well. Brother Kenneth Gieske had left the Christian Brothers Order in 1984 and had returned years later as Mr. Gieske the teacher. Although he had left the order, his calling as a teacher remained, and the revitalized DeLaSalle continued in its mission of making Christian citizens. Gieske said, "We are saving young lives, both in terms of salvation and citizenship. The things that the children learn at DeLaSalle will serve them well in life." He notes that classes and assemblies begin with the prayer, "Let us remember we are in the holy presence of God." Sometimes the end of a class or assembly is signaled by the prayer, "St. John Baptiste pray for us, live, Jesus, in our hearts" to which the voluntary response is "forever."

Mike O'Keefe, a 1978 graduate of DeLaSalle and current vice president of planning, is an example of the family traditions that are an important part of the school. Mike's father graduated from DeLaSalle in 1936, his brother was class of 1967, and his three children the classes of 2001, 2003, and 2008. O'Keefe returned to DeLaSalle in 1990. "Our mission, "he says, "is to graduate young men and women who are literate, engaged, service-oriented people, specifically, they are prepared for further education." In the graduating class of 2008, 147 of the 149 students went on to higher education with one of the remaining two going to work and the other joining the United States Marine

Corps. According to O'Keefe, the success of DeLaSalle students comes from the fact that their parents make an effort to have their children go to school there and are predisposed to the DeLaSalle experience, the structured environment and the demanding but not overwhelming routine.[39]

Along with the renewed vigor of DeLaSalle came the widespread desire for a better athletic field. DeLaSalle had been a football powerhouse in the 1950s and many of the alumni (including President Collins himself, who had graduated from DeLaSalle in 1955) remembered those days, and thought the school deserved a football field better than the one they currently had, which was suitable only for practices. A plan for a multi-purpose athletic field suitable for football, soccer, and physical education, was drawn up and presented to the Park Board, with $3 million in funding for the project being generously provided by a 1958 DeLaSalle alumnus, Skip Maas.[40]

As envisioned by Brother Collins, the athletic field would be not only for the DeLaSalle players but for their families and the community at large. It fulfilled an aspect of the life-changing educational mission DeLaSalle had dedicated itself to. Brother Collins stated:

We want to find ways to develop the essential sense of community and teach people to work together. It particularly matters in a school with diversity, to learn to work together for a common purpose. We have to find a variety of ways for kids to respect and appreciate differences. You find out that there is a commonality between people, but you have to have a place to learn that. That's the reason DeLaSalle is here in the city, that's why I'm here. If we don't save them now someone else is going to have to pick up the bill. We are writing future history in the lives of these kids. We are talking about the culture and life of a city and the caliber of its citizens. We are a community of people who share a certain faith, a certain mission, and a certain dream.

DeLaSalle's practice field lay over the foundation of the W.W. Eastman mansion on land the school had acquired decades earlier. Over the years, home football games had been played there when other facilities were unavailable, but the construction of the A building in 1960 had created problems, making it dangerous when a player ran out of bounds. The field was also short, and players running into the end zone on one side hit a slope until it was finally leveled in 1982 with dirt brought in from a monster truck rally at the Metrodome stadium.

The only land adjacent to DeLaSalle that could be turned into an athletic field was over a portion of Grove Street and onto park land where the Park Board had built tennis courts for $1.1 million. The Basset and DeLaittre mansions had once stood there, and later the Island Tile and Marble building. Though not indicated by signage, the tennis courts were open to the public according to a shared use agreement with the Park Board, though the DeLaSalle tennis team had priority. In exchange, the Park Board was allowed to use the DeLaSalle parking lot on occasion.[41]

DeLaSalle began planning for the athletic field around 2004, though it rose to the top of Brother Collins's priorities only when local political lobbyist and DeLaSalle graduate John Derus informed him that there were enough sympathetic votes on the Park Board to raise the proposal.[42] The plan aroused opposition from a number of groups, including the majority of the island's residents, historical preservationists, Indian representatives, the Sierra Club, the Friends of the Mississippi River, and the National Park Service.

For DeLaSalle, having allies on the Park Board was merely the first step, and did not insure success, as Nicollet Island's development over the years had left a tangled and often contradictory legal legacy.

The ensuing battle focused primarily on two contradictory contracts concerning the development of Nicollet Island. The first was the January 23, 1979, agreement between the Metropolitan Council and the Minneapolis Park and Recreation Board to turn parts of Nicollet Island into a regional park. The Metropolitan Council committed $4.6 million, which grew to $19.5 million, to buy land which the Park Board agreed was to be "devoted exclusively to the purposes for which they were acquired, namely, regional recreational open space for public use."[43]

The second was a 1983 settlement between the Park Board and the MCDA which required the Park Board to "use its best efforts to construct upon property adjacent to the DeLaSalle property an outdoor neighborhood recreational and athletic facility (the "Athletic Facility"), which at a minimum shall consist of a full (regulation) size football field and no less than two full (regulation) size tennis courts."[44]

Between these two agreements was a large gap giving free play to conflict. For DeLaSalle, the approval process was cumbersome, due to the historic status of the area in question. One of the first approvals needed was from the Historic Preservation Commission (HPC), the watchdogs of preservation in Minneapolis.

Both sides made their case, and the HPC voted unanimously against the DeLaSalle proposal. Although the HPC gave summary rulings, it was possible to appeal the decisions to the city council, which could overrule it. They did. Controversy erupted in the city council as well when Barbara Johnson, its president, did not recuse herself from decision making even though she was an officer on the DeLaSalle Board of Trustees. Johnson defended herself, saying that she had consulted with an ethics officer who cleared her for voting because she had no financial interest in the school. (Johnson did step down from the DeLaSalle Board of Trustees before making some later decisions pertinent to the athletic field.)[45] Preservationists also pointed out that several members of the Park Board had connections with DeLaSalle, to no effect.[46] Another HPC permitting meeting was held to evaluate the athletic field proposal with more refined plans, and again the HPC unanimously voted against it. The ruling was appealed to the city council again and the council again approved the field.

M ike O'Keefe attributed the city council's favor for the project to support that came from the councilmen's constituents. O'Keefe believes that in Minneapolis there was a general desire for the project as evidenced by letters of support written to DeLaSalle High School: "These people were not connected with the political process and didn't show up at hearings, but these families wanted a field. This project was an expression of our roots on the island, our desire to stay planted and to make a difference here."

Both of the decisions by the city council were appealed by the preservationists to the Minnesota Court of Appeals where they were consolidated into one argument. The preservationists argued that the Minnesota Environmental Rights Act (MERA) provided that historic resources are protected against impairment or destruction and that the destruction of a portion of Grove Street violated this provision. The burden under MERA was on the developer to show that there was no feasible or prudent alternative. Another lawsuit along similar lines was introduced in Hennepin County District Court. This was done by the preservationists as more expansive evidence could be introduced than in the other lawsuit, due to the other lawsuit being limited to evidence related to the appeal of the city council.[47] Both lawsuits were eventually dismissed or decided in favor of DeLaSalle.

Before the conflict got into full swing in the winter of 2006, landscape architect Ted Wirth, grandson of Theodore Wirth, who built the Minneapolis Park system, proposed an alternative site: the undeveloped B.F. Nelson park site owned by the Park Board, which was just a short walk over the Nicollet Island/ Boom Island pedestrian bridge. (Ted Wirth had designed Boom Island Park.) Wirth presented a sketch of a 1,050 seat stadium tucked into a berm on the site, with canoe access, nearby parking, and a downtown view. The Park Board was uninterested in the proposal.[48]

Meanwhile, the Metropolitan Council had to approve a land exchange since public park land was involved. Official policy stated that park land could not be converted to other uses unless the council approved an exchange for equally valuable land somewhere else.

The policy initially proved problematic for the DeLaSalle advocates, who hit upon the notion of removing the regional park restrictive covenants on the Nicollet Island parcel in exchange for the Minneapolis Park and Recreation Board agreement to place a restrictive covenant on equally valuable land.[49]

Although the Park and Recreation Board was still to own the land, the Nicollet Island parcel had to be freed from a restrictive covenant, after which DeLaSalle could then modify and use the land for 80 years. This restrictive covenant had to be replaced by restrictive covenants on equally valuable land. The Park Board had a parcel of land upriver on the west bank which they sought to exchange. When preservationists successfully argued that the parcel in question was encumbered by restrictions and could in no way be considered equal in value, the Metropolitan Council delegated the responsibility and power to one of its members, regional administrator and chair Peter Bell, to find additional parcels to increase the value of the land the Park Board was offering. Bell came up with four parcels in addition to the one initially offered to increase the value of the exchange.[50] The preservationists appealed the Metropolitan Council's actions to the Minnesota Court of Appeals on grounds of improper process, meaning delegating a responsibility of the Metropolitan Council to one man, Peter Bell, and arguing that the parcel the Park Board was offering for the land for DeLaSalle was not equal in value.[51] While the lawsuit was pending, on Oct. 10, 2007, to the chagrin of the preservationists, the Metropolitan Council approved the five-parcel-for-one-parcel covenant exchange, which totaled 9.2 acres for the one 2.89 Nicollet Island parcel, undercutting one of the preservationists' arguments.[52] An appeal of the decision of the Metropolitan Council action was taken by the preservationists on November 13, 2008, and the petition for review to the Minnesota Court of Appeals was dismissed.

A second battle between the two

groups also took place in the court of public opinion. Both sides were tarred and public figures weighed into the fray. Radio personality Garrison Keillor of *A Prairie Home Companion*, and a columnist for the *Minneapolis Star Tribune*, briefly took the side of the preservationists, before retiring from the conflict under pressure. Nick Coleman, a columnist for the *Minneapolis Star Tribune* and Joe Soucheray, AM radio talk show host of *Garage Logic* and a columnist for the *St. Paul Pioneer Press*, strongly advocated for the DeLaSalle faction.

Lisa Hondros and Chris Steller, two of the leaders of the preservationists, stated:

We have consistently argued that local government should fairly examine potential alternative sites with less severe impacts on fragile historic and natural resources. The development's proponents paint this as NIMBYism [Not in my backyard]. But agencies and organizations that advocate for the public's interest in the St. Anthony Falls Historic District and the Mississippi National River and Recreation Area joined the effort to show the decision makers that Nicollet Island is everyone's backyard.

The project site along the Mississippi River raises issues of appropriate riverfront development, and has drawn environmental as well as historic preservation organizations to the cause of advocating for an exploration of alternatives. The Preservation Alliance, the National Trust, the National Park Service, the Sierra Club's Northstar Chapter, Friends of the Mississippi River and Minneapolis Park Watch all played vital roles.

Local government bodies composed of appointed citizen-experts, such as the city's HPC and planning commission, found the project unfit for its historic setting and turned it down. Nonetheless, political factors trumped evaluation of the merits of allowing a private institution to build a new stadium over an historic street and public land in a national historic district and a national park along the Mississippi River. [53]

Hondros later remarked, "We were very naïve about the whole process and had to figure it out as we went along." President Collins has a different perspective. In a November 11, 2005 interview, Brother Collins, himself a Democrat, spoke about the conflict with neighbors whom he described as "liberal, Democratic activists who know how to play the political game," but "...they underestimated power and the influence of DeLaSalle not, necessarily the DeLaSalle of 2005, but

In 1991 a new Hennepin Avenue Bridge was completed, the fourth bridge at this location. This bridge with its lighted towers stylistically echoes the first two suspension bridges at this site.

DeLaSalle from 1900 to 2005."[54] Brother Collins's conclusion had proven accurate. Beyond public opinion, celebrity advocacy, and the legal challenges, in the final equation, the conflict was settled through politics, and DeLaSalle's connections and influence won the day.

By 2008, the fight was over, and a groundbreaking ceremony for the new facil-

ity took place on October 16, 2007. The field was essentially completed in late 2008. The eastern section of Grove Street was demolished, the old Eastman mansion foundation which had been revealed under the old DeLaSalle football field was analyzed and dismantled, and the tennis courts were torn down. A projectile point Indian artifact was found north of Grove Street by the archeological survey. The ground where the Eastman, Nimocks/Bassett, DeLaittre, Calladine, and Rea/Secombe homes had once stood and where some of their remains were found was reconfigured, with the Eastman and Nimocks/Basset homes' remains being removed entirely.[55] A new athletic field, stadium lights, and bleachers were provided for DeLaSalle.

The legal conflict, like most legal conflicts, primarily enriched the lawyers. DeLaSalle had spent around $4 million for the field, about $500,000 of that being for their legal expenses. The preservationists spent a similar amount on legal fees.[56]

Today Nicollet Island is a place of beauty and history. The southern tip boasts the Nicollet Island Inn and Nicollet Island Pavilion where gatherings can look upon the beauty of the Mississippi, old St. Anthony Main, St. Anthony Falls, and the skyline of downtown Minneapolis. Dakota people still come to the island and to the falls to offer tobacco to their ancestors and the spirits. Horse-drawn carriages await passengers outside the Nicollet Island Inn for a tour around the island and throughout the area. People visit the area on Segways, tours starting in the restored St. Anthony Main area. In the middle section sits DeLaSalle High School, where the Christian Brothers have been educating young lives since 1900, and the lovingly restored Grove Street Flats, the Truck Building, and the West Island Condos. Stairs lead down to a boat launch on the river where boats can tie up and people can fish. At the upper tip, a village of architectural gems dating back 150 years has been restored. The island is crossed by walking, bike, and running trails, and lovely bridges. Bald eagles, beaver, blue heron, raccoons, woodchucks, and the occasional deer are seen. The beauteous array of flora that once attracted Thoreau can still be seen in every season except winter, when the island turns into a winter wonderland. From Indian times immemorial, through explorer, pioneer, Gilded Age, hippie, and restoration days, Nicollet Island has remained the gem of the Mississippi, *Wita Waste*, the beautiful island.

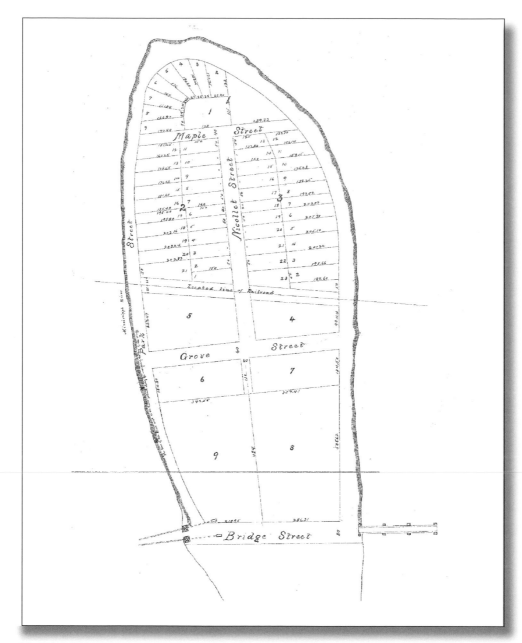

This plat of Nicollet Island was registered in April of 1866. It was created by surveyor Franklin Cook for W.W. Eastman, J.L. Merriam and their wives. It depicts the lots on which the houses and other structures on Nicollet Island began to be built shortly after it was made.

6

The Architecture of Nicollet Island

One of the things that draws people to Nicollet Island is the variety of historic homes and diverse architectural styles that can be found there. At the northern tip, there are a variety of Romantic and Victorian era or Victorian–styled homes which were either built on the island or moved there to complete the neighborhood village. Most of the residences have been added to at one time or another and all have benefited from significant restoration. In the island's central section the Grove Street Flats, built in the Second Empire Style, is a highlight. The West Island Condos were built in imitation of the Second Empire Style, while the strictly utilitarian Truck Building exhibits some unusual and distinctly modern features. The nearby DeLaSalle High School buildings feature mid-century modern and other styles.

At the southern tip, the Nicollet Island Inn and the Nicollet Island Pavilion operate in buildings built in the late 1800s. The following history and descriptions of these buildings are derived primarily from the Miller-Dunwiddie study of 1974, the National Register of Historic Places files, and observations by Todd Grover, architect and restorationist.

Most of the houses on Nicollet Island fall into the Greek Revival and Italianate styles. One of the houses and the Grove Street Flats falls into the Second Empire style. Queen Anne and Folk Victorian styles, which became popular from 1860 to 1900, are also represented. Minor elements from other styles are displayed in some of the houses.

The Greek Revival style became popular during the eighteenth century in Europe, part and parcel of an aristocratic neo-classical style and mindset that survived the French Revolution. In the United States it shed its aristocratic overtones, being considered a "democratic" style that harkened back to Republican Rome and fifth century Athens.

The Greek Revival style is identifiable by gables or hipped roofs with a low pitch. The cornice line of the main roof and porch roofs often carries a wide band of trim to mimic the entablature above classical columns. It is usually split into the frieze above and the architrave below. Entry or full width porches supported by rounded or square Doric columns are also characteristic of the style. The front door of a Greek revival home is often surrounded by narrow sidelights and a rectangular line of transom lights above. The doors and lights are usually incorporated into a more elaborate door surround.[1]

The Italianate style usually features a house with two or three stories and a low-pitched roof with widely overhanging eaves with decorative branches beneath tall narrow windows, which are often arched or curved on top. The windows frequently have elaborate crowns in an inverted U shape. Italianate houses can feature a square cupola or tower.[2] This style was popular in Minneapolis during the late nineteenth century.

The Victorian style of architecture is named after Queen Victoria's reign, 1837 to 1901. Victorian architecture drew freely from features and details adapted from both medieval and classical buildings. During this period industrialization led to the mass production of complex house components. The balloon frame, held together by two-inch boards joined by wire nails, began to replace heavy-timber framing, which were suitable only for box-like shapes; as a result, house plans became more elaborate and irregular. The fact that pre-made building materials such as doors,

windows, siding, and decorative components were becoming cheaper and easier to acquire added further to the extravagant house shapes and detailing.

Architectural historians further classify the Victorian style into Second Empire, Queen Anne, and Folk Victorian styles. The Second Empire style is defined by a mansard or double pitched roof with dormer windows on a steep lower slope both above and below with decorative brackets usually present beneath the eaves.[3]

The Queen Anne style is typified by steeply pitched roofs of irregular shape, usually with a front facing gable. Patterned shingles, cutaway bay windows, and other devices are used to avoid a smooth-walled appearance. An asymmetrical façade with a partial or full width porch, one-story high and extended along one or both side walls, can be used to create this effect.[4]

The Folk Victorian style is identifiable from spindlework detailed porches or flat, jigsaw cut trim appended to National Folk (post-railroad) house forms that feature six distinctive house shapes. Folk Victorian houses often feature a symmetrical façade (excepting those houses of the gable-front-and-wing subtype). Cornice-line brackets are common features.[5]

The following descriptions of individual buildings include information about their early histories.

95 West Island Avenue, Block 2, Lot 14
The Baker House

A Folk Victorian style house featuring a cross-gable and an open one-story front porch with a small gable dormer. It has a hood over the second floor window and a bay window on the side.[6]

The house was most likely built by Jason Baker between 1885 and 1888. Baker was a wholesale confectioner and fruit dealer who was also involved in real estate purchases, sold several lots on Nicollet Island, and built 95 West Island Avenue to sell. Baker's home was located at 93 West Island Avenue. In 1888 Baker sold lot 14 to William C. Leber for $8,000, a price which indicates that most likely a house was built on it by then. Leber was a self-employed jeweler and continued to own the house through 1929.[7]

101 West Island Avenue
The R.M.S. Pease House

A wood-frame one-and-a-half story house in the Greek Revival style featuring a high pitched gable roof with cross-gable. The gable roof has a simple cornice with eave returns and has a simple frieze board. The

The Baker house, 95 West Island Avenue

entrance is off center and recessed, framed by pilasters and capped by a simple architrave. Corner boards capped by plain moldings frame the building. Six-over-six windows are arranged symmetrically and are capped by simple moldings.[8]

The building was most likely built around 1864 for a bookkeeper named Roger M. S. Pease. It originally stood at 814 University Avenue SE, Minneapolis. Fred Rollins purchased the home in 1915 and his family lived in it until 1986.[9] In 1987 it was moved to its present location on Nicollet Island and restored by Jeffrey Siegel and Dorothy Sams.

The Meader-Farnham house

103/105 West Island Avenue
The Meader-Farnham House

A two-story wood-framed house in the Italianate style. The front façade has three wide bays with narrow rectangular windows with a four-over-four sash. The simple porch that runs along the front façade has square columns topped by decorative brackets. A double-leaf entry door with arched lights is centrally placed. The center bay features a pedimented gable with oeil-de-boeuf window. The other windows are narrow, paired rectangles in wooden frames.[10]

The house was originally constructed at 913 5th Avenue South, Minneapolis, around 1870, by an unknown builder who was most likely a carpenter. W. F. and Jennie Meader purchased the home for $2,000 and sold it to George and Mary Farnham in 1876. George Farnham worked for W. F. Meader, who owned a dry goods and millinery store on Washington Avenue. The house was moved by Jeff Siegel, Dorothy Sams, and John Kerwin from its original location in July 1985 and emplaced in its present location in 1986. It was restored under the guidance of Roark, Kramer, and Roscoe Design.[11]

107/109 West Island Avenue
The Second Griswold Queen Anne

A two-and-a-half story house in the Queen Anne style. It has a corner turret and a central gable with a decorative wood frieze. The porch has a decorative spindle architrave. It features low relief carved wood plaques over the entrance, pattern shingles on the gable ends, and stained glass windows. The four corner fireplaces have imported tile hearths and facings. At an unknown time the duplex was split into a fourplex.[12]

The house was built in 1890 on a lot purchased by Franklin C. Griswold in 1884, after Griswold had moved the house that was on the lot to 177 Nicollet Street. It was probably designed by Frederick Garner Corser, a noted

Minneapolis architect, and a friend and relation of the Griswolds. Griswold moved his family into the 107 half of the home in 1891 and rented the 109 portion. Franklin C. Griswold was a Dakota War soldier who fought in the battle of Birch Coulee and rose to the rank of 1st Lieutenant. Griswold eventually became one of the major landlords of Nicollet Island. One of his sons became an opera singer and another invented a railroad warning signal that was sold worldwide.[13] (For details see pages 72-73.)

111-113 West Island Avenue
The Burnett Tenement
A two-story, simple Italianate style, wood-frame house finished with clapboards and cornerboards. The center gable projection has a diamond window, decorative frieze board, and brackets. The doorway is flanked by Queen Anne plate glass windows with sidelights and tri-part transoms. The current porch, finished with a lattice porch skirt, extends across the front of the building and features square and chamfered porch posts. The windows are one-over-one on both stories and the second story windows have a simple carved top surround. The chimneys are buff brick with corbelled caps. At an unknown point the residence was divided into four units.[14]

The 4,800-square-foot house was built

The Burnett Tenement

by William P. Burnett in 1881 as a double tenement. It's designed in the "dumbbell" style developed by the Field and Son New York firm of architects. This style permitted light and ventilation to enter the building at the recessed porch located midway along the sides of the building. This was the first house intended solely for rental purposes and the first multi-unit dwelling on the island.[15]

115 West Island Avenue
The Peter Weinard House - Reproduction
This square-shaped frame two-story house is in the Italianate style, as evidenced by the

low hipped roof with a gabled pediment on the front façade, eared window frames, and brackets appearing under a substantial overhang. The open-single story porch spans the front façade.[16]

The current home is a reproduction of the original, which burned down in 1991 in a fire of unknown origin. The house was rebuilt in 1992 with the addition of some north side windows, but otherwise is a near match to the original. The original was probably built by Peter Weinard in 1872 on a lot that his brother John Weinard purchased in 1868. Peter Weinard was a fresco painter for Weinard Brothers painters and decorators. He lived in the house from 1873 to 1894. The original house had no windows on the north face and that may have been where Weinard painted his frescoes. Afterwards he appears to have rented it to Benjamin F. Butler, a foreman, and Herman C. Grote, a printer. Weinard continued to own the home until he died in 1914 or 1915 when the home passed to his son John Weinard.[17]

15-17 Maple Place, Block 2, Parts of Lot 10 & 11
The First Griswold Queen Anne

A two-story Queen Anne terminated in towers, this house has spires, peaked gables, pillars, arches, pattern shingles and low relief wood plaques. Significant details on the house include elaborate drop brackets and angled cornice boards, basketweave detailing on both ends, and rakes on gables on the front façade. It has segmental arched panels at the cornice on the front façade, a dormer with a jerkin roof located between the matching gables, and an elaborate Palladian balcony centrally located in the roof of the southeasterly façade. Original stained glass remains on the front of the building. One-over-one light sash is common throughout the remaining elevations. The four chimneys display elaborate brickwork. At some point the house was subdivided into four units.[18]

The house was built by Franklin C. Griswold as a rental property in 1886. It may have been designed by the architect Frederick

The first Griswold Queen Anne

Garner Corser, who was a friend and relation of the Griswold family. It was originally numbered 11-13 Maple Place, but superstitious tenants did not wish to rent a property numbered 13, so Griswold changed it to 15-17. [19] Griswold bought two lots for the building. Lot 10 was purchased from Charles Johnson in 1882 for $2,500 and lot 11 was bought from Andrew Finnegan the same year for $1,500. At the time, Johnson resided at 99 Nicollet Street at the front of lot 10. He was a clerk at Fuller and Simpson's Men's Furnishings. Finnegan was a plumber. Griswold used the equity he accrued in the property to fund other investments. The Griswold family lived in unit 15 from 1887 to 1889; unit 17 was divided into two apartments. In 1891, the Griswold family moved into the house at 107-109 West Island Avenue. Griswold and his family owned 15-17 Maple Place through 1929. Unit 15 was subdivided into two units some time later. [20]

18-20 Maple Place

A Folk Victorian style one-and-a-half story wood-frame house built around 1881. It has a cross-gable roof with jerkinhead and a pedimented dormer caps the house, and features rectangular window openings and a pedimented architrave. The structure may have been two separate houses that were joined together at an unknown date and remodeled in 1955 with an addition built on the rear. [21] It appears to have been owned by Franklin C. Griswold for use as a rental property. [22]

97 Nicollet Street
The Nadeau House

Designed by Bob Roscoe in the Victorian style, this two-story house has a gabled wood shingle roof, a simple front façade with contemporary columns, doors, and vertically-oriented windows. The windows on the second floor are arched. It was built in 1996 on a lot won by a Park Board lottery winner (the only empty lot available) to fill a gap created by the demolition of the Conway House, which was severely deteriorated and had suffered from a fire that destroyed part of the second floor.

93 Nicollet Street, Block 2, Lot 8
The Mayall House

A two-story house that has elements of both Italianate and Greek Revival styles. The gabled roof, cornice, and corner boards reflect a Greek Revival influence. This house has a porch, above which is a pair of arched windows on the second floor, crested with a little scroll-sawn ornament of twin circled stars. The front door on the porch has twin arched windows repeating the theme of the windows above the bracketing on the porch. The round-headed windows located in the second story front façade, and another window in the northwesterly façade, have Italianate details. There is a 2007 addition on the rear of the house. The front door is Italianate with two arched lights over two panels framed in molding. Two-over-two light windows are found throughout.[23]

The house was built by Francis Higgins, probably in 1873, on lot 8, which he purchased with lot 7 from W. W. Eastman and J. L. Merriman for $1,000 in 1868. Higgins was a cooper and partner at the firm of Cook and Higgins. In October of 1873, Jason Baker purchased lot 8 from Higgins for $1,000 and sold it two months later to George F. Wyman. Three months after that, Wyman sold the property to William A. Barnes. Barnes sold the property to John and Myra Mayall in April, 1874. The Mayalls used the house as a residence in 1874, with John Mayall apparently dying that year. Myra Mayall, then a widow, appears to have moved off the island. In 1882, Franklin C. Griswold bought the property for $2,000. Griswold used the equity he accrued in the property to fund other investments.

Griswold wanted to clear the lot at 107 West Island Avenue of a house that he owned in order to build a new family home there. Thus, Griswold arranged a trade with Adolph Barquist. Barquist moved his house, then located at 177 Nicollet Street, to the rear of 93 Nicollet Street, and gave it to Griswold. Griswold connected the two houses and created a double house with the address 91-93 Nicollet Street. In exchange, Barquist received Griswold's house at 107 West Island Avenue. This house was moved to 177 Nicollet Street and relinquished to Barquist. The exchange occurred in the summer of 1887.

In 1901, Griswold divided 91-93, moving the house at the rear of 91-93 Nicollet Street to the front of the same lot on the south side of current 93 Nicollet Street. Prior to this move, 93 Nicollet Street had been called 91 Nicollet Street and 91 Nicollet Street had been called 93 Nicollet Street.[24]

91 Nicollet Street
The Backe-Barquist House

A simple one-and-a-half story wood framed house in the Italianate style, with a front porch showing narrow siding and some Italianate brackets. Window openings are rectangular, double hung, and the lights are divided in a two-over-two style.[25] There is an addition built on the rear of the house.

The house was originally constructed at 177 Nicollet Street by Mathias T. Backe, a carpenter, in the year 1872 or 1873. Backe had entered into an agreement for deed with W.W. Eastman in May 1871; he received title two years later. Backe apparently resided on Nicollet Place (now called Nicollet Street). Adolph Barquist, a clerk for Janney, Semple, & Co., bought the house from Backe in 1882. Barquist apparently resided at 177 Nicollet Street until his death in 1889.[26]

Griswold wanted to clear the lot at 107 West Island Avenue of a home that he owned in order to build a new family home there. Thus, Griswold arranged a trade with Adolph Barquist. Barquist moved his house, then located at 177 Nicollet Street, to the rear of 93 Nicollet Street, and gave it to Griswold. Griswold connected the two houses and created a double house with the address 91-93 Nicollet Street. In exchange, Barquist received Griswold's house at 107 West Island Avenue. This house was moved to 177 Nicollet Street and relinquished to Barquist. The exchange occurred in the summer of 1887.

In 1901, Griswold divided 91-93, moving the house at the rear of 91-93 Nicollet Street to the front of the same lot on the south side of current 93 Nicollet Street. Prior to this move, 93 Nicollet Street had been called 91 Nicollet Street and 91 Nicollet Street had been called 93 Nicollet Street.[27]

177 Nicollet Street
The Adams-Barquist House

A one-and-a-half story wood-frame house done in a simplified version of the Greek Revival style. The rectangular house plan has a front gable and the primary entrance is on the side sheltered by a roof. It features a symmetrically fenestrated front face with two-over-two rectangular windows on the first and second stories.[28]

The house was built in 1873 by Charles E. Adams at 107 Island Avenue. Adams was at various times a sewing machine salesman, a flour mill proprietor, and a travel agent. Franklin C. Griswold bought the house in 1884 and moved it to its present location in June of 1887 as part of a deal with Adolph Barquist. Barquist, a clerk for Janney, Semple, & Co., lived in the house until his death in 1889, when his wife Sarah inherited the property. Sarah Barquist moved out in 1892 and rented the property to William T. McGann, an engineer, who lived there from 1894 to 1896. The house remained in Sarah Barquist's possession until 1929.[29]

167-169 Nicollet Street
The Barquist-Holmberg House

Details of this two-story brick Italianate structure include a low hipped roof with a central gable, a bracketed wood frieze located under a substantial overhang, a second frieze worked into the brick on the second story, round arched window and door openings, and an elaborate bracket hanging from the crown of the gable. The bracketed porch posts and bay windows are arranged symmetrically on the front and are Italianate in character. A decorative wood frieze pattern appears on the cornice. Windows on the first story have brick segmental arches. The wood porch spans the front façade and shelters the double door entry that is flanked by bay windows. The porch elements are bracketed chamfered porch posts with stair newels and plain square balusters.[30]

The house was probably built by both Andrew Barquist and Jonas P. Holmberg in 1881-1882. Harvey L. Brookins sold them each one half of the lot in 1881. Barquist was a clerk for Janney, Semple, & Co. He lived at 169 Nicollet Street from 1883 to 1889 or 1890. Holmberg was a tailor and cutter for J. H. Thompson. He apparently lived at 167 Nicollet Street from 1884 to 1889. Barquist and Holmberg evidently retained 167-169 Nicollet Street and used it as a rental property. Alexander McDonald, a packer, lived at 167 Nicollet Street from 1892 to 1896. Samuel Holt, a barber, resided at 169 Nicollet Street from 1895-1896.[31]

The Brookins House

163 Nicollet Street
The Brookins House

This one-and-a-half story simple Greek Revival house is based on a gable-front rectangular plan. The house has a symmetrically fenestrated front façade with two-over-two vertically-oriented sash windows on the first and second stories. The front door is a single-light over two panels. The rear addition has a single-story gabled roof.[32]

163 Nicollet Street was built in 1873 by George W. Brookins, a Civil War veteran, lumberman, surveyor, and well driller. Franklin C. Griswold bought and lived in the house in 1883. He moved out the following year, making 163 Nicollet Street a rental. Griswold's wife maintained custody of the property until 1937.[33]

27 Maple Place

A simple one-and-a-half story house in the French Second Empire style. It is the only single-family dwelling of this style on Nicollet Island. The second story is covered by a mansard roof with rounded arch dormers. Window sashes are double hung with two-over-two lights. Window trim is eared. It was built in 1888 by Franklin C. Griswold, who used it as a rental property.[34]

163 East Island Avenue
The Pye House

A wood-frame two-story house capped by a cross-gabled roof built in the Folk Victorian style. On the front gable there is a contemporary wood bracket. The north and south façades have projecting bays that create a cruciform pattern. Windows are rectangular

27 Maple Place

and an enclosed porch and kitchen have been added to the house.[35]

This two-story frame house was built in 1880 by James Pye, a "draughtsman" for W.F. Gunn and Company. Pye was an assistant engineer under William F. Gunn, designer of the Pillsbury A Mill. The lot for this home was purchased by Pye in 1880 for $1,000 from Amy Hepp. The house was built on the lot and was sold in 1883 for $2,500.[36]

167/169 East Island Avenue
The Murphy House

A two-story Italianate style house with a low pitched hip roof. The axial plan of the wood-framed building is a gradual progression of four narrowing cubes with the last cube being only a single story. The house features a projecting central gable with an oeil-de-boeuf attic window emphasizing the main entrance bay. Wide eaves over the two-story sections have denticulated cornices with paired corner brackets. On the two-story sections, shaped architraves are highlighted by flat-hood moldings on the first story, arched hood moldings at the second story, and eared trim.[37]

The house appears to have been built around 1870 for "Captain" Edward Murphy, one of Minneapolis's original pioneers, who settled in the Riverside Park area. He came to Minneapolis in 1859 and platted "Murphy's

The Murphy house

171 East Island Avenue
The Loberg House

A two-story wood-frame Greek Revival house with a rectangular front gable, this residence features a symmetrically fenestrated façade with eared window trim and eave treatment, including boxed eaves and eave returns. It features an oeil-de-boeuf window in the gable peak. The main entry is located on the front façade and has a two-over-two panel door with a plain rectangular glass transom. The simple front porch features square chamfered columns and an open balustrade. The house differs from its twin, 175 East Island Avenue, in that it has a small gable in the south slope of the gabled roof containing a window.[39]

This house was built at 1814 Cedar Avenue around 1875 by two Norwegian carpenter brothers named Andrew and Ole Loberg.[40] In 1990 it was moved with its mirror-image twin, 175 East Island Avenue, by the Minneapolis Community Development Agency (MCDA), and offered for sale. The move was not immediate as the house was plucked from its original location, where a planned parking lot was threatening it, and put on blocks for six months while the Hennepin Avenue Bridge was being rebuilt. In 1991 it was restored by its new owners.[41]

addition" to Minneapolis. In 1855, he donated the city's first park, named Murphy Park. 167/169 East Island Avenue appears to have been primarily a rental property. In 1988, it was moved to its present location from its original location of 716 Twenty-First Ave S., across from Augsburg College, where it served as student housing. The owners who moved the property restored it.[38]

The Loberg twins

175 East Island Avenue
The Loberg House

This house is a mirror-image twin of the one at 171 East Island Avenue—a two-story wood-frame Greek Revival structure. The main entry is located on the front façade and has a two-over-two panel door with a plain rectangular glass transom. The simple front porch features square chamfered columns and an open balustrade. This house features a symmetrically fenestrated façade displaying eared window trim and eave treatment including boxed eaves and eave returns. It features an oeil-de-boeuf window in the gable peak.[42]

The house was built at 1812 Cedar Avenue around 1875 by two Norwegian carpenter brothers named Andrew and Ole Loberg.[43] In 1990 it was moved with its mirror-image twin, 171 East Island Avenue, by the Minneapolis Community Development Agency (MCDA), and offered for sale. Like its twin, the house was put on blocks for six months while the Hennepin Avenue Bridge was being rebuilt. In 1991 it was restored by new owners.[44]

183-184 East Island Avenue
– The Woodward Flats

The building at 183-184 East Island Avenue is a wood-framed, two-story duplex with an asymmetrical plan. The low-pitched hip roof is evocative of the Craftsman style. An open wrap-around porch with simple square columns fronts the primary façade. Windows have double-hung, one-over-one light sash, and are rectangular in shape. Contemporary renovations have made this building one of the few on Nicollet Island displaying the post-Victorian simple lines of the Craftsman style.[45]

It was designed by the architecture firm of Bertrand and Chamberlin in 1898, and constructed for Austin M. Woodward, the President of A.M. Woodward Co., a grain company, as a rental property for $2,800 the same year. This building is set on the lot of the Meyers house, which is now at 185/186 East Island Avenue.[46]

185-186 East Island Avenue
O'Brien-Meyers House

This house was originally two separate structures that were moved by the housemover F. W. Pratt and joined into the present duplex in 1898. The northern portion of the home, at 185, is the oldest structure on the island, dating from around 1866. It is the original Meyers house. It was built in the Greek Revival style indicated by the simple cornice returned around the gable ends and supported by a simple frieze. An exterior door was cut into the primary façade, probably when the houses were joined.[47]

The other portion of this house, the original O'Brien house, is also in the Greek Revival style. It has a frieze on the front façade similar to that on the other attached home, and is framed by non-capped pilaster strips. The windows are in the two-over-two style. Doors were added to the combined structure when it was joined are in the Italianate style.[48]

John Meyers built 185 East Island Avenue in about 1866 on a lot which he purchased from Eastman and Merriam for $375. Meyers, an expressman, appears to have lived there from 1873 to 1874. He died around 1875 and his wife Julia inherited the property. She and her daughter Clarissa lived there until 1878. In 1882, the property was sold, through a guardian, to Hannah Woodward for $2,420. Woodward's son, Austin, received the property upon her death in 1899. The Woodwards don't appear to have lived in the home; rather, they lived at 189 Island Avenue from 1882 to 1885. After this time they appear to have moved to St. Anthony Park, St. Paul. In 1899, the structure was moved to the rear of the lot to make room for 183-184 East Island Avenue.

Henry O'Brien built the original house at 186 East Island Avenue in 1872, on a lot he purchased from Alonzo M. Caswell in 1871. O'Brien mortgaged his property and lost it in foreclosure to Martin Johnson of New York in 1873. Woodbury Fiske, an investor, bought the property from Johnson in 1873, and A.M. Woodward purchased the house from him in 1883, putting it in his wife's name. At some point the house had a fire that may have been a factor in joining it with the Meyer's house.[49] Woodward evidently rented the property and in 1898 had the building moved to the rear of the lot and attached to the Meyers house so 187-190 East Island could be built.[50]

187-190 East Island Avenue
The Woodward Flats fourplex

A two-story wood-frame fourplex decorated with classical elements. It is composed of rectangular masses that flank a two-story interior stairwell. The flat roof is accentuated by a Greek geometric-style frieze below a plain wooden cornice. This motif is continued in the entry design that includes paired wood columns and a recessed entry which support wood crossbeams on the beadboard entry ceiling. A simple 2x2 balustrade completes the recessed entry. The overall composition of the front façade was inspired by the style of 16th century Italian architect Andrea Palladio.

Standard window configuration on the side elevations is two-over-two wood sash. Select first and second story windows on this home have a simple decorative wood panel between them. A centered wooden stair accesses the front entry.[51]

The building was designed by the architecture firm of Bertrand and Chamberlin in 1898, and constructed for Austin M. Woodward, the President of A.M. Woodward Co., a grain company, the same year for rental purposes. It cost $4,000 to build.[52]

20 Grove Street
The Truck Building

This utilitarian building is brick with inset wood panels and windows. The building features bay doors that were originally garage doors and have since undergone modification. The roof is a distinctive hyperbolic paraboloid shape used by Frank Lloyd Wright and other mid-century architects.

The building was designed by Harry Garrish in the 1950s and built in 1960 on the site of the R.P. Upton house.[53] For years it served as a Hertz truck rental garage. The developer John Kerwin attempted to turn the building into condos, but was refused by the Minneapolis Historical Preservation Commission (HPC). Nonetheless, in violation of city code, artists began moving into the building with

The Grove Street Flats

their workshops, and eventually city approval was given for tenancy. The Truck Building remains an artists' haven and workshop.

2-16 Grove Street
The Grove Street Flats

A limestone tenement-style structure in the French Second Empire style capped by a mansard roof with arched dormer windows. It was built from limestone quarried on Nicollet Island. The Flats were originally built as an eight-unit complex. The primary façade features segmental arch windows on the lower level and flat windows on the second level. The complex features skylights and roof gardens. A system of stairways and platforms was added to the rear of the structure sometime after it was built. There is a thirteen-bay

wood garage to the rear of the Flats. In the Flats restoration in 1981, the complex was divided into 18 living units.[54]

Originally built by W.W. Eastman in 1877 for $5,000 each, these four-story tenement houses were one of the most fashionable addresses of the time and the last remaining structure in the Eastman Flats development that spanned Nicollet Island. As the area declined, the Flats were subdivided into apartments and further subdivided after World War II. As the Flats were subdivided, stairways and platforms were added to provide access to the new subdivided areas.[55] By the 1960s the property had been abandoned and was occupied by transients; in 1972 it was condemned. By the late 1970s the building was collapsing due to neglect. In 1980, the city council was meeting to approve final demolition of the Flats when developer John Kerwin announced that he had a purchase agreement for the Flats and that he intended to restore them. The city delayed demolition and Kerwin restored and sold individual flats.[56]

39-61 West Island Avenue
The West Island Condos

Built in imitation of the Second Empire style and facing westward towards the Mississippi River, this three-story, mansard-roofed building houses nine condominiums. It was completed in the summer of 1984. John Kerwin, restorer of the Grove Street Flats, was the developer, overcoming objections from the Park Board and the city for his use of outparcel land.

1 DeLaSalle Drive
DeLaSalle High School

The original DeLaSalle High School building, known as the C building, was built in 1900 on the west side of the island. It was then called the DeLaSalle Institute. By 1907, an addition had been built, and by 1914 the Loring/King property had been acquired for room to expand due to the school's growing enrollment. By the 1920s there was a desire for a college preparatory school and a new high school, so building B was built on the grounds of the Loring/King mansion in 1922. The Christian Brothers

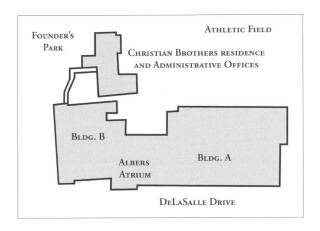

lived in the Loring/King mansion until the 1950s when they moved into a new Brother's residence that now includes administrative offices. The Loring/King mansion, Blakely house, and the William W. Eastman carriage house were demolished for various expansions.[57] Building B has a double-loaded corridor design, typical for schools at the time. The B building features full height windows, now partially covered with an opaque panel because of a drop ceiling in the classrooms. The entrance to the B building is ornamented with sandstone carvings and decorative pilasters that terminate above the second story. The façades are ornamented with a contrasting sandstone belt course, corner quoins, and a second story band above the windows. A carved crest with the motto *Signum Fidei* is over the entrance, and there is a carved frieze depicting Saint Jean-Baptiste DeLaSalle above

DeLaSalle High School

the second floor terminating in a shell motif at the top.

When World War II ended, the Baby Boomers caused another expansion of the school, and in 1959 building A was opened. Building A is a mid-century modern brick building with more recent red-brick entry additions. In 1971 the original DeLaSalle building C burned down. A statue of Saint Jean-Baptiste DeLaSalle was moved into a courtyard area where the building once stood. In 2000 the Albers atrium was added, connecting building A and building B, replacing a skyway, creating office space, adding an elevator for disabled access, and creating a new main entry for the building. In 2008 the DeLaSalle athletic field was expanded over a portion of Grove Street and tennis courts that had previously occupied the area.

51-53 Merriam Street
The Nicollet Island Inn

A three-story structure built from limestone quarried on Nicollet Island, the building features a full basement and two-foot-thick limestone relieved by narrow window openings. The wrap-around glass-encased porch is a more recent addition, as is the glass elevator in the interior. It is currently home to the Nicollet Island Inn, a Victorian-era-style inn and restaurant.[58]

In 1893, Kenneth McDonald and Fred Delamater purchased the lot for the building from William Eastman for $10,000. They had been operating a sash, door, and blind manufacturing business on the site previously. Construction on the current building had just begun when the Great Fire of 1893 swept through the area, but the building was not

The Nicollet Island Inn

significantly affected. McDonald and Delamater's company failed in 1895 and the factory reopened in 1896 under new management as the Island Sash and Door Company. It continued operations until 1899, and afterwards the building served several milling companies.[59] It fell into disrepair and was fixed up by the Salvation Army in 1913, and served as a men's shelter for the next 60 years. In the 1970s the Park Board bought the building, and it fell into neglect.[60] In 1981, suitable developers were found. The financial investors were Ron Jacob and Alan Fishlowitz, who hired architect David Shea to design a plan for a restored restaurant and inn. Restoration was completed, and the Nicollet Island Inn opened and has continued under varying ownership to the present day.

40 Power Street
The Nicollet Island Pavilion

A one-story building built with a gabled roof and articulated with brick pilasters and a corbelled cornice. The building has multiple arched openings on the eaves sides. It features a centrally located tower. It has a deck that overlooks the Mississippi River and St. Anthony Falls.

Perched on the southern tip of the island and overlooking the upstream side of St. Anthony Falls, the building housing the

The Nicollet Island Pavilion

Nicollet Island Pavilion was originally the William Bros Boiler Works, built c. 1892, and damaged by the Great Fire of 1893, after which it was repaired. It was subsequently added onto, and the expanded building became the Durkee-Atwood complex in 1923. In 1984, the Hennepin County Historical Society made a bid to transform the old Durkee-Atwood complex into a glass interpretive center, with the theme of the urbanization of Hennepin County. This plan failed, and the property came into the possession of the Minneapolis Park and Recreation Board, which restored the William Bros building and demolished the remainder of the Durkee-Atwood complex in the mid 1980s. Of note, the Arnold Schwarzenneger film *Jingle All the Way* had a scene filmed here. The Nicollet Island Pavilion is available for event rental.

Architectural Terms

Arch – a curved structure that supports the weight of the material above it.

Architrave – the lowest part of an entablature resting on the capital of a column.

Balloon Frame – a system in framing a wooden building in which vertical structural elements of the exterior walls and partitions consist of single studs, which extend the full height of the frame.

Balustrade – an entire railing system, including a top rail, balusters and often a bottom rail.

Balusters – small posts that support the upper rail of a railing.

Beadboard – wood paneling that is routed vertically so that parallel lines span the height of the board, often used as wall or ceiling material.

Brackets – a decorative horizontal support for an overhanging weight.

Capital – the top part of a pillar or column.

Chamfered – cut off at an angle, usually forty-five degrees, used for porch posts.

Clapboard – a narrow board with one side thicker than the other, used for external horizontal siding.

Corbel – a projection from a wall that some-times supports or appears to support vaults, arches, and roofs.

Corner Board – a board, which is used as trim on the external corner of a wood framed structure.

Cornice – an ornamental molding at the meeting of the roof and walls, usually consisting of bed molding, soffit, fascia, and crown molding.

Cross Gabled Roof – a gabled roof parallel to the roof-ridge of the main part of a building.

Crown – the highest portion of an arch.

Cupola – a roof or ceiling in the form of a dome.

Denticulated - having a fine toothed margin.

Doric – the first and simplest of the three Greek orders; normally does not have a base.

Dormer Window – a small window with a gable or triangular top projecting from a sloping roof.

Eaves – the lowest part of a pitched roof projecting beyond the wall.

Elevations – the architectural drawing of a side of a building.

Entablature – the upper horizontal part of an order, between the capital and the roof, consisting of the architrave, frieze, and cornice.

Façade – the face of a building; often refers to the front with the main entrance.

Fenestrated – architecture having windows or window-like openings.

Frieze – the middle part of an entablature, often decorated with spiral scrolls.

Gable – the vertical triangular wall between the sloping ends of a gable roof.

Hip Roof – a four-sided roof, having sloping ends and sides.

Jerkin Roof – a gable roof, truncated or clipped at the apex.

Lattice Board – an openwork structure of crossed strips or bars of wood.

Lights – small panes of window.

Low relief wood plaques – sculptural relief that projects a little from the background.

Mansard Roof – a hip roof, having two slopes on each side, with the lower slope much steeper than the upper slope, which has minimal pitch.

Moldings – a strip made of wood or other structural material, used to decorate or finish a surface.

Oeil-de-Boeuf – a small circular or oval window, usually on an upper story.

Order – one of the original three styles of Greek architecture, distinguished by the type of column and entablature used.

Palladian Balcony - a platform projecting from the wall of the building, stylistically derived from the work of 16th-century architect Andrea Palladio.

Pediment – the triangular segment between the horizontal entablature and the sloping roof; also, a surface used ornamentally over doors or windows.

Pilaster – an ornamental rectangular or round column with a capital and base; projects slightly from a wall.

Pillar – a slender freestanding vertical support, a column.

Pitch – the angle at which a roof rises from its lowest to highest point.

Quoins – angular courses of stone at the corner of a building.

Spire – a tall, tapering, acutely pointed roof of a tower, as in the top of a steeple.

Stair Newels – a post supporting the handrail of a staircase.

Surround – the molding that outlines an object or opening.

Transom – a window above a door, usually hinged to a horizontal crosspiece over the door.

Window Sash – a framework that holds the panes of a window in the window frame.

Appendix

Fanny Ellis, you remember,
That unclouded afternoon,
When the groves of Nicollet Island
Wore the livery of June,
And we walked beneath their shadow
While the light-winged moments sped,
And our thoughts were bright and cloudless
As the bright sky overhead.

Fanny Ellis, Fanny Ellis!
Lovingly you will recall,
Where, upon the green sward seated,
I repeated "Locksley Hall."
Then the whisper of the South Wind
Was not softer than your sighs,
Nor the far-off blue of Heaven
Deeper than your liquid eyes.

Never had so bright a verdure
Clothed the grass beneath our feet,
Never had the happy wild birds
Sang so merrily and sweet;

Never had the blushing flowers
Breathed such fragrant breath away;
Never were our lives so holy,
As they seemed that Summer day.

Seated there, beside the river,
Listening to the cataract's roar,
While the restless waves below us
Tossed their foamy crests ashore;
We forgot that aught of sorrow
Could to human lives belong;
And the music floating round us,
Seemed an angel's triumph song.

Fanny Ellis, Fanny Ellis!
Through the blissful years to come,
We shall talk of this together,
In the tranquil light of home.
Since the ties that then were woven,
Time can never rend apart;
Since the love that day unfolden,
Binds us ever, heart to heart.

Notes

CHAPTER 1

1. Father Louis Hennepin, *Description of Louisiana: Newly Discovered to the Southwest of New France by Order of the King*, trans. Marion E. Cross, intro. Grace Lee Nute (Minneapolis: University of Minnesota Press, 1938), 90.

2. Hennepin, 117.

3. Frank G. O'Brien. *Minnesota Pioneer Sketches: From the Personal Recollections and Observations of a Pioneer Resident* (Minneapolis, Minnesota: H.H.S. Rowell, Publisher, The Housekeeper Press, 1904), 155.

4. Samuel W. Pond, *The Dakota or Sioux in Minnesota As They Were in 1834*, intro. Gary Clayton Anderson (St. Paul: Minnesota Historical Press, 1986), 71.

5. Pond, 87.

6. Much information about the early history of the villages that developed around the falls can be found in Lucille Kane, *The Falls of St. Anthony: The Waterfall That Built Minneapolis* (St. Paul: Minnesota Historical Society Press, 1987), especially pages 2, 6-7, 9, 12-14, 176-7, 185.

7. John–Ryan Paprock and Teresa Peneguy Paprock, *Sacred Sites of Minnesota* (Black Earth, Wisconsin: Trail Books, 2004), 4.

8. as quoted in Harriet E. Bishop, *Floral Home; or, First Years in Minnesota* (New York: 1857), 198.

9. archeological information comes from Scott Anfinson, "Archaeology of the Central Minneapolis Riverfront Part 1: Historical Overview and Archaelogical Potentials," *The Minnesota Archaeologist* 48, 1-2 (1989); Michelle M. Terrell, Ph.D., RPA interview, October 27, 2008.

10. James Anderson, interview, October 27, 2008.

11. Dave Wiggins, interview, October 27, 2008.

12. Johnathan Carver. *Travels Through The Interior Parts of North America in the Years 1766, 1767 and 1768* (Minneapolis, Minnesota: Ross & Haines, Inc., 1956, 3rd ed.), 66, 69-70.

13. Carver, 71.

14. Elliott Coues, ed., *The Expeditions of Zebulon Montgomery Pike Vol. 1* (New York: 1895), 1: 83, 227.

15. Quotations from Pike's journal can be found in Zebulon Montgomery Pike, *The Journals of Zebulon Montgomery Pike with Letters and Related Documents, Vol 1.*, ed. and annotated Donald Jackson (Norman: University of Oklahoma Press, 1966), 40, 41-2, and 201.

16. A. Hermina Poatgieter and James Taylor Dunn, eds. *Gopher Reader II: Minnesota's Story in Words and Pictures* (St. Paul: Minnesota Historical Society Press, 1975), 249-253.

17. Kane, 12-14.

18. Maj. R. I. Holcombe and William H. Bingham, eds., *Compendium of History and Biography of Minneapolis and Hennepin County, Minnesota* (Chicago: Henry Taylor and Co., 1914), 60-1.

19. For more information of the ox cart trails see Rhoda R. Gilman, Carolyn Gilman, and Deborah M Stultz, *The Red River Trails, 1820-1870, Oxcart Routes between St. Paul and the Selkirk Settlement* (St. Paul: Minnesota Historical Society Press, 1979), especially p. 18.

CHAPTER 2

1. Rufus J. Baldwin, A.M., "Bridges," in *History of Minneapolis and Hennepin County, Minnesota, Vol.1.*, eds. Judge Issac Atwater and Col. John H. Stevens (New York and Chicago: Munsell Publishing Co., 1895), 349.

2. See *Minneapolis, City of Opportunity: A Century of Progress in the Aquatennial City 1856-1956* (Minneapolis, Minnesota: T.S. Denison and Company, 1956); June D. Holmquist and Sue E. Holbert, *A History Tour of 50 Twin City Landmarks*, Minnesota Historical Site Pamphlets Series No. 2 (St. Paul: Minnesota Historical Society, 1966), 33.

3. John H. Stevens, *Personal Recollections of Minnesota and Its People, and Early History of Minneapolis* (Minneapolis: Marshall Robinson, 1890), 194-5.

4. See Rodney C. Loehr, "Caleb D. Dorr and the Early Minnesota Lumber Industry," *Minnesota History Magazine* Vol. 24, Issue 2 (1943): 125-130; Holcombe and Bingham, 250.

5. Stevens, 84-5.

6. Ibid, 184-5.

7. Merlin Stonehouse, *John Wesley North and the Reform Frontier* (Minneapolis: University of Minnesota Press, 1965), 37.

8. The letters from Ann Loomis North to her parents can be found in the collections of the Minnesota Histoical Society. The passages reproduced in the text came specifically from letters dated November 8, 6, 12-13, and 13,1849; December 6, 9, 16, 28, and 30, 1849; and March 3, 1850.

9. Stonehouse, 35.

10. Lucy Leavenworth Wilder Morris, ed., *Old Rail Fence Corners* (Austin, Minnesota: F H McCulloch Printing, 1914), 224.

11. For details see Rebecca Marshall Cathcart, *A Sheaf of Remembrances* (St. Paul: Minnesota Historical Society Collections, 1915), 520-3, 532-3.

12. See Cathcart, 523.

13. Cathcart, 533.

14. Stonehouse, 25.

15. Cathcart, 533.

16. Ann Loomis North to parents, Oct. 20, 1850.

17. Frederika Bremer to H.C. Örsted, St. Paul's, Minnesota, October 25, Letter XXVII (New York: Harper Brothers, 1853 v. 2).

18. Morris, 224.

19. Stonehouse, xii-xiii.

20. Holcombe and Bingham, 150.

21. Ann Loomis North to Brothers, March, 14, 1850, Minnesota Historical Society.

22. Cathcart, 527-8.

23. Loehr, 138.

24. *Ballou's dollar monthly magazine*, 12-1 (Boston: Elliott, Thomes and Talbot, July 1860), 416.

25. Frank G. O'Brien, *Minnesota Pioneer Sketches: From the Personal Recollections and Observations of a Pioneer Resident* (Minneapolis: H.H.S. Rowell, Publisher, The Housekeeper Press, 1904), 234-5.

26. O'Brien, 158-9.

27. Franklin Benjamin Sanborn, ed., *The First and Last Journeys of Thoreau Lately Discovered Among His Unpublished Journals and Manuscripts, Vol. 2*, (Boston: The Bibliophile Society, 1905) 32-3.

28. Winthrop Eastman interview, August 18, 2009.

29. These descriptions are derived from a pamphlet printed for Snyder, McFarlane & Cook, Bankers, *Minneapolis and St. Anthony Falls with a Description of the Country Above the Falls, From Authentic Sources* (Philadelphia: Joseph M. Wilson, Publisher, 1857), 6-7; Holmquist and Holbert, 33; Larry Millett, *Lost Twin Cities* (Minneapolis Historical Society Press, 1992), 71-2; Carole S. Zellie and Amy M. Lucas, *Minneapolis Riverfront as Birth Place and First Place* (Minneapolis: Saint Anthony Falls Heritage Board, 2008), 23.

30. "Celebrating at the Opening of the Mississippi Wire Suspension Bridge," *Minnesota Republican*, Jan 23, 1855, 2.

31. *New York Evening Mirror* February 16, 1855 "From Our Correspondent of the Far West."

32. Morris, 28-9.

33. Ann Loomis North to brothers, March 15, 1850, Minnesota Historical Society.

34. Morris, 27-29.

35. Stevens, 288.

36. O'Brien, 312.

37. Harlow Gale, *Minneapolis, A Short Reversal of Human Thought: Being the Letters and Diary of Mr. Harlow A. Gale 1857 to 1859* (Minneapolis: printed privately for His Grandchildren, 1922), 32-33.

38. O'Brien,143-5.

39. Gale, 29.

40. This account is largely based on details found in Mike Anderson, "Nicollet Island, capitol of Minnesota?" *Northeaster*, March 23, 1999, 8-9.

41. Gilman, et al., 18.

42. Anderson, 9-10.

43. *Minneapolis and St. Anthony Falls*, 5-6.

44. http://www.rotsweb.ancestry.com/-msissap2/winston.html.

45. Judge Issac Atwater and Col. John H. Stevens, eds., *History of Minneapolis and Hennepin County,*

Minnesota, Vol. 1 (New York and Chicago: Munsell Publishing Co., 1895), 100.

46. Honorable David Headon, *Summary Statement of the General Interests of Manufacture and Trade Connected with the Upper Mississippi* (Minneapolis: State Atlas Book and Job Print, 1862), 5.

47. *Faribault Central Republican*, June 5, 1861.

48. Information about Griswold derives largely from Charles C. Griswold, *As the River Flows: A Memorial to Franklin Clinton Griswold*, (Published in 1939), 35-36.

49. Kathy Davis Greaves and Elizabeth Ebbott, *Indians in Minnesota* (Minneapolis: University of Minnesota Press, 2006), 28.

50. John Chaffee, *History of 163 Nicollet Street*, 2006.

CHAPTER 3

1. Accounts of the final tally differ. See Edward C. Gale, "Loss of Nicollet Island Recounted," *Minneapolis Journal*, February 23, 1913; Theodore Wirth in *Minneapolis Park System 1883-1944* (Minneapolis: The Minneapolis Parks Legacy Society, 2006), p. 17, puts the tally at 552 nay votes and 467 yeas; Charles M. Loring, in "Memories of 60 Years in Minneapolis Recounted by Charles M. Loring, 87," *Minneapolis Journal*, December 9, 1906, says that the measure failed by 83 votes.

2. Loring, op. cit.

3. Charles M. Loring, "Looking Through A Vista of Fifty Years," in *History of Minneapolis and Hennepin County, Minnesota*, Vol.1., eds. Judge Issac Atwater and Col. John H. Stevens (New York and Chicago: Munsell Publishing Co., 1895), 157.

4. Two Pines Resource Group, *Literature Search for Archaeological Potential, DeLaSalle High School Athletic Field, Nicollet Island, Hennepin County, Minnesota* (Minneapolis: Two Pines Resource Group, 2005), 10.

5. Agreement between Minneapolis Bridge Company and Merriam, Eastman, et al., 1866.

6. Greg Brick, *Subterranean Twin Cities* (Minneapolis, University of Minnesota Press, 2009), 147-152.

7. This and following accounts can be found in *Minneapolis Chronicle*, December 28, 1866; December 29, 1866; January 1, 1867.

8. See Florence Lehmann, "First White Woman to Live On Nicollet Island Wants Never to See Place Again," *Minneapolis Journal*, July 3, 1927; Michelle M. Terrell, Ph.D., Archaeological Potential, DeLaSalle High School Athletic Field, Nicollet Island, Hennepin County, Minnesota, (Two Pines Resource Group No. 01-15, 2005), 22; *History of Hennepin County and City of Minneapolis* (North Star Publishing Co., 1881), 524; Lehmann, *Minneapolis Journal*, July 3, 1927.

9. For details about the brewing industry on Nicollet Island see Doug Hoverson, *Land of Amber Waters: The History of Brewing in Minnesota* (Minneapolis: University of Minnesota Press, 2007), 17-18, 249; Catherine Burke, "Gluek Family Retains Leadership in Brewery, Oldest Business in City," *Minneapolis News*, May 29, 1947; Gluek Brewing Company, http://www.gluek.com;

10. See Gluek Tunnel Easement, Book 17, Deeds, City of Minneapolis, 406.

11. Burke, "Gluek family..."

12. See Kane, 71-2, 75-76; Lehmann, *Minneapolis Journal*, July 3, 1927.

13. W. W. Eastman, "The Tunnel Company, A Full Statement From Mr. Eastman," *St. Anthony Falls Democrat*, Vol. 1, April 15, 1870.

14. "W. W. Eastman Dead," *Minneapolis Journal*, July 26, 1902.

15. *Saint Anthony Falls Rediscovered*, (Minneapolis Riverfront Development Coordination Board, 1980), 61.

16. "W.W. Eastman Dead," *Minneapolis Journal*, July 26, 1902.

17. Details are derived from Loring, "Memories of 60 Years," 38; "Charles M. Loring is Dead," *The Minneapolis Journal*, March 19, 1922; Theodore Wirth, "Honorable Charles M. Loring, Our Venerable Tree Planter," *The Minnesota Horticulturist* Vol. 50 No. 6 (June 1922), 163.

18. "Charles M. Loring is Dead," *The Minneapolis Journal,* March 19, 1922.

19. Ibid.

20. "Island Improvements," *Minneapolis Tribune,* March 13, 1878, 4; "The Star Block," *Minneapolis Tribune,* June 16, 1877, 4.

21. E. T. Abbott, "Old Time Reccolections [sic] Minneapolis-St. Paul 1871-1937.

22. Horace Bushnell Hudson, ed., *A Half Century of Minneapolis* (Minneapolis: The Hudson Publishing Company, 1908), 218.

23. Hudson, 219-20, 231-32;Two Pines, 27.

24. Details are taken from "She Would Be Free: The Eastman Divorce Case Comes Up Before Judge Russell," *MSP Journal,* June 18, 1895; "The Eastmans Reconciled," *Minneapolis Journal,* July 23, 1895; "Fred Eastman Fined," *Minneapolis Journal,* April 3, 1896; "Divorced At Last," *Minneapolis Journal,* May 23, 1896; "Fred Eastman At Liberty," *Minneapolis Tribune,* June 11, 1896.

25. Two Pines, 32-3.

26. Details about the Noonan case are taken from "Kate Noonan's Case," *The Minneapolis Tribune,* June 4, 1877; "A Sensational Tragedy in Minneapolis: William H. Sidle Shot and Killed by one Kate Noonan," *Lake Superior Review and Weekly Tribune,* February 23, 1877; "The Old Story," *Indianapolis Sentinel,* February 23, 1877; State of Minnesota ex rel. Kate Noonan vs. Sheriff of Hennepin County, 24 Minn. 87, Supreme Court of Minnesota, August 11, 1877; "The Law of Homicide," *Minnesotian Herald,* June 16, 1877; *Lake Superior Review and Weekly Tribune,* June 15, 1877; "Murder, And Worse," *Inter Ocean,* December 19, 1877;"The World's Doings," *Minnesotian Herald,* December 29, 1877.

27. *Saint Anthony Falls Rediscovered: the Architectural Heritage of Minneapolis's St. Anthony Falls Historical District,* (Minneapolis: Minneapolis Riverfront Coordination Board, 1980), 63.

28. Territorial Pioneers, *Proceedings and report of the annual meetings of the Minnesota Territorial Pioneers, May 11, 1899 and 1900* (St. Paul: Pioneer Press Company, 1901), 154.

29. "W.W. Eastman Dead," *The Minneapolis Journal ,* July 26, 1902.

30. Mildred Schlener to Barbara Flanagan, Special Collections, Hennepin County Library, 1974.

31. Kathryn Strand Koutsky and Linda Koutsky, *Minnesota State Fair: An Illustrated History* (Minneapolis: Coffee House Press, 2007), 9.

32. "With the Long Bow: Bill King's Fair in 1881," *The Minneapolis Journal,* 1937.

33. Hudson, 486; "Col. W.S. King Gone," *The Minneapolis Journal,* February 24, 1900.

34. "Mrs. King Wins Suit, Hudson Denounced As A Blackmailer," *The Minneapolis Journal,* Dec 24th, 1914.

35. Atwater and Stevens, 539-542.

36. John DeLaittre, *The Reminiscences of John DeLaittre,* 1910, 82.

37. Aaron Hanauer, City of Minneapolis CPED Planning Division Heritage Preservation Commission Staff Report, 500 3rd Street North, November 25, 2008.

38. *Saint Anthony Falls Rediscovered,* 73.

39. See "Noted Minneapolis Opera Singer Dies After Operation in New York," *Minneapolis Journal,* February 26, 1914; 88 "Frank Griswold," *Star and Tribune,* January 8, 1992.

40. Barbara Flanagan, "Nicollet Island children recall the good old days," *Minneapolis Star,* October 10, 1974.

41. Judy Vick, "Ex-Librarian to Recount Story of Old Minneapolis, *Minneapolis Sunday Tribune,* Jan. 6, 1963, 4.

42. Augusta Starr, "Nicollet Island," given as a speech of paper 1958, collated by Kathryn Johnson and C. Rafter, April 1959.

43. Millett, 72-3.

44. *Evening Journal,* Feb 7, 1883.

45. Details derive from Theodore Wirth, *Minneapolis Park System 1883-1944* (Minneapolis, The Minneapolis Parks Legacy Society, 2006),19, 20, 22, 26.

46. Millett, 178-9.

47. "Mr. Eastman's Bluff," *Minneapolis Journal,* October 26, 1899; "Rights of Islanders," *Minneapolis*

Journal, November 23, 1899.

48. Richard Heath, *The Extra Alarmer* Vol 20, No 2, June-July 1993 and *The Extra Alarmer* Vol. 20, No. 3, August-September 1993 (Extra Alarm Association of the Twin Cities).

CHAPTER 4

1. *Minneapolis – A Plan and Program for River Development* (City Planning Commission, Autumn, 1972), 9.

2. "A Remarkable Civic Plan," *Minneapolis Journal*, December 2, 1906, 1.

3. Edward H. Bennett, Andrew Wright Crawford, ed., *Plan of Minneapolis*, 1917, 160.

4. Ibid., 161-2.

5. *Saint Anthony Falls Rediscovered*, 62, 65.

6. Anfinson, 103.

7. "Anthony Kelly's Estate," *Minneapolis Journal*, June 9, 1899.

8. Atwater and Stevens, 388.

9. "Nicollet Island Landmark Doomed by School Project," *Minneapolis Tribune and Star Journal*, August 2, 1942.

10. "Eastman Flat Tenants Stymied for Place to Live, They Complain," *Minneapolis Star Journal*, August 13, 1942.

11. "Council Will Get Eastman Flats Protest," *Minneapolis Star Journal*, August 5, 1942, 4.

12. Frank Schneider to Brooks Cavin, "My Memories of Nicollet Island," Special Collections, Hennepin County Library, September 1975.

13. Barbara Flanagan, "A Nicollet Island Pioneer Remembers," *Minneapolis Star*, Variety, March 26, 1971.

14. Martin and Pitz & Associates, Landscape Research, Schoell & Madson Engineers, *The Nicollet Island Master Plan*, for The Minneapolis Park and Recreation Board, 1996, 7.

15. Kit Neville, "Tenants, traffic and transience," *Minnesota Daily*, February 12, 1969, 8.

16. Ibid., 9.

17. Information about the Lerner store can be found at Harry Lerner, *Tenacity Well Directed: The Inside Story of How A Publishing House Was Created And Became A Sleeping Giant In Its Field – Well, Not Exactly* (Minneapolis: First Avenue Editions, 2009), 20-24.

18. Ibid, 20-24.

19. Information from Clague Hodgson comes from an interview, September 26, 2008.

20. State of Minnesota v. Diamond No. 45204. Supreme Court of Minnesota. April 9, 1976.

21. Ellen Stewart, interview, October 4, 2008.

22. Ibid.

23. Paul McLeete (formerly Massnick), interview, June 22, 2009.

24. McLeete, June 22, 2009; Stewart, Oct 4, 2008.

25. Stewart, October 4, 2008.

26. Ibid.

27. Cindy Gentling, interview, October 23, 2008.

28. John Heiman, interview, June 29, 2009.

29. John Chaffee, "Sheba knew she was the queen of Nicollet Island," *Southeast*, 28-8, November 2002, 1, 7.

30. Patricia Ohmans, "At Home on Nicollet Island, *City Pages*, Vol 4, No 130, June 1, 1983.

31. Ned Pratt, "Island in the River," *Common Ground*, 5 (Summer, 1975): 66.

CHAPTER 5

1. Millett, 268.

2. "City Planner Urges Park on Nicollet Island," *Minneapolis Tribune*, May 12, 1957.

3. "For Nicollet Island," *Greater Minneapolis,* June 1962, 48.

4. Martin & Pitz, 7.

5. David Nimmer, "Group Presents Plan for Nicollet Island," *Minneapolis Star*, August 5, 1965.

6. "Bridges Approved," *Minneapolis Star*, January 5, 1968.

7. Riverfront Advisory Committee, *Mississippi/Minneapolis-A Plan and Program for Development* (Minneapolis: City Planning Commission: Autumn 1972).

8. Larry Maddox, "Nicollet Island Park: A Work in Progress," *People for Parks News*, July 1995, 10.

9. Mildred S. Friedman, "Nicollet Island: A New View."

10. *Island in the River*, Project Area Committee of the Nicollet Island-East Bank Urban Renewal Area, 1972.

11. Mark Lerner, interview, June 29, 2009.

12. Kane, 191-2.

13. "Historic Preservation Feasibility Study/Nicollet Island and East Bank Urban Renewal Project," (Minneapolis: Minneapolis Housing and Redevelopment Authority, 1974).

14. Steve Brandt, "Three for the future on Nicollet Island," *Minneapolis Tribune*, December 19, 1976.

15. "Agencies Tangle over Nicollet Island," *Minneapolis Tribune*, December 6, 1980.

16. Direction for Development of Nicollet Island-A Proposed Position Statement by the City of Minneapolis.

17. Details about the purchase of the Flats comes from an interview with John Kerwin, October 15, 2008.

18. Barbara Flanagan, "Island Inn limestone causes quandary," *Minneapolis Star*, March 5, 1982.

19. Martha S. Allen, "Kahn accused of coercion in plan for Nicollet Island," *Minneapolis Star Tribune*, May 12, 1983.

20. Two Pines, 11.

21. Kerwin interview.

22. Thorbeck & Lambert, Inc. and Virginia M. Westbrook, *Nicollet Island Interpretive Center*, (Minneapolis: Hennepin County Historical Society.)

23. Bob Roscoe, interview, September 15, 2008.

24. Maddox, 12.

25. Laurie Michael, "Couple's castle: Blueprint for island kingdom?" *Skyway News*, Vol 17, No 88, November 4, 1986.

26. Glenn Gordon, "At Home on the Island," *Minnesota Monthly*, March 1992.

27. Details about the move come from Bill Beyer, "The odyssey of a bridge: An essay in steel floats downstream," *Architecture Minnesota*, July/August 1987, 44;

Kate Perry, "Bridge christening thrown overboard by series of miscues," *Minneapolis Star and Tribune*, September 3, 1986; "Broadway bridge finally reaches new home," *Minneapolis Star and Tribune*, Sept 7, 1986.

28. "New RY Terminals," *Minneapolis Journal*, November 30, 1901.

29. http://www.mrdbridges.com.

30. John Chaffee, interview, June 29, 2009.

31. Rosalind Bentley, "Animal control unit kicks donkey off island," *Minneapolis Star and Tribune*, June 21, 1984.

32. "Animal control officer met with human resistance when they removed donkey," *Northeaster*, September 7, 1988, 6.

33. Details about the sign come from Tim Lyke, "Light Beer," *Skyway News*, May 23, 1989 and "Grain Belt sign to shine again," *Star Tribune*, May 24, 1989; "Grain Belt neon glows anew in Minneapolis," *Star Tribune*, February 19, 1992; Michelle Bruch, "Plans to restore Grain Belt sign," *Downtown Journal*, December 21-January3, 6; Eastman interview.

34. Mike Anderson, "Larger bridge could disrupt Nicollet Island's '19th-century' life," *Northeaster*, August 21, 1995.

35. Chaffee interview.

36. François Medion, interview, November 12, 2008.

37. http://www.ci.minneapolis.mn.us/news-release/20010724-20010922-(2001-7-24)-sculpture-from-minneapolis-city-sister-to-be-dedicated-on-July-22.html.

38. Brother Michael Collins, interview, February 2, 2009.

39. Mike O'Keefe, interview, October, 17, 2008.

40. Collins interview.

41. Scott Russell, "Envisioning an Island: How Nicollet Island became what it is today – a park with homeowners, and, perhaps, a private school's athletic fields," *Skyway News*, March 14-20, 2005, 14.

42. Collins interview.

43. Grant Agreement Between the Metropolitan Council and the City of Minneapolis by and Through the Minneapolis Park and Recreation Board for Rec-

reation Open Space Acquisition, Contract No. 7902, 1979, 5.

44. Nicollet Island Agreement -1983, Contract for Acquisition and Transfer of Lands for Redevelopment by Public Bodies, 2.

45. Terry Collins, "Update: DeLaSalle Athletic Field; In a summer rerun, council to revisit decision on playing field," *Star Tribune*, August 17, 2007.

46. http://buzz.mn, "Council does double-reverse on historic preservation," November 26, 2009.

47. Lisa Hondros, interview, November 12, 2008.

48. Linda Mack, "Wirth-y alternative," *Star Tribune*, Arts Section, March, 5, 2006, 2.

49. Steve Dornfeld, "Re: Review of draft," email message to author, December 8, 2008.

50. Ibid.

51. Hondros interview.

52. Metropolitan Council Meeting, October 10, 2007, 2.

53. Lisa Hondros, "Re: Review of draft," email message to author, March 5, 2009.

54. *Born by the River*, Brother Michael Collins interview, November 11, 2005, 88.

55. Michelle Terrell, "Re: Nicollet Island Literature Search," email message to author, December 22, 2008.

56. Collins interview; Hondros interview.

CHAPTER 6

1. Virginia and Lee McAlester, *A Field Guide to American Houses* (New York: Alfred A. Knopf, 1986), 179.

2. Ibid., 211.

3. Ibid., 241.

4. Ibid., 263.

5. Ibid., 309.

6. Todd Grover, interview, November 15, 2009.

7. Miller-Dunwiddie Architects, Inc., *Historic Preservation Feasibility Study Nicollet Island & East Bank Urban Renewal Project: Report Two of Preliminary Survey and Evaluation Phase* (Minneapolis: Minneapolis Housing and Development Authority,

1973), 3.

8. Camille Kudzia, Minnesota Historic Properties Inventory Form: 101 West Island Avenue (Minnesota State Historic Preservation Office, October 1988).

9. Ibid.

10. Camille Kudzia, Minnesota Historic Properties Inventory Form: 103-105 West Island Avenue (Minnesota State Historic Preservation Office, October 1988).

11. Ibid.

12. Camille Kudzia, Minnesota Historic Properties Inventory Form: 107-109 West Island Avenue (Minnesota State Historic Preservation Office, October 1988).

13. Miller-Dunwiddie report abstract, March 29, 1974, 2.

14. United States Department of the Interior National Park Service, National Register of Historic Places, Burnett Tenement.

15. *Saint Anthony Falls Rediscovered*, 63.

16. Miller-Dunwiddie, *Historic Preservation*, 7.

17. Ibid., 6.

18. Ibid., 8.

19. Camille Kudzia, Minnesota Historic Properties Inventory Form: 15-17 Maple Place (Minnesota State Historic Preservation Office, October 1988).

20. Miller-Dunwiddie, *Historic Preservation*, 8.

21. Camille Kudzia, Minnesota Historic Properties Inventory Form: 18-20 Maple Place (Minnesota State Historic Preservation Office, October 1988).

22. Ibid.

23. Camille Kudzia, Minnesota Historic Properties Inventory Form: 93 Nicollet Street (Minnesota State Historic Preservation Office, October 1988).

24. Miller-Dunwiddie, *Historic Preservation*, 12.

25. Ibid., 14.

26. Ibid., 13.

27. Ibid., 12.

28. Camille Kudzia, Minnesota Historic Properties Inventory Form: 177 Nicollet Street (Minnesota State Historic Preservation Office, October 1988).

29. Miller-Dunwiddie, *Historic Preservation,* 17.

30. Camille Kudzia, Minnesota Historic Properties

Inventory Form: 167-169 Nicollet Street (Minnesota State Historic Preservation Office, October 1988).

31. Miller-Dunwiddie, *Historic Preservation*, 15.

32. Camille Kudzia, Minnesota Historic Properties Inventory Form: 163 Nicollet Street (Minnesota State Historic Preservation Office, October 1988).

33. Ibid.

34. Camille Kudzia, Minnesota Historic Properties Inventory Form: 27 Maple Place (Minnesota State Historic Preservation Office, October 1988).

35. Camille Kudzia, Minnesota Historic Properties Inventory Form: 163 East Island Avenue (Minnesota State Historic Preservation Office, October 1988).

36. Ibid.

37. Camille Kudzia, Minnesota Historic Properties Inventory Form: 167-169 East Island Avenue (Minnesota State Historic Preservation Office, October 1988).

38. Ibid.

39. Camille Kudzia, Minnesota Historic Properties Inventory Form: 171 East Island Avenue (Minnesota State Historic Preservation Office, October 1988).

40. Ibid.

41. Roscoe interview.

42. Camille Kudzia, Minnesota Historic Properties Inventory Form: 175 East Island Avenue (Minnesota State Historic Preservation Office, October 1988).

43. Ibid.

44. Roscoe interview.

45. Camille Kudzia, Minnesota Historic Properties Inventory Form: 183-184 East Island Avenue (Minnesota State Historic Preservation Office, October 1988).

46. Miller-Dunwiddie, *Historic Preservation*, 19.

47. *Saint Anthony Falls Rediscovered*, 71.

48. Camille Kudzia, Minnesota Historic Properties Inventory Form: 185-186 East Island Avenue (Minnesota State Historic Preservation Office, October 1988).

49. *Saint Anthony Falls Rediscovered*, 71.

50. Miller-Dunwiddie *Historic Preservation*, 18.

51. Camille Kudzia, Minnesota Historic Properties

Inventory Form: 187-190 East Island Avenue (Minnesota State Historic Preservation Office, October 1988).

52. Miller-Dunwiddie *Historic Preservation*, 19.

53. Two Pines, 11.

54. Camille Kudzia, Minnesota Historic Properties Inventory Form: 2-16 Grove Street (Minnesota State Historic Preservation Office, October 1988).

55. *Saint Anthony Falls Rediscovered*, 69.

56. Kerwin interview.

57. Two Pines, 11.

58. Camille Kudzia, Minnesota Historic Properties Inventory Form: 51-53 Merriam Street (Minnesota State Historic Preservation Office, October 1988).

59. Miller-Dunwiddie report abstract, enclosure 3.

60. http://NicolletIslandInn.com

Photo Credits

Minnesota Historical Society
14 Franklin Steele
33 The first bridge ever to span the Mississippi River,
    (William Henry Illingsworth, photographer).
47 The First Minnesota Regiment on Nicollet Island
50 Little Crow (John L. Gravenslund, photographer).
51 Franklin C. Griswold (Joel Emmons Whitney, photo).
57 John L. Merriam (Whitney's Gallery)
65 The Loring/King mansion
67 The Eastman Flats
74 Colonel William S. King
85 The 1876 bridge (William Henry Illingsworth, photo).
92 The Great Fire of 1893
104 The southern tip of Nicollet Island
125 Gateway Urban Renewal

Northfield Historical Society
22 John Wesley North
22 Ann Loomis North

Hennepin County Library,
Minneapolis Collection
Cover: Bird's eye view of the city of Minneapolis - 1885.
2 Map of St. Anthony by Private R.A. Colby - 1848.
4 Father Hennepin
5 Dakota Indians
9 A sketch of St. Anthony Falls c. 1766
13 Joseph N. Nicollet
18 Captain John Tapper and Caleb Dorr
19 Milling operations near Nicollet Island
60 A 1866 etching of Minneapolis, Nicollet Island, and St.
Anthony
63 The tunnel collapse
86-87 Panoramic View of Minneapolis c.1874 by George H.
Ellsbury and V. Green
94 1914 Map of Nicollet Island

Hennepin History Museum
36 The Red River carts
56 William W. Eastman
134 The Island Sash and Door Company building

DeLaSalle High School
100 entrance to DeLaSalle High School building B
101 Eastman Flats being demolished

Harry Lerner
108 Morris Lerner

Clague Hodgson
111 Sam Valen, the Wolf-Man of the Pracna

Ellen Stewart
114 Steve Arhelger and Ellen Stewart

Judy Richardson
118 Sheba and Pearl with their owner Doris Park

Christopher and Rushika Hage
106 The iconic Grain Belt Beer Sign
132 The Grove Street Flats
143 The Merriam Street Bridge
156 The new Hennepin Avenue Bridge
162 The Meader-Farnham House
164 The first Griswold Queen Anne
168 The Brookins House
169 27 Maple Place
175 DeLaSalle campus plan
176 DeLaSalle High School

GIS, City of Minneapolis
122 orthophotographic map of Nicollet Island

Nicollet Island, A New View
126 One of many imaginative plans for Nicollet Island

Hopkins Atlas
54 1885 map of Nicollet Island

City of Minneapolis
16 1865 plat of Nicollet Island
158 1866 plat of Nicollet Island

John Chaffee
71 The Griswold house
139 Loberg houses being moved
140 Houses undergoing restoration

John Toren
149 Bell of Two Friends
170 Murphy House
171 Loberg Twins

Selected Bibliography

Atwater, Judge Issac and. Stevens, Col. John H. eds., *History of Minneapolis and Hennepin County, Minnesota, Vol. 1*. New York and Chicago: Munsell Publishing Co., 1895.

Baldwin, A.M., Rufus J. "Bridges." In *History of Minneapolis and Hennepin County, Minnesota, Vol.1.*, eds. Judge Issac Atwater and Col. John H. Stevens. New York and Chicago: Munsell Publishing Co., 1895.

Bennett, Edward H. and Crawford, Andrew Wright, eds. *Plan of Minneapolis*, 1917.

Bishop, Harriet E. *Floral Home; or, First Years in Minnesota*. New York: 1857.

Brick, Greg. *Subterranean Twin Cities*. Minneapolis: University of Minnesota Press, 2009.

Carver, Johnathan. *Travels Through The Interior Parts of North America in the Years 1766, 1767 and 1768*. 3rd ed. Minneapolis, Minnesota: Ross & Haines, Inc., 1956.

Cathcart, Rebecca Marshall. *A Sheaf of Remembrances*. St. Paul: Minnesota Historical Society Collections, 1915.

Coues, Elliott, ed., *The Expeditions of Zebulon Montgomery Pike Vol. 1*. New York: 1895.

DeLaittre, John. *The Reminiscences of John DeLaittre*. Privately printed, 1910.

Gale, Harlow. *Minneapolis, A Short Reversal of Human Thought: Being the Letters and Diary of Mr. Harlow A. Gale 1857 to 1859*. Minneapolis: Privately printed for His Grandchildren, 1922.

Gilman, Rhoda R., Gilman, Carolyn and Stultz, Deborah M. *The Red River Trails, 1820-1870, Oxcart Routes between St. Paul and the Selkirk Settlement*. St. Paul: Minnesota Historical Society Press, 1979.

Greaves, Kathy Davis and Ebbott, Elizabeth. *Indians in Minnesota*. Minneapolis: University of Minnesota Press, 2006.

Griswold, Charles C. *As the River Flows: A Memorial to Franklin Clinton Griswold*, Privately printed, 1939.

Headon, Honorable David. *Summary Statement of the General Interests of Manufacture and Trade Connected with the Upper Mississippi*. Minneapolis: State Atlas Book and Job Print, 1862.

Hennepin, Father Louis. *Description of Louisiana: Newly Discovered to the Southwest of New France by Order of the King*. Translated by Marion E. Cross, with an introduction by Grace Lee Nute. Minneapolis: University of Minnesota Press, 1938.

Historic Preservation Feasibility Study/Nicollet Island and East Bank Urban Renewal, Project. Minneapolis: Minneapolis Housing and Redevelopment Authority, 1974.

History of Hennepin County and City of Minneapolis. North Star Publishing Co., 1881.

Holcombe, Maj. R. I. and Bingham, William H. eds., *Compendium of History and Biography of Minneapolis and Hennepin County, Minnesota*. Chicago: Henry Taylor and Co., 1914.

Holmquist June D. and Holbert, Sue E. *A History Tour of 50 Twin City Landmarks*, Minnesota Historical Site Pamphlets Series No. 2. St. Paul: Minnesota Historical Society, 1966.

Hoverson, Doug. *Land of Amber Waters: The History of Brewing in Minnesota*. Minneapolis: University of Minnesota Press, 2007.

Hudson, Horace Bushnell. ed., *A Half Century of Minneapolis*. Minneapolis: The Hudson Publishing Company, 1908.

Island in the River. Project Area Committee of the Nicollet Island-East Bank Urban Renewal Area, 1972.

Kane, Lucille. *The Falls of St. Anthony: The Waterfall That Built Minneapolis*. St. Paul: Minnesota Historical Society Press, 1987.

Koutsky, Kathryn Strand and Koutsky, Linda. *Minnesota State Fair: An Illustrated History*. Minneapolis: Coffee House Press, 2007.

Lerner, Harry. *Tenacity Well Directed: The Inside Story of How a Publishing House Was Created and Became a Sleeping Giant In Its Field – Well, Not Exactly*. Minneapolis: First Avenue Editions, 2009.

Loring, Charles M. "Looking Through A Vista of Fifty Years," In *History of Minneapolis and Hennepin County, Minnesota, Vol.1.* eds. Judge Issac Atwater and Col. John H. Stevens. New York and Chicago: Munsell Publishing Co., 1895.

McAlester, Virginia and Lee. *A Field Guide to American Houses*. New York: Alfred A. Knopf, 1986.

Martin and Pitz & Associates, Landscape Research, Schoell & Madson Engineers. *The Nicollet Island Master Plan*, for The Minneapolis Park and Recreation Board, 1996, 7.

Michaels, David. *Schulz and Peanuts: A Biography*. New York: HarperCollins Publishers, 2007.

Miller-Dunwiddie Architects, Inc. *Historic Preservation Feasibility Study Nicollet Island & East Bank Urban Renewal Project: Report Two of Preliminary Survey and Evaluation Phase.* Minneapolis: Minneapolis Housing and Development Authority, 1973.

Millett, Larry. *Lost Twin Cities.* Minnesota Historical Society Press, 1992.

Minneapolis – A Plan and Program for River Development. City Planning Commission, Autumn, 1972.

Minneapolis, City of Opportunity: A Century of Progress in the Aquatennial City 1856-1956. Minneapolis, Minnesota: T.S. Denison and Company, 1956.

Minnesota Historical Society. *Minnesota in the Civil and Indian wars, 1861-1865, Vol. 2.* St. Paul: Pioneer Press Company, 1936.

Moe, Richard, *The Last Full Measure: The Life and Death of the First Minnesota Volunteers.* With a foreword by James MacGregor Burns. New York: Henry Holt and Company, 1993.

Morris, Lucy Leavenworth Wilder, ed., *Old Rail Fence Corners.* Austin, Minnesota: F H McCulloch Printing, 1914.

O'Brien, Frank G. *Minnesota Pioneer Sketches: From the Personal Recollections and Observations of a Pioneer Resident.* Minneapolis, Minnesota: H.H.S. Rowell, Publisher, The Housekeeper Press, 1904.

Paprock, John – Ryan and Paprock, Teresa Peneguy. *Sacred Sites of Minnesota.* Black Earth, Wisconsin: Trail Books, 2004.

Pike, Zebulon Montgomery. *The Journals of Zebulon Montgomery Pike with Letters and Related Documents, Vol 1.*, Edited and annotated by Donald Jackson. Norman: University of Oklahoma Press, 1966.

Poatgieter, A. Hermina and Dunn, James Taylor, eds. *Gopher Reader II: Minnesota's Story in Words and Pictures.* St. Paul: Minnesota Historical Society Press, 1975.

Pond, Samuel W. *The Dakota or Sioux in Minnesota As They Were in 1834.* With an introduction by Gary Clayton Anderson. St. Paul: Minnesota Historical Press, 1986.

Riverfront Advisory Committee. *Mississippi/Minneapolis-A Plan and Program for Development.* Minneapolis: City Planning Commission: Autumn 1972.

Saint Anthony Falls Rediscovered: the Architectural Heritage of Minneapolis's St. Anthony Falls Historical District. Minneapolis: Minneapolis Riverfront Development Coordination Board, 1980.

Sanborn, Franklin Benjamin, ed. *The First and Last Journeys of Thoreau Lately Discovered Among His Unpublished Journals and Manuscripts. Vol. 2.* Boston: The Bibliophile Society, 1905.

Snyder, McFarlane & Cook, Bankers. *Minneapolis and St. Anthony Falls with a Description of the Country Above the Falls, From Authentic Sources.* Philadelphia: Joseph M. Wilson, Publisher, 1857.

Stevens, John H. *Personal Recollections of Minnesota and Its People, and Early History of Minneapolis.* Minneapolis: Marshall Robinson, 1890.

Stonehouse, Merlin. *John Wesley North and the Reform Frontier.* Minneapolis: University of Minnesota Press, 1965.

Terrell, Ph.D., Michelle M. *Archaeological Potential, DeLaSalle High School Athletic Field, Nicollet Island, Hennepin County, Minnesota.* Two Pines Resource Group No. 01-15, 2005.

Territorial Pioneers. *Proceedings and report of the annual meetings of the Minnesota Territorial Pioneers, May 11, 1899 and 1900.* St. Paul: Pioneer Press Company, 1901.

Thorbeck & Lambert, Inc. and Westbrook, Virginia M. *Nicollet Island Interpretive Center.* Minneapolis: Hennepin County Historical Society.

Two Pines Resource Group. *Literature Search for Archaeological Potential, DeLaSalle High School Athletic Field, Nicollet Island, Hennepin County, Minnesota.* Minneapolis: Two Pines Resource Group, 2005.

Wirth, Theodore. *Minneapolis Park System 1883-1944.* Minneapolis: The Minneapolis Parks Legacy Society, 2006.

Zellie, Carole S. and Lucas, Amy M. *Minneapolis Riverfront as Birth Place and First Place.* Minneapolis: Saint Anthony Falls Heritage Board, 2008.

Index

About the Authors

Christopher and Rushika Hage first met in a history class while attending St. John's University and the College of St. Benedict. History has been a life-long passion for both of them, and each has a B.A. in history. Christopher also has a master's degrees in criminal justice and Rushika in medieval history.

The couple first discovered Nicollet Island more than a decade ago and fell in love with the place, like so many people had before them. When they moved back to Minneapolis from California a few years ago they began doing research on the island—an effort that led eventually to the creation of this book.

Christopher's other interests include jousting, martial arts, yoga, glassblowing, ceramics, reading, and travel. He is a United States Marine Corps Reserve Officer, an Iraq veteran, and also works for the U.S government helping people reflect on life choices. Rushika also enjoys flamenco, belly dancing, yoga, knitting, sewing, and teaching classes on church history.